Beyond Companionship—
Christians in Marriage

Beyond Companionship—
Christians in Marriage

Diana S. Richmond Garland
and David E. Garland

Wipf and Stock Publishers
EUGENE, OREGON

Wipf and Stock Publishers
199 West 8th Avenue, Suite 3
Eugene, Oregon 97401

Beyond Companionship
Christians in Marriage
By Richmond Garland, Diana S. and Garland, David E.
Copyright© January, 1986 Richmond Garland, Diana S. and Garland, David E.
ISBN: 1-59244-131-9
Publication Date: January, 2003
Previously published by Westminster Press, January, 1986 .

Contents

We wish to thank President Roy L. Honeycutt and the trustees of the Southern Baptist Theological Seminary for granting us a sabbatical leave for 1984–85, which enabled us to complete this book. We are grateful to the Education Commission of the Southern Baptist Convention and a friend of the seminary for providing financial assistance. We owe a debt of gratitude to the Auslandsamt of Eberhard-Karls Universität, Tübingen, for making our year in Germany such a pleasant experience, and to the Diakon of the Evangelische Fakultät for providing an Arbeitszimmer in the Theologicum for our research. We also thank the many friends who have encouraged us.

1

The Challenge of Marriage for Christians Today

Many books about marriage for Christians begin with alarm: the institution of marriage is in trouble because of the climbing divorce rate. Few people today have not been touched in some way by divorce, either their own or that of a close relative or friend. Despite the outcry over the increasing number of divorces, however, statistics lend themselves to a more positive interpretation of the state of marriage. It is projected that the majority (60%) of persons born in the United States in the 1970s who marry will remain married until the death of one partner (Glick and Norton 1977), and they will remain married longer, about ten years more than a marriage in 1869, since people today live longer. At the turn of the century, a wife could expect the death of her husband before the last child left home; now most couples plan for— and have reason to expect—many years of married life after the children have left the roost. The chance that today's bride and groom will both survive and stay married until their golden wedding anniversary is more than twice as great as it was in 1900 (Laslett 1977). Even those who divorce have not lost their belief in marriage; over 80 percent remarry (Broderick 1979).

This interpretation of the statistics should not, however, be used to ignore the suffering of those who have experienced the grief and hurt of a marriage that ended in divorce. And many others suffer through the misery of marriages that have failed to measure up to wedding-day dreams but never venture into a divorce court. Living happily ever after is, for them, something that happens only in fairy tales. For many, marriage has seemed all too formidable a task.

The primary concern of those who marry today is not just how to stay married till death do them part but how they can be happy together. Most Americans (other than statisticians) do not measure the strength of marriage by the ability to ward off divorce. National census statistics recede into the background when we examine the challenges for married couples. For most of us, the criteria of a strong marriage are well-being and happiness, and the social science literature is filled with studies of the factors that contribute to marital adjustment. Women's magazines and best-sellers popularize these studies and offer helpful hints on how to have a happy marriage.

Marriage in the lives of Christians, however, has special challenges that transcend these criteria. Meeting the challenge of marriage issued to Christians entails something more than being able to stick it out, or even to attain happiness. It boils down to a challenge to live Christlike lives through the marital relationship. This is easier said than done, and it means that "success" cannot be measured by scales of marital satisfaction or happiness but is dependent on the degree to which partners are enabled to "lose their lives in order to save them." The challenge is not to find personal happiness but to give of one's self to another. The Christian does not marry to be served but to serve, to be fulfilled but to fulfill, to be made happy but to make happy.

It is those who struggle with the summons of Christlike living in their marriages who may experience happiness as a by-product. Studies have found consistently that the most significant factor in the happiness of marriage is "religiosity," a factor usually ignored and not even measured in most social science research (Filsinger and Wilson 1984). "Religiosity" as measured by the social sciences usually refers to a variety of factors such as church attendance and opinions about the importance of faith in one's life. These cannot be equated with Christlike living; nevertheless, this consistent finding certainly deserves more attention. Significant religious experience and experiencing a fulfilling marriage are in some way related to each other. A critical question from a social science perspective, then, is how a religious definition of marriage differs from other definitions, and how this definition might explain this research finding. What is characteristic of marriage in the lives of those with religious commitment? Behind this question is perhaps the more pressing one for Christians in marriage: What characterizes marriage relationships that reflect the living-out of Christians' commitment to one another and to God?

Defining the challenge of marriage for Christians is our purpose here. How does the Christian calling transform the definition and purpose of this essentially secular institution? In this book we attempt to understand what the Bible says about marriage for the lives of God's people. Using also our knowledge of the social sciences, we attempt to determine specific implications for Christians living in today's world: how biblical insight may be applied in marriages in our society today. This work is based on the premise that biblical study must challenge the social scientific understanding of persons and their culture, and that the social sciences must leaven biblical scholars' interpretation of the scripture so that it can speak effectively to modern needs. Both our understanding of our own experiences and our understanding of God's Word are subject to error; by examining each in the critical light of the other, we may come closer to realizing what God intended for marriage.

Whether you bought this book in a bookstore or borrowed it from a library, you should know that its premises differ from most of the other books on the same shelf, whether those other books address the social scientific perspectives on marriage, the need to change problematic marital relationships, or the attempt to define or strengthen the marriages of Christians. In many ways this book is written in reaction to those others. Some assumptions floating around about marriage have received much support, both from church leaders and from social scientists and marriage counselors and therapists. Our premises, and the underlying themes for this book, are that these assumptions are actually myths that misrepresent what the challenge of marriage is for Christians.

Myth No. 1: There is *one* pattern of marriage that is right for all time and all people.

The social sciences study relationships as they occur in a particular context, and most research studies carefully outline the limits of applying findings to different cultural contexts. Yet, as these findings are popularized, they are often presented as if they were absolute principles universally applicable. The danger exists that the study of "what is" in a particular setting will be turned into principles for "what ought to be," not only in that setting but in all marriages in all contexts. This danger is even more pronounced when one attempts to present *the* biblical teaching about marriage and family in a popular form.

The Bible was not intended to provide us with a marriage manual. No biblical writer treats marriage systematically. In the Old Testament, it was taken for granted as a secular reality that the prophets used as a poignant example of the ups and downs in the relationship between God and Israel (Isa. 50:1; 54:6; Jer. 3:1, 7–8, 20; Ezek. 16:23; Hos. 2:19–20). Jesus' only lengthy discussion of the subject was precipitated by a test question from the Pharisees about the grounds for divorce (Matt. 19:3–12; Mark 10:2–12). Combining texts from Genesis 1:27, 2:24, and 5:2, he argued that marriage has its basis in God's act of creation—male and female he created them—and that the two become a one-flesh unity. He asserted that God has joined the two together, and therefore the bond should not be broken. Jesus said nothing, however, about the way this one-flesh unity was to be lived out, and presumably he accepted the marital pattern of his first-century Jewish culture. In fact, he said nothing on the subject of preparation for marriage, sexual relations in marriage, birth control, roles of the spouses, quality of the relationship, or how to strengthen a marriage—subjects that preoccupy many today.

Paul dealt with the issue of marriage at length in 1 Corinthians 7 only because of the congregation's confusion over it, particularly concerning matters of sex and the Christian, and because they had asked him to respond specifically to particular issues (1 Cor. 7:1; see D. E. Garland 1983). Paul responded ad hoc to specific difficulties and aberrant attitudes in Corinth and was not trying to offer a complete systematic guide to married life. One cannot, therefore, heedlessly translate what Paul wrote here into a universally applicable marital code, although what Paul wrote was profound and insightful and will provide the basis of much of our discussion later in the book.

The Bible also records many marital patterns and practices that would not only be socially unacceptable today in America but in some cases illegal—for example, the polygynous marriages of such biblical notables as Jacob (Gen. 29:15–30), David (1 Sam. 25:39–43; 2 Sam. 5:13; 11:26–27) and Solomon (1 Kings 11:1–8). The number of wives and concubines was limited only by the resources required to maintain them. Even Yahweh's relationship to Northern and Southern Israel was likened to a marriage to two wives (Ezekiel 23), but this polygynous pattern can hardly be considered exemplary for us. And what wife today would offer her maid to her husband as a second wife as Sarah and Rachel did (Gen. 16:1–3; 30:1–5, 9)?

Most Christians today would also find levirate marriage unacceptable. This is the marriage, enjoined in Deuteronomy 25:5–10, between a woman whose husband has died without offspring and the brother of the dearly departed. Its purpose was to perpetuate the name of the deceased as well as to keep his property in the family. The failure to comply with this practice proved fatal to Onan and mortally embarrassing to Judah (Genesis 38). Jesus seems to have tacitly accepted this marital practice when the Sadducees tried to trip him up with their stock anti-resurrection anecdote about the woman who married seven brothers in succession. Jesus rebuked them for knowing neither the scriptures nor the power of God who raises the dead, not for talking about levirate marriage (Mark 12:24–27).

These patterns of marriage, which would be considered strange if not aberrant today, indicate the importance of discerning the message of the Bible in its cultural setting. Marital customs and outlook change within the Bible and have continued to change throughout history. What we can find in scripture is not a prescribed biblical pattern of marriage but resources for discussing how God's will is to be lived out in marriage in our time and place. The message of scripture is timely as well as timeless, but its meaning for persons has different emphases and import in their context than it has for others in different times or places. As we determine what that message is, it must then be applied to our own ways of living together, in our own culture. An understanding of what marriage for Christians is must be addressed from within the experience of Christians in each age and culture.

This book is therefore not about all marriages in all places, but about marriage as we have experienced it in middle-class American culture —in our own relationship, in the relationships of friends, and in the relationships of couples we have known in churches, marriage enrichment groups, and counseling. It is the responsibility of you, the reader, to determine how our reflections from these experiences may be useful as you discern God's purposes in *your* life, in different circumstances from ours. We hope that, with a critical approach from the individual reader, the book may have applications in quite different contexts from our own.

Myth No. 2: If you are determined to hang in there and if you work hard enough, you can have a good marriage.

The assumption is that people give up too soon on their marriage and put out too little effort to keep it alive. They do not work hard enough to make their marriage succeed—thus the high divorce rate. This assumption guides our church programs and influences our thinking about people who are divorced. We often assume that marriages in trouble are experiencing trouble because one or both partners have not done their part to make the marriage work. Notice the language— "*make* the marriage work." One may hear the remark, "I can't believe John and Beth are separated. They seemed so happy. If they could have just stayed with it longer."

We label this attitude the "bent-arm hang" approach to marital relating. When Diana was in junior high school gym class, she had to go through the President's Physical Fitness tests, which included several skills and tests of strength. She was not particularly athletic, did not enjoy sports, and had particular difficulty with activities requiring skill. One required throwing a softball a certain distance. Despite her father's patient practice sessions with her, she flunked that one. To pass the tests —and the course—she had to do well on at least one of the remaining activities. Fortunately, at least in this case, she is a willful and determined person; and one test—the bent-arm hang—called for just those qualities. It required no real skill except the ability to hang one's chin above the bar for as long as possible. And so she hung, gritting her teeth and shaking all over, until she had earned an A and had passed the course. The purpose of the tests was to promote physical fitness and to involve children in athletics so that they might continue to be physically active. The result for Diana, however, was that she learned to hate athletics even more. It reinforced her belief that she was no good at sports.

The same false premise lies behind this myth of marriage—that if people are given standards to meet and encouraged to try to meet them, they will learn to appreciate their marriage and will want to invest more of themselves with their marital partners. The divorce rates are thought to signify that people "give up" too soon and that we have become "soft" on marriage. Some authors even imply that people get into marriage banking on getting out if they are not happy. One has written, "For most people today, a covenant is a mutually convenient arrangement that automatically dissolves when it fails to meet the needs of one party" (Snow 1974, 281).

This attitude toward the marriage commitment has been poked fun at by the cartoon strip *Funky Winkerbean*. The character named Ann has finally become engaged but confides to a friend over coffee, "You know, Heather, it's odd . . . but now that I'm actually engaged I'm starting to feel nervous about getting married!" The friend sympathizes. "I know what you're thinking, Ann, and it's only natural to be nervous! Marriage is a big commitment! Seven or eight years can be a long time!"

Despite this myth, only a few couples marry thinking that the marriage is anything but permanent. But as difficulties begin to mount and they feel the strain in their emotional muscles from doing the marital bent-arm hang, we call out to them, "Hang in there! Keep struggling and things will work out!" The problem is, they are often already doing that, and the words "hang in there" are like salt in open wounds. It is like saying, "Be warmed and filled," to a cold, hungry person (James 2:16). Instead of helping, we have added to their frustrations and their load of guilt for the sensed failure of their marriage. The marriage may be legally intact—they passed the course—but it misses the mark. The alienation and hurt are not what God intended.

Working at marriage does not necessarily create a joyful, vital relationship. This is not to say that couples ought not to work at communicating with each other, to work through conflict and all those other tasks that contribute to marital strength. It is a dangerous assumption, however, to promise marital happiness as a result of more skillful interacting. Often the marital enrichment programs and family ministries of the church unwittingly promote this very assumption. The words of the psalmist, "Unless the LORD builds the house, those who build it labor in vain" (Ps. 127:1), might well be applied also to the house and home of the marital couple. We can work as hard as we like at our marriage, but labor alone will not ensure success.

There are therefore three basic problems with the belief that hard work and commitment to hang in there will lead to a successful marriage. First, most people who have experienced marital failure have indeed struggled to hang on and have done everything they knew to do to salvage the relationship. Although little research has been conducted on the struggle of persons who are enduring difficult marriages, what is available indicates that even their physical well-being is undermined by the struggle. Unhappily married persons are less healthy than divorced or happily married persons. (Renne 1971). As these persons go through the process of divorce and remarriage, health indicators improve. The experience of a failing marriage is rarely casual; it is a physical and emotional trauma.

Second, this myth ignores the imperfection of persons, who can rely only on God's grace to lift them out of their unsuccessful attempts to perfect themselves and their relationships. No matter how hard we try, the maintenance of the covenant of marriage cannot be guaranteed by our own hard work. People who are flawed cannot form a perfect relationship. Kolbenschlag (1979, 138) contends that "the permanence of the marriage bond is its fruit, not its root." When we assume that the root of a strong marriage is our promise to each other on our wedding day, we are doomed to fail. It is not something we can assure, but it is the fruit that comes in the process of relating to each other in the grace of God.

It is no doubt true that working on the marital relationship has merit, as shown by the strongly positive outcomes of marriage enrichment programs in improving the happiness of couples. The problem arises when this assumption is reversed, and it is assumed that, if enrichment programs and increased communication skills *prevent* problems, it is a lack of such training—not enough work by the couple in exploring and using all the resources available to them—that *causes* the problems. To illustrate, "people who get frequent headaches may learn that if they take aspirins at the first sign of the headache they can then *prevent* the headache from developing. But this does not mean that lack of aspirin causes "headaches" (Markman, Floyd, and Dickson-Markman 1982). It should also be noted that programs designed to enrich marriages most often discourage couples having difficulties from participating, sending them to counseling instead. The results of most marriage enrichment research is based on work with good relationships, not couples in difficulty.

The third problem with this myth is the assumption that a marriage is the result solely of the actions and attitudes of the partners themselves. It assumes that a marriage is a "closed system," responding only to what the partners do or do not do. Many factors other than the personalities and behaviors of the two partners affect a marriage—for example, children, extended family, neighborhood, employment, income, health or illness, even such factors as the physical space and privacy of the home or natural events and disasters. An examination of divorce statistics, for instance, reveals that divorce rates are much higher among the poor and, in particular, among the unemployed (Cutright 1971; Ross and Sawhill 1975; Cherlin 1979). Poverty and economic uncertainty are usually out of the control of the spouses, yet they create conditions that make marital survival more difficult. Of course, not all poor people have poor marriages, but they are more likely to experience chronic marital distress from the strain of not having enough in an affluent society. To tell them to hang on and work harder is to blame them for the stress with which they must live. For those who believe that marital problems are symptoms of sin, this can even lead to the conclusion that poor people are more sinful than the rest.

Myth No. 3: Marriage is the most important relationship in life.

Marriage is extremely popular in our culture. Although people are now tending to wait until they are a little older to marry (Melville 1980), about 96 percent of men and women eventually marry, and this percentage has steadily increased since the turn of the century (Saxton 1980). Of those who divorce, 80 percent remarry (Visher and Visher 1979), indicating that the divorce was seen as a failure of a relationship with one particular partner and not a reflection on the desirability of marriage itself. The upshot is that few people choose to live life alone without marrying, and the marital relationship is often seen to be a key to whether, in the end, life is good or not. Myth No. 3 is the value premise on which Myth No. 2 is based—that one must work hard at marriage because it is all-important. Nothing should come before the work on the marital relationship—not children (couples are told to keep the demands of parenting secondary to building their own relationship), not work (we are admonished not to bring work home but to recognize the need for "quality family time"), not even church (family ministry approaches often argue that church activities should not be allowed to detract from family marital time). This relationship called marriage must be important indeed.

We would argue, however, that this emphasis on the importance of marriage often becomes an endorsement of the myth that the marital relationship *should* always receive highest priority. Perhaps what many couples need, however, is to give less attention to their marital relationship and more attention to the family and social network they need to keep their relationship alive. It is true that parents need time with children and with each other and that the clutter of activities needs to be cleared away to allow this time together. For many, however, busyness is a way of filling time because meaningful relationships with others beyond the spouse are absent. In our mobile society, couples are often far removed from their families; if they do live in the same town, they are cautioned not to allow parents and other family to interfere in their own nuclear family life. Churches are often so large that they can no longer meet the needs of individual family members for community, especially in a one-hour worship service spent in anonymity. As a result, the need for community and belonging, for family, must be met within the martial relationship itself. In the lives of many, the spouse is the only person with whom to share lasting friendship and the feelings of being a family. No one person, however, can meet all the needs for intimacy and family relationships of another. Hunt writes, "Throughout most of human history men and women have depended on a whole network of close relationships to satisfy their many emotional needs. Today we depend on a single relationship to do so" (Hunt 1977, 23). Margaret Mead has claimed that our culture places a greater burden of expectation on marriage than any other society at any time.

One might even argue that much of the current emphasis in churches on family ministry may serve not to strengthen families but to raise the stakes even higher. Not only do Christians get the message that they are supposed to honor their marital commitment, but they are supposed to have enriched and fulfilling marriages. The Marriage Encounter movement within the Roman Catholic Church advocates a process of daily dialogue in which spouses write their private thoughts or feelings in a journal, share what they have written with each other, and then discuss what they have read (National Marriage Encounter 1978). Although this kind of intimate sharing of thoughts, feelings, and experiences can be of great benefit to couples, it poses the danger—borne, out in research on the effects of this approach to enrichment—that couples will become disillusioned and frustrated when they are unable to experience this intimacy in the press of daily life (Doherty, McCabe, and Ryder 1978; DeYoung 1979; Doherty and Lester 1982). Couples are left with the heavy expectation that for their spiritual well-being they should not only have daily dialogue with God but also meaningful dialogue with the marital partner. (Parents also live with the responsibility for having "quality" time with their children.) Commitment is no longer enough; we are supposed to be on a perpetual interpersonal "high" in our marital relationship. Inevitably, doubts arise. "What's wrong with our marriage that we go for days without having a single, intimate, meaningful, soul-searching conversation?" When these days stretch into weeks or months, despair is almost inevitable.

From this perspective, our attempts to help strengthen marriage and family relationships may serve only to increase the stress and at times precipitate crises in already overloaded families. Doherty and Lester

(1982) have reported that ten years after participating in Marriage
Encounter, 19 percent of the couples reported more frustration because
of awareness of unmet needs, 14 percent reported conflict over Marriage Encounter itself, and 9 percent reported greater discomfort in
discussing feelings with their spouses. Similar findings might be suspected from other such family ministry programs, although the research
examining these factors of disillusionment and frustration has not been
conducted. (See D. S. R. Garland 1983 for a comprehensive review of
this research.)

One problem, then, with all the attention given to marital relationships is that people begin to expect to live day in and day out with one
another in an emotional hothouse modeled on the empathic listening,
sharing of self, and collapse of individual boundaries that they may have
experienced in a marriage retreat or similar program provided by those
intending to enhance marital relationships. Certainly these programs
have been a great help to many couples, but they must be balanced with
two guidelines. First, days will come—most days—when marriage partners will not experience this level of intimacy with each other, and these
days may at times stretch into longer periods of relative distance—"dry
spells." Second, this is to be expected because, as important as it is, the
marriage is not the most important relationship in life, and our attention cannot always be primarily given to our marriages. In addition to
the inevitable failure that results when the marital relationship is made
the primary relationship of life, the spiritual significance of doing this
needs to be examined. David Elkind writes perceptively:

> [People] want something permanent and beautiful to believe in. The
> current escalating divorce rate reflects, at least in part, this search. Just as
> the child gives up a succession of heroes because he or she discovers each
> of the hero's faults, people today are willing to give up marriage if the
> partner is not perfect. In effect, therefore, the search for the God-like
> person who will be perfect in every way has shifted from the church to
> the family. Partners now seek in their mates the qualities once sought in
> God. . . . Among the stresses of contemporary marriages are the tremen-
> dous demands that were once fulfilled by a vital belief in God. (Elkind
> 1981, 102)

Put more bluntly, the emphasis on marriage is dangerously close to
becoming idolatry of marriage. Clinebell and Clinebell (1970, 205)
define family idolatry as "families who treat themselves as their own
objects of ultimate concern." The primary relationship of our life is our
relationship with God, not with our marital partner. Yet many couples
enter marriage thinking that in this way they can escape their aloneness
(Napier 1980) and implicitly that they can escape their need for God.
This does not mean that Christians are not to be concerned with

marital communication and intimacy, but that these are not goals in and of themselves. Marriage is not ultimate. The Bible keeps marriage in proper perspective; it deals with it almost incidentally. It recognizes that marriage is an institution of this world that does not carry over to the next (Mark 12:25). It is not an end in itself. In marriage, the two are to become one flesh, but flesh is one of those things that are passing away (1 Cor. 15:50). Jesus clearly recognized that the obedience to the kingdom might necessitate leaving wives and families (Luke 18:29). Some will be eunuchs for the sake of the kingdom of heaven (Matt. 19:12). Paul was not anti-marriage, as some of his interpreters have unfairly labeled him, but he did recognize that devotion to the spouse was secondary to devotion to the Lord. Certainly the husband and wife are to be anxious to please each other (1 Cor. 7:33–34), but what is primary is undivided loyalty to the Lord (1 Cor. 7:35). Marriage, as an institution of this world, is something destined to pass offstage (1 Cor. 7:31).

As a consequence, the marital relationship for Christians involves two dynamics, neither of which can be ignored. The vertical dynamic is the relationship of each partner individually with God and their calling to ministry as partners. The horizontal dynamic is the relationship of partners with each other. It is their need to care and be cared for, to share joys and sorrows, to be intimate with another, and to accept and feel acceptance. This dynamic enhances their ability to go out from a home base of acceptance and love into the service and sacrifice for which they are called.

Myth No. 4: An ideal marriage for Christians is one in which the partners can talk endlessly about their relationship with each other.

It is wonderful, of course, for marital couples to be able to share their deepest hurts and longings, their most profound joy and appreciation of each other. Wonderful, but not the ultimate goal in marriage. In many cultures, a husband and wife would not dare to share this kind of intimate knowledge of themselves with a member of the opposite sex, including their spouse, yet they may consider their marriage to be fulfilling and perhaps "ideal." A serious risk lurks in American culture to take research that identifies the characteristics of "healthy" marital relating (as opposed to couples having difficulties and consequently in marriage counseling) and turn these characteristics—derived from white middle-class American couples—into what is ideal. This is a mistaken use of psychology, not only when such findings are applied to population groups other than middle-class Americans but even when applied to the couples involved in the study. It is unsound because it is based on the faulty premise that characteristics associated with psychological or interpersonal health are the same thing as the ideal, the goal for which to strive. By analogy, people who are in excellent physical shape are found to need less sleep than those who are sedentary and overweight. To conclude from this that one can achieve better physical well-being by sleeping less is fallacious. We would hardly make less sleep an ideal of physical health. A similar logic is applied to the goal of marriage using characteristics associated with marital health. One must be mindful that interpersonal relationship factors that are correlated with marital health nevertheless may be useful tools for developing greater intimacy and companionship among partners. But they are not in and of themselves ultimately valuable and should not be considered as a description of the ideal marital relationship.

If clear communication, good conflict management skills, and mutually agreed-on roles are not the ideal, what, then, is the ideal for Christians in marriage? The Bible makes clear that marriage is part of God's created order (Gen. 1:27–28). It has existed from the beginning, when God said, "It is not good that the man should be alone" (Gen. 2:18). Persons have a deep-seated need for relationships with others. Many feel an essential incompleteness as solitary beings (see 1 Cor. 11:11–12), and so they seek out another who, they hope, will become a source of wholeness, tranquillity, and joy. When the Bible speaks of the two becoming one flesh, it might be suggested that "only the two together can be thought of as fully one" (see Hoskyns and Davey 1981, 241). So it was that man was given a companion with whom he could become intimate. But in the creation narratives, God never told Adam and Eve to sit down, knee to knee, and look meaningfully into each other's eyes. He gave them—us—work to do. This keeps the marriage relationship from becoming an end in itself.

If we can use Christ's relationship with the church as an example of the marriage relationship (Eph. 5:32), we find that Christ did not love the church and give himself up for her only to have intimate fellowship and forever to stroll together through the garden while the dew is still on the roses. Christ nourishes and cherishes the church in order that, through it and its mission, "the manifold wisdom of God might now be made known to the principalities and powers in the heavenly places" (Eph. 3:10).

Similarly, Jesus did not say, "Come sit down with me and rest under a shade tree." Instead, he offered us a share of his work load. He offered a yoke, not a chaise lounge on which to repose (Matt. 11:28). In the same way, marriage is not a retreat into intimacy with another away from the rest of the world. Instead, partners have committed themselves to work together in a joint task set before them by God. The Clinebells state the importance of a joint task for marriage well:

"Spiritual growth in marriage occurs as the couple become co-creators of newness" (Clinebell and Clinebell 1970, 197).

In the social sciences, a fundamental principle in the study of human groups has been the need to attend to both the purposes of the group —its tasks—and the relationships of the members—building community and dealing with interpersonal conflict. Without attention to the relationships of the members, the group's tasks are often not accomplished because of unresolved conflicts, hidden interpersonal agenda, and confusion about even the definition of the task. Without attention to the group's tasks, however, the group may dissolve in frustration and resentment over its purposelessness and lack of direction. These two dynamics—the group's work and the relationships between members —are interdependent. The current focus of ministry with marital couples is in peril of ignoring the significance of a common task in marriage that gives direction and meaning to the interpersonal relationship. For example, marriage enrichment programs may concentrate solely on developing more effective communication between partners, including listening to one's partner and sharing of self one with the other. Handling conflict, sexuality, and marital roles may also be addressed. While these things are important, the question of the meaning of the marriage, its ultimate function, is often not even asked, much less answered.

In Erikson's stages of individual development, the task during the early adult years is intimacy. Erikson was describing the development of individuals, not marriages, so his work must be used with caution. Nevertheless, an important parallel exists between individual development and the development of a marital relationship. The stage of intimacy, learning to share the self with another, is significant, yet only one stage in the path of growth. In our understanding of marriage, however, we appear to have become stuck here. The next stage of growth is generativity, the transcendence of self in the rearing of children or the accomplishment of other life-centering tasks (Erikson 1968). One cannot move to the stage of generativity without developing intimacy, but intimacy is not an end in itself.

It is often stated that the couple, the dyad, is the basic unit of society, and that the purpose of marriage is for two people to meet each other's needs for intimacy and companionship. Several family theorists, however, are operating on another premise, that the triad is the basic interpersonal unit. Bowen states that "the triangle, a three-person emotional configuration, is the molecule or the basic building block of any emotional system, whether it is in the family or any other group. The triangle is the smallest stable relationship system" (Bowen 1976c, 75–76). Unfortunately, since this concept was developed in the study of troubled families, family theorists usually identify the triangle of interpersonal relating as though it operates only dysfunctionally. An example of this kind of dysfunctional triangle would be parents who channel their anger at each other into conflicting demands on their child. The process of "triangling," however, occurs in all interpersonal relationships, including well-functioning marriages. As we talk with each other, the two of us tend to draw in a third—a person or a task that we discuss. In this way, we form a triangle with that person or task, even though the third party is not even present. When we work out our differences, usually we bring in our relationship with a third person: "That isn't the way my dad did it" or "We need to work out a different way of handling our anger that will be a good example for the kids." Dad and the kids have been a part of our relationship without even being present. Guerin says:

> Think of your best functioning personal relationship. Now imagine isolating that relationship in time and space. Having done that, imagine attempting to confine all communication to personal thoughts and feelings about your own self and the other. It won't be long before you are talking about the Mets, Aunt Suzie, or somebody or something else. The process in the relationship has moved to stabilize itself by triangulating in a third person and/or object. (Guerin 1976, 484–485)

"You-me talk," the discussion of our thoughts and feelings about each other that excludes other topics and persons, is emotionally highly charged and cannot be maintained over a period of time. Sadly, many couples see the inability to maintain that level of relationship intensity as an indication that their relationship is less than adequate. This expectation may inadvertently be encouraged by programs designed to improve marital communication. Spouses do need to talk together about thoughts and feelings regarding their relationship; but they also need to discuss their children, their work, their parents.

We would suggest, then, that there is an optimum amount of couple relating (that which focuses on us), and that there is a curvilinear relationship between marital well-being and "you-me talk." (See Figure 1.) Not enough focus on our interpersonal relationship is dysfunctional, but so is too much. Said another way, too much reflection on our joint navels can be just as unhealthy as too little.

One might compare a marriage that is concerned only with itself to a church that ministers only to its own members, neglecting others outside and concentrating on building bigger and better barnlike sanctuaries with recreational facilities that rival the YMCA. Both a church and a marriage that place all the emphasis on "us" have misconceived and strayed from their purposes. When the marriage relationship becomes turned in on itself, it is unable to gain a clarity of purpose that comes from moving outside its own system. Even though the spouses are involved in their work and friendships outside the marriage, they may have difficulty using these experiences to expand the marital relationship itself. If the relationship becomes closed to outside involvement, it will die from starvation of purpose.

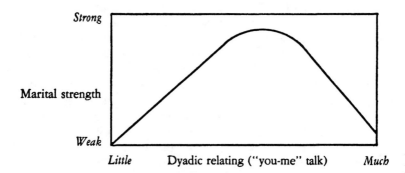

Figure 1. The relationship between dyadic relating
and marital strength

It is impossible to separate what comes first, the overemphasis on the couple or the downward spiral of alienation from each other. Often couples experiencing difficulty seem caught in a pattern in which every mood, every comment, every stray look is personalized and taken as a commentary on the marital relationship. When the wife comes home after her carefully prepared proposal was rejected by the boss, and after being stopped for speeding, to find that the neighbor's dog has torn up the front flower bed, she may well slam through the door muttering to herself. Her husband reacts. "What are you mad at me for now?" She yells, "Nothing! Just leave me alone!" Not reassured, he responds with anger. "Sure, you bet! Who could get near you? No matter what I do, it's wrong." She snaps back, "All you can think about is yourself. If you could just care about me for a change." She has not told him why or how she needs care. He has not attempted to find out why she is upset. Both have focused only on their relationship: if you are angry, it must be at me; if I am hurting, it is because you have not done anything to make me feel better. They only see themselves and the marital relationship. They do not recognize the influence of other relationships on their marriage—the inevitable and beneficial ones as well as the stressful relationships with work and neighbors.

The triadic pattern is suggested in the two primary covenants understood by Karl Barth, the "vertical" covenant with God and the "horizontal" covenant with neighbor (used in McLean 1984). Barth's understanding of two covenants causes a great deal of trouble, however, because the interrelationship between them is lost. The three elements —self, neighbor (in this case, spouse), and God—must be envisioned in a stable state as a triangle. We have come close to this concept in our marriage manual triangles, with God on the top point and husband and wife forming the base points, but this is more a recognition that the marriage is "under God" and subject to biblical teachings than a relational diagram. We believe, however, that our relationship with our spouse takes on meaning only as it transcends itself in relationship with God and God's purposes. Our relationship with God has substance only when we move beyond into service to neighbor/spouse.

The marital covenant, therefore, is based on the triangle of husband, wife, and their commitment to a joint task. One source of instability in marriages is the exclusive attention to the couple that ignores the importance of their joint task. The problem of the wife's putting the husband through school and his outgrowing her was the expression of this problem in the 50s and 60s. "He outgrew her" meant that the life activities from which he derived meaning no longer included her. They did not share what was important to each that was *outside* the marriage. One latent motivation for women to enter careers may be the search not only for personal fulfillment but also for restoration of meaning, the task and purpose, lost from the marriage relationship.

A career or joint work cannot alone be identified with the totality of the "calling" of a marital couple to a task beyond themselves. Most of us are familiar with the problem of workaholism and the confusion of work and career with meaning in life. Work may be a part of this calling, but God's purposes for us are larger. We are called to care for God's creation and to be companions to one another (Gen. 1:28; 2:18). That which goes on between us and that which pulls us outward are both in tension with each other and interdependent.

These tasks will be explored in the remaining chapters of the book. Chapters 2 through 4 look at our call to the task of caring for God's creation. In chapters 2 and 3, the biblical and sociological issues of roles and power in marriage are discussed. Chapter 4 explores further what it means to couples to be called by God to a joint work. Chapters 5 through 7 look at our call to the task of companionship, discussing the functions of anger and conflict in marriage (chapter 5), sexuality and intimacy (chapter 6), and divorce (chapter 7).

The premises of this first chapter underlie all that will be said in this book. In summary, they are:

1. No single model of marriage exists for Christians applicable in all times and all places. This book was written to provide help for today's American couples and those who minister with them; it addresses the questions that they bring to the scripture and, sometimes,

to the counselor. For that reason, this book is not a comprehensive model of marriage for all Christians.

2. No amount of hard work and determination can assure a happy marriage. Some forces at work in marriage are outside the power of spouses to control. Implicit in the ideal of marriage as created by God is the need for God's grace.

3. Marriage is not the most important relationship in life. Our most important relationship is with God, and we grow in that relationship through relating to our neighbors, including our spouse.

4. An ideal for marriage includes not only communion with each other (whatever that may mean in any given relationship) but also a joint commitment to God's purposes that transcend the earthly institution of marriage.

Some limitations should be clear. This book does not provide how-to hints for couples searching for guidance with problems such as destructive conflict patterns, sexual difficulties, or divorce. Instead, we attempt to provide a biblical and cultural perspective on the issues and problems that couples face to provide a helpful context in which to attempt problem-solving and evaluation of the marital relationship.

This book is not comprehensive; much more can (and has) been said about every one of the topics discussed. We have chosen to highlight some of the prevalent themes in understanding marriage in our Christian context embedded in American culture and to challenge them.

Finally, even though this book incorporates social science research and theory in the discussion of marriage, it does not attempt to be objective or value free, as is often expected in scientific discussion. The book is primarily an exploration of Christian beliefs and values about marriage. We have not only defined what these are but have also argued for particular value-based responses to the topics discussed. In so doing, we have described research and theory from the social sciences that are relevant and shed light on the issues. We believe that this is an acceptable approach to the use of the social sciences as long as we acknowledge that this is what we are doing and that others may interpret the implications of social science research differently. God continues to be revealed to us through the world that is still in the process of creation. The sciences are one source of perception of this ongoing revelation about ourselves and our Creator.

2

Biblical Perspectives
on Marital Roles

The first myth named in chapter 1 was the belief that one pattern of marriage is right for all time and all people. In that discussion, we mentioned the importance of cultural context in understanding patterns of marriage and described briefly the variety of marriage forms that can be found even in the Bible. This of course does not imply that anything goes for Christians in marriage; the Bible does speak to the nature of the relationship between men and women and should influence any form marriage may take for Christians in a particular cultural context.

A volatile issue in the church today revolves around what the Bible says to us about the basic relationship between husband and wife. Is it ordained by God that man is to outrank his wife and that her role requires complaisant submission to his authority? Or is the relationship between husband and wife to be one of partnership so that they not only stand together on an equal footing before God (Gal. 3:28) but also are to relate to one another as equals? In an age of choices and a variety of alternative marital forms, many Christian spouses have struggled to discern the biblical message about marriage. This chapter is an examination of the key biblical passages that bear on the topic of the husband-wife relationship. Before turning to the biblical texts, we will survey briefly the current debate about the proper roles for men and women in marriage.

Marriage as Chain of Command or Equal Partnership?

One of the most popular teachings about the relationship between man and woman has alleged that man is the woman's "head" and that she is forever to submit to his authority. Bill Gothard, an ardent proponent of this view, estimated in 1977 that over a million people had attended his seminars (Bayly 1977). Gothard's platform is that the husband is God's hammer and his wife is the chisel; by the action of the hammer on the chisel, the children (considered diamonds in the rough) are shaped. The passivity of the chisel as opposed to the activity of the hammer makes clear the wife's subordinate role in the home (Mollenkott 1977). Using a military analogy, Gothard contends that the family ought to be ordered by a chain of command in which everyone in the home is under authority, and that God deals with family members through these channels of authority. This authority is not considered domination so much as protection. When persons get out from under this "authoritative umbrella," they expose themselves to unnecessary temptations that they are too weak to overcome. In other words, the husband's authority protects the woman from Satan (Howell 1979).

> "Before the fall," says Gothard, "Eve had a different relationship. Satan came directly to Eve instead of through Adam. When the woman was beguiled, God put a restriction on her. 'Thy desire shall be to thy husband, and he shall rule over thee' (Gen. 3:16). But this restriction was for her own protection. Now Satan can no longer get through to her unless he goes through the husband." (Bockelman 1976, 74)

Many others, including women, espouse this kind of hierarchical relationship. Maxine Hancock writes that the husband's judgment is the absolute norm for the wife: We do not submit to our husbands because they are gentle and kind, or good, or godly, but because they are our husbands (Hancock 1975, 38). Judith Miles has stated that women are "in-carnate models of submission and loyalty" (Miles 1975, 151). She argues that it is through the woman's submission that the man learns how to submit himself to God. Even though a man has thoroughly corrupted his potential to be an image of God, the godly wife is still to submit to him, and her submission to him is to be a model of the kind of relationship that he is to have with God. In a revealing passage, she describes how this view influenced her own marriage:

> One day this familiar verse acquired a heightened meaning for me, "Wives be subject to your husbands, as to the Lord" (Eph. 5:22). It could not mean *that!* Not as to *the Lord!* But here it was. I was to treat my own human husband as though *he* were the Lord, resident in our own humble home. This was truly revelatory to me. Would I ask Jesus a basically maternal question such as "how are things at the office?" Would I suggest to Jesus that he finish some task around the house? Would I remind the Lord that he was not driving prudently? Would I ever be in judgment over my Lord, over His taste, His opinions, or His actions? I was stunned—stunned into a new kind of submission. (Miles 1975, 44)

This kind of teaching can easily lead to an idolatrous submission to the husband. Marabel Morgan verges on this in her best-seller *The Total*

Woman when she writes, "It is only when a woman surrenders her life to her husband, reveres and worships him, and is willing to serve him, that she becomes really beautiful to him" (Morgan 1975, 96–97). *The Total Woman* has been taught as gospel in churches for a decade and has convinced many. Others (Foh 1979; Hurley 1981) who view submission of the wife and headship of the husband as divinely ordained find some of the popularized statements of the position extreme; they make more moderate applications from the same theological presuppositions about the biblical texts.

The supremacy of the husband has been taken for granted by the male-dominated church for centuries (see Fiorenza 1984) and has been expounded by notable theologians such as Aquinas, Luther, Calvin, and Barth (see Jewett 1975, 61–82). Only because this position has been challenged by radical changes in our culture and by accompanying changes in attitudes have so many risen to try to defend this traditional hierarchical pattern of the husband-wife relationship.

One of these changes is the increasing number of theologians who call for equal partnership between husband and wife and argue that submission is a mutual responsibility required of both. Both husband and wife are to submit individually to God as sovereign and to place the needs of their spouse above their own. That men and women are to function as equals does not mean that they are to lose their distinctiveness as male and female; instead, they are to complement each other's strengths and challenge each other to growth and change (Clinebell 1973).

Biblical texts have been bandied about to support each point of view, but simply compiling an arsenal of scripture passages does not clinch the argument. As Hull recognizes:

> The dominant fact about this subject is its notorious difficulty. In the face of bristling controversy among Bible believers, it would be folly to assume that any well-intentioned investigator need only open the pages of Scripture, assemble the pertinent texts, and draw the obvious conclusions which they support. Rather we find ourselves in a situation where students of equal scholarship and of equal piety have appealed to the same ultimate Source in defense of incompatible positions. (Hull 1975, 5)

Some have tried to take a mediating approach to avoid argument over which view is right:

> Both [views] have worked well for Christians at different periods of history. So instead of arguing about one being right and the other wrong the best conclusion probably is that a Christian couple may take their choice; but they had better make quite sure, from the beginning, that they are both making the same choice! (Mace and Mace 1976, 30)

Is it, however, simply a matter of a young couple's choosing a pattern of marriage as they would choose a china pattern? If we recognize that a variety of patterns of marriage can be found in the scripture, on what basis do we claim that one pattern is more right than another? In spite of the difficulties and with due respect to those who have struggled with this question before us, we will join the fray and engage the biblical text in an attempt to discern what God's intention is for married couples today.

Male and Female He Created Them

When Jesus was challenged with a question about the grounds for divorce, he responded by citing God's intention for marriage from the beginning (Gen. 1:27; 2:24; Matt. 19:4–6), and the creation account has continued to be a starting point for wrestling with the issues of male and female relatedness. An understanding of husband-wife relationships as hierarchical is derived primarily from the Genesis 2 account. Stitzinger (1981) provides a representative example of this view. He has outlined eight points from Genesis 2 that he thinks prescribe "definitely" and "clearly" a hierarchical role relationship. First, he notes that the man was created before the woman (Gen. 2:7). Second, the man was designated as "Adam," the term used also to describe all humankind. Because the man is given this name rather than the woman suggests to Stitzinger that he occupies the position as head. Third, Adam was given a position of leadership and authority before Eve's creation (Gen. 2:15); he was cultivator and keeper of the garden, and he was the one restricted from eating of the tree (Gen. 2:16–17). Fourth, he exercised his authority without Eve's involvement in the naming of the animals (Gen. 2:19–20). To give a name is to have authority over that which is named. Fifth, his leadership role is clear since it was he who needed a "helper" (Gen. 2:18, 20). God met this need by custom designing a subordinate who would assist him in carrying out God's commands. Sixth, he again exercised authority in designating his helper's name, his first act of rule over her (Gen. 2:23). Seventh, that he is to leave his mother and father and cleave to his new wife (Gen. 2:24) means that he is the one to act, to take initiative, to lead. Finally, the man is the spokesperson for the relationship, since it is he whom the Lord addresses in the garden (Gen. 3:9, 11). Stitzinger concludes that subordination of the woman was a divinely intended part of the created order; it preceded the fall from grace.

Others have interpreted the creation narrative differently. Even if one must resort to the kind of exegesis that marks the approach of Stitzinger to the creation account, it is not difficult to reach other conclusions. Had women been the predominant shapers of theological thought over the centuries instead of males, these conclusions would probably be the prevailing views of today. That man was created prior to woman proves nothing. If we look at creation proceeding in an ascending order of superiority with man as the crowning touch, as in Genesis 1:26, it would follow that woman, created after man, would be foremost. God saved the best for last. The order of the creation of the man and the woman, however, has nothing to do with male authority and female submission. Nor does the fact that the woman was built from the rib of the man. The man was created of the "dust from the ground" (Gen. 2:7), but that does not make him subordinate to the earth; on the contrary, he has power over the earth to till it (Gen. 3:23). By the same token, it would follow that the woman should have power over the man from whom she was taken (Trible 1978, 101).

The arguments about the leadership priority of the man totally ignore Genesis 1:26–31. The use of the plural in these verses indicates that God did not design a hierarchical relationship between the male and female when he created them: "So God created man in his own image, in the image of God he created him; male and female he created them" (Gen. 1:27). He created *them;* he blessed *them* and gave *them* dominion (Gen. 1:28); and in Genesis 5:1–2 he also named *them*. They were created as equals. The man and the woman were intended by God to correspond to each other. The woman was not created simply to be a "helpmeet," as the venerable King James Version has it. The term "helper" suggests in English that one is an assistant and subordinate, but it does not connote inferiority; it is also used in the Old Testament for God who creates and saves Israel (Trible 1978, 90). The key for understanding the meaning of the woman as "helper" is the phrase "fit for him," literally, "opposite to him," or "corresponding to him." This means that she was to be like him, his counterpart, yet at the same time differentiated from him. She was created to be "a partner for him" (NEB). What the man needed was a soul mate, not a servant. This is why the animals, although also helpers, failed to pass muster. He established his supremacy over the animals but failed to find a helper fit for him. In the woman he met his equal, a helper who was not his subordinate but who corresponded to him.

A rabbinic legend accords well with this line of interpretation. It imagined that Adam complained, when all the creatures were paraded before him, "Everyone has a partner, yet I have none." According to the story, this lack was not because of God's oversight but because of God's foresight. He knew that the man would bring charges against the woman (see Gen. 3:12) and therefore did not create her until Adam expressly yearned for her (*Gen. Rab.* 17:4; see also the view of Cassuto 1961, 128). The text in Genesis makes clear that when God saw it was not good for man to be alone, he created for him a companion with whom he could be intimate, not an assistant whom he could dominate. She was formed from him; and immediately he recognized her to be his counterpart: "This at last is bone of my bones and flesh of my flesh" (Gen. 2:23; see B. *Yebam.* 63a). In their union the man and woman supplement each other physically, socially, and spiritually. The woman is a bone-and-flesh mirror image of the man, who remains incomplete without her. It is not insignificant that she was taken from man's side, for she was to be his partner. She is therefore no mere appendage to the man; as one flesh they are a part of each other's being.

Those who see marriage as a chain of command have also argued that the Tempter approached the woman because she was the weaker and more vulnerable. Eve's encouragement to her husband to partake of the fruit is interpreted as an act of insubordination; her sin of disobedience to God was in part her self-assumed position of leadership above her husband. Adam listened to his wife and, by allowing her to have authority over him, sinned in distorting the natural hierarchy. When God came, he called to the man, not the woman, thus placing primary responsibility on him (Gen. 3:9).

If one cares to engage in this kind of psychological exegesis, it is just as logical to argue that the woman was tempted first because she was more sensitive and thoughtful than the man. She, at least, engaged in theological dialogue with the serpent; Adam dumbly accepted the offered fruit ("she gave some to her husband, and he ate," Gen. 3:6). She was beguiled by a creature "more subtle than any other wild creature" (Gen. 3:1, 13); what was Adam's excuse? Was he still groggy from the deep sleep? The order of the temptations does not suggest anything about the vulnerability of the woman or the natural superiority of the man. Both were equally guilty of disobedience to God, and it had nothing to do with violating supposed role assignments.

The key passage for our concerns, however, is Genesis 3:16. The actions of both the man and the woman have corrupted the "very good" of God's creation. Their sin resulted in dire consequences for their relationship: the husband now shall rule over the wife. This new development implies that it was *not* what God had originally determined for their relationship, and Trible points out that the dominance of the husband in 3:16 is *de*scribed, not *pre*scribed (Trible 1973, 41). It is the upshot of their joint disobedience. Brueggemann comments:

> In God's garden, as God wills it, there is *mutuality and equality.* In God's garden now, permeated by distrust, there is *control and distortion.* But that distortion is not for one moment accepted as the will of the Gardener. (Brueggemann 1982, 51).

Seeing the rule of man over woman as a result of sin and viewing the "wholesomeness of the relation between male and female [as] corrupted because we deny our relationship with God" (Achtemeier 1976, 74) makes the hierarchical pattern of marriage something less than God's intention for humanity. For this reason one can hardly appeal to Genesis 2–3 as the biblical warrant for it. If anything, the hierarchical pattern is a perversion of God's intention.

The Household Rules of the New Testament

The pivotal passages in the New Testament for the argument that God has ordained the relationship between husband and wife to be hierarchical are Ephesians 5:22–33, Colossians 3:18–19, Titus 2:4–5, and 1 Peter 3:1–7. In these passages the wife is admonished to be subject to her husband. One must be cautious in interpreting these admonitions and must examine them carefully in light of the historical context that evoked them (largely ignored by those espousing a hierarchical model of marriage).

The first thing to be noted is that each of these injunctions is embedded in larger units that Luther christened *Haustafel*, a list of rules for the household. Generally, they consist of a string of admonitions to family members, wives and husbands, children and parents, slaves and masters. Parallels to these lists of duties have been noted in Stoic moral philosophy, Hellenistic Judaism, and Aristotelian political thought; consequently, competing theories exist about the precise background of the household rules in the New Testament. Nevertheless, studies have shown how the household rules were formulated in conformity to the conventional ideals of the ancient world. Rordorf reflects the consensus of scholarly opinion:

> These lists of domestic duties reflect the social structures and the rules of good conduct of their age. The Christian message is not interested in changing them. Rather it teaches the Christian to live "in the Lord" within the ordinary framework of his culture. (Rordorf, 1969, 198)

In the first century, the ordinary framework of culture accorded great and unquestioned power to the father and the husband (see Leipoldt 1962). Consequently, "the predominance of the husband was part of the cultural environment of the early Christians, not one of their creations" (Rordorf, 1969, 200). Often cited is the opinion of Plutarch in his *Advice to Bride and Groom:*

> . . . if they [wives] subordinate themselves to their husbands, they are commended, but if they want to have control, they cut a sorrier figure than the subjects of their control. And control ought to be exercised by the man over the woman, not as the owner has control of a piece of property, but as the soul controls the body, by entering into her feelings and being knit to her through goodwill. As, therefore, it is possible to exercise care over

the body without being a slave to its pleasures and desires, so it is possible to govern a wife, and at the same time delight and gratify her. (142E; see also Martial, *Epigrams* 8.12)

In Hellenistic Judaism this idea was expressed more heavy-handedly by Philo of Alexandria: "Wives must be in servitude to their husbands, a servitude not imposed by violent ill-treatment but promoting obedience in all things" *(Hypothetica* 7.3). In the same vein Josephus wrote, "The woman it [the Law] says, is in all things inferior to the man. Let her accordingly be obedient, not for her humiliation, but that she may be directed; for the authority has been given by God to the man" *(Against Apion* 2.201).

Although it would seem to be the case that the lists of duties in the New Testament reflect the conventional tried-and-true wisdom of how members of a household are to relate properly to one another, the New Testament writers did not simply siphon off this worldly wisdom without discrimination or purpose. The duties were modified by Christian perceptions and recast to speak to particular needs in the Christian communities. They have been influenced by the Old Testament and have been qualified by a distinctive Christian motivation. These things were to be done "in the Lord" (Eph. 5:22; 6:1,5,6,7; Col. 3:18, 20,22,23; 1 Peter 3:4). Nor is it the case in the New Testament that certain members have rights and others duties. The lists of duties normally occur in pairs and are considered reciprocal. Consequently, when we examine these passages we can expect to find reflections of the way things were between husbands and wives in the ancient world from centuries of cultural conditioning, but we can also expect to find flashes of a distinctively Christian vision of the way things ought to be between husbands and wives that transcends cultural conditions.

The question of why the domestic codes are found in the New Testament at all is another issue. They were not designed to provide a theological justification for the existing social order from a Christian perspective. The New Testament authors were motivated on the one hand by a desire to conciliate public opinion; on the other, they aimed to induce Christians to lead irreproachable lives as a witness to heathens: when they see the reverent and chaste behavior of their wives, husbands might be won to the Lord (1 Peter 3:1-2).

The early Christians wished to avoid being vilified as a politically or socially revolutionary movement. They were not intent on revamping the social order. There was an apparent need, however, to quench the excesses of fanatics and mystagogues who, swept away by their new-found freedom and equality in Christ, breached the conventions of society in such ways as to bring discredit to the name of Christ and even to miss the mark of Christian calling. Owing to an uncontrolled spiritism, some tried to make changes too fast and often ended by going too far in upsetting the conventions of the social order. Marriage relationships were undermined. The duties of family life were being disregarded. Sexual decorum was ignored in public settings (1 Cor. 11: 2–16).

The early Christians were concerned with being well thought of by outsiders (see 1 Cor. 10:32; 14:23; 2 Cor. 8:21; 1 Thess. 4:12; 1 Tim. 3:7). Since the patriarchal order of the household was widely believed to underpin the stability of society, they attempted to rein in the enthusiasts so as not to be lumped together with other Oriental religions that were blamed for sapping the foundations of this order. This can be seen clearly from Titus 2:5: wives are to be subject to their husbands, *"that the word of God may not be discredited"* (emphasis added). Hoskyns summarizes the situation well:

> What we may forget is that in all these instances, "subjection" is the alternative not to more liberal conceptions of the relations between husband and wife, parents and children, employers and employees but to wholesale repudiation of those relationships by men and women carried away by the demands of the gospel. These injunctions originated in a situation in which marriage bonds were being disregarded, families broken up, and social or economic obligations ignored, in the belief that only so could Christ's calling be given the priority it deserved. (Hoskyns and Davey 1981, 352).

In Colossians 3:18 we find a rejoinder to this impatience with the restraints of society that seemed to curb the newfound freedom and equality in Christ. The wife's submission to her husband was "fitting," "proper," not only according to society's expectations but also "in the Lord." It would be dangerous, however, to think that this state of affairs was intended to be permanent or that it should be eternalized. Ideas about what is fitting have changed across the centuries as the gospel has moved across lands and cultures. As societal pressures changed, for example, the leaven of the gospel permeated and slowly altered Christian attitudes toward the institution of slavery. The same thing should be said for the view of the hierarchical subordination of the wife in the marriage relationship. We can see this leaven already beginning to transform the attitude toward the relationship of husband and wife in the New Testament. Even though we read that the wife is exhorted to be submissive to her husband, when the commands to the husband are carefully studied we see that his role is not that of overlord. The call to love his wife as his body and as Christ loves his church, and to bestow honor on her as a coheir of the grace of life, entails a submission on the part of the husband. The Christian ideal of marriage is not hierarchy, in which the husband is to rule the roost and the wife is born to submission. To interpret the New Testament as such is, to our mind, to pervert the truth of the gospel proclaimed by Jesus Christ, who treated tax collectors and Pharisees, prostitutes and pietists, maimed and whole, slaves and free, rich and poor, males and females as equals.

Ephesians 5:22–33

The section of household rules in Ephesians begins with instructions to wives and husbands. Many have tended to read this passage as if only the first three verses were important. They are satisfied that the gist of what husband-wife relations are to be is found here—the husband is to be the head and the wife is to be subject in everything. Some readers have concluded from this that the wife is to heed the husband's rebukes, obey his commands, fulfill his desires, and follow his lead in all things. But when one reads the text without patriarchal blinders, a different picture emerges. The ideal is not masculine rule and feminine compliance but mutual surrender in commitment to Christ and to the needs of others.

Instructions to the wife. In Ephesians 5:22, the wife is instructed to be subject to her husband as to the Lord. Actually, no verb occurs in the Greek text of verse 22. It reads, literally, "Wives to your own husbands as to the Lord." The verb "be subject" must then be supplied from 5:21: "be subject to one another out of reverence for Christ." This verb is also found in 5:24, "As the church is subject to Christ, so let wives also be subject in everything to their husbands." A number of things require our attention.

The first is the implication of the fact that the verb "be subject" *(hypotassomai)* is never used specifically with wives as the subject. In 5:22, the reader is consequently required to refer back to 5:21 to supply the verb. Although it is possible grammatically for verse 21 to begin the new section with the domestic code, it is more probable that it completes the thought begun in 5:18b. The readers are challenged to "be filled with the Spirit, addressing one another in psalms and hymns and spiritual songs, singing and making melody to the Lord with all your heart, always and for everything giving thanks in the name of our Lord Jesus Christ to God the Father. Be subject to one another out of reverence for Christ" (5:18b–21). Since 5:22 must be read in light of 5:21, the notion of the wives' subjection is transformed. It is not simply a demand for the wife to assume her divinely ordained role of underling. Her submission to the husband must be viewed as part and parcel of the Christian calling. Mutual submission is evidence of being filled with the Spirit and is expected of everyone regardless of age, station, or gender. All Christians are to be subject to one another in the fear of Christ (see also 1 Peter 5:5; *1 Clement* 38.1).

This exhortation to be subject to one another reiterates a theme found throughout the teaching of both Paul and Jesus that Christians have been called to serve others and not to assert their own rights (see Rom. 12:18b; 15:1–3; 1 Cor. 10:33–11:1; Gal. 5:13; Phil. 2:3–4; and Matt. 23:11–12; Mark 10:42–45; John 13:14–15). What is obligatory for Christians is an unconditional surrender of self that mirrors that of Christ (see Eph. 4:32). Personal interests are to be subordinated for the sake of others, but that does not make a person subordinate in the kingdom of God. Others are to be considered better than oneself, but that does not mean that one is inferior to others; it means that those in Christ are to seek first the welfare and interests of others and to do nothing from selfishness (Phil. 2:3–4). The call to be submissive to others is therefore similar to the call to be humble (Eph. 4:1–3). This basic truth must color how one interprets the subjection of the wife in Ephesians in 5:22. If all Christians are to be subject to one another, the wife's subjection to her husband is not some role unique only to her in God's scheme of things.

A second thing to be noted about verse 22 is that the word "obey" is *not* used, and the King James Version has erroneously introduced it into its translation. In the continuation of the household rules, children are instructed to obey their parents (6:1), and slaves are told to obey their masters (6:5), but wives are not commanded to obey their husbands. That leaves us to ponder the role of children and slaves, but those are other issues. What is pertinent is that the wife is not asked to be servile before her husband or to knuckle under to his will. She is not the husband's vassal, and marriage is not servitude for the wife.

A third point is that wives are to be subject to their husbands *as to the Lord*. This does not mean that they are to be subject as if their husbands were their lords, for this would require the plural, "as to their lords." The husband is not the wife's lord or savior (5:23), and she is not to genuflect before him. Nor does this mean that the husband somehow becomes the representative of Christ for her, or that her submission to him is an occasion for demonstrating her allegiance to Christ, as is the case with the slaves' submission to their masters (Eph. 6:7; Col. 3:23; see Barth 1974, 612). "As to the Lord" has to do instead with the motivation of her submission. We are responsible to Christ in all aspects of life, including the intimacy of marriage (Friedrich 1977, 58), and the wife's commitment to Christ is therefore to be the ground of her commitment to her husband. What is interesting is that nothing is said about the wife's complying with the natural order of things in the universe, which was an argument appealed to by other writers in the ancient world (see Schweizer 1983, 216). The wife's voluntary submission to her husband simply reflects her calling (and every Christian's calling) to relate to others by Christ's standard of love and humility.

Instructions to the husband. Far more is demanded of the husband in Ephesians 5:25–33 as "the head" of his spouse. This no doubt is because in the cultural context the husband had far greater power and autonomy. The commands directed to the husband are clear, but what it means for him to be designated as "head" is less clear.

The headship of the man is mentioned also in 1 Corinthians 11:3, "But I want you to understand that the head of every man is Christ, the head of every woman is her husband, and the head of Christ is God." The meaning of "head" in this passage is not "chief" or "ruler" but "source" or "origin" (see Bruce 1971, 103; Bedale 1954, 211–212). That Christ is head of every man means that he was the source of every man's existence as the agent of creation (see 1 Cor. 8:6; Col. 1:16). By the same token, according to the creation account in Genesis 2 (alluded to in 1 Cor. 11:8, 12), man was the source of woman's existence. She was called wo-man because she was made from man. Now, Paul pointed out, men and women are interdependent since "man is now born of woman" (1 Cor. 11:11–12). Finally, the source of Christ was God, since all things are from God. This concept of headship as source is therefore not a real parallel to Ephesians 5:23. Paul was not dealing with marriage and the relationship between husband and wife in 1 Corinthians but with problems that had emerged in the community's worship surrounding issues of the differences between male and female. For this reason, Paul appealed to the creation accounts, which affirm that man was created male and female.

To understand what is meant by the phrase in Ephesians 5:23 that "the head of the wife as Christ is the head of the church," one must turn to Ephesians itself. The headship of the husband is carefully qualified. He is the head of the wife *in the same way* that Christ is the head of the church. The term "head" was used earlier in 1:22 and 4:15 to describe Christ. It was asserted in 1:22 that Christ is head over all things, but he is head over all things *for* the church. The headship of Christ is a source of life and vitality for the church. The head fills the body with its fullness (1:23). It is the source of the body's development and growth (4:15–16), and in Colossians 2:19 the head is said to nourish the body. In Ephesians 5:23, Christ as head of the church saves his body. This is where the analogy between the husband as head of his wife and Christ as head of his church breaks down, since the husband is no more able to save his wife than himself. The husband as head of his wife, however, *is* able to nurture his wife, his body (5:28). It is precisely this idea that is pursued in verse 29. The husband as head is to nourish and cherish his wife, his body, just as Christ does the church, his body.

The passage as a whole was therefore not intended to set out the order of preeminence in the marriage relationship but to show how the husband was supposed to relate to his wife. Christ does not relate to his church as an Oriental potentate tyrannizing his subjects or a five-star general domineering over buck privates. Instead, he nourishes, cherishes, and loves. In our culture, in which marriage is idealized as the caring for and emotional nurturing of each other, this expectation seems unnecessary. In the cultural context of Ephesians, however, this expectation was revolutionary. Marriage was not centered on the emotional and spiritual nurturing of each other; wives were considered by many to be property, inferiors with whom some husbands would rarely even converse.

If the husband was to be the head of his wife as Christ is head of his church, he was to love his wife *just as* Christ loves his church (see Eph. 5:2). It was certainly nothing new to tell the husbands to love their wives, but this love is given a new dimension when the standard is Christ's love for his people. The husband was to learn how he was to love his wife from the concrete example of how Christ expressed his love. Christ gave himself up in behalf of his church (see Gal. 2:20; Phil. 2:6–11), which was precisely how he became the head of it. He did this, according to Ephesians 5:26–27, that he might sanctify her and present her spotless and glorious before his throne—that she might be holy and blameless. It was a love that aspired to what was best for the beloved. Christ loved through his sacrifice; he was willing to pay the supreme cost and cherish the beloved even when she was unworthy of that love (Rom. 5:8). He loved without conditions. He experienced the failings of the beloved and yet gave of himself to overcome them. This is the kind of love that the husband is expected to have for his wife, and it is an awesome demand without parallel in the ancient world.

The conclusion is reached in 5:28: "Even so husbands should love their wives as their own bodies." Again, the example is Christ. *Just as* Christ nourishes and cherishes the church, his body (5:29–30), so must the husband nourish and cherish his wife. It is not that the husband is to love his wife as he loves his own body, but he is to love her *as* his body. She *is* his body. As one flesh (5:31), the two have become a part of each other. With this statement the dichotomy of superior/inferior is erased completely. This is not subordination but identification (Caird 1976, 89). The relationship of love regards the spouse as an equal, and any chain of command authority is destroyed.

Since the emphasis on one flesh is the climax of the argument, it deserves attention. The first thing we should clarify is that becoming one flesh does not imply that in marriage the husband and wife "become an amalgamation in which the identity of the constituents is swallowed up and lost in an undifferentiated unity" (Bailey 1952, 44). Each retains individual identity, but each person is strengthened and enlarged by the new life together.

More significant, however, is the fact that the quotation comes from Genesis 2:24 and thereby refers back to the original state of things between man and wife. As noted earlier, Jesus quoted this verse to repudiate the evolution of divorce that was permitted by Moses because of man's hardness of heart. Divorce was not God's intention from the beginning, for he had joined the two together into one flesh (Matt. 19:4–8). After the fall, however, the relationship between husband and wife was disfigured by their sin. Hardness of heart took root: "Your husband . . . shall rule over you" (Gen. 3:16). Dominance and subservience, and eventually divorce, where the husband had the absolute power to dispose of his wife whenever he wished, became normative, even though this was not God's desire for marriage in creation. Christ, however, has reversed the consequences of the fall (see Rom. 5:1–21). Those who were dead in their sin have been made alive in Christ (Eph. 2:5). We are new creations, created in Christ Jesus for new works (Eph. 2:10). As Christ's death and resurrection made possible the reconciliation of Jew and Gentile, begetting in himself one new humanity and putting to death enmity and effecting peace, so it is also the case between husband and wife (Stauffer 1964, 1:648). The relationship between husband and wife is restored in accordance with the intention of the Creator. In Christ the old tensions are resolved and the marriage relationship acquires a new norm—no longer antagonism and rule but union and equality as God intended from the beginning. The dominance/subservience pattern has passed away; a new order has come into being. The touchstone of the husband's relationship to his wife is now to be Christ's sacrificial nurturing love for his people.

It is clear from these instructions to the husband that he is not authorized to lord it over his wife. It is the pagans who lord it over one another; it is not to be so among you, Jesus warned (Matt. 20:25–26). If Christ is the husband's model, he must seek out ways to give himself up for his spouse, not give himself airs as the head of the spouse. The husband's own example of sacrifical *submissive* love is to elicit whatever submission the wife entrusts to him. If the wife's submission is to be likened to that of the church to Christ (Eph. 5:24), it is a "submission to redemption and redemptive love" (Quesnell 1968, 354). It is to be inspired and can never be demanded. Ephesians 5 therefore characterizes marriage as "an experience of surrender without absorption, of service without compulsion, of love without conditions" (Richardson 1958, 258) for both the husband and the wife. The Christian marriage is to be distinguished by partnership.

1 Peter 3:1-7

The injunctions to wives in 1 Peter 3:1–6 need to be understood in light of their context in the epistle as well as the historical context. The passage appears in the midst of a series of exhortations beginning in 2:11. A basic premise of the exhortations is that by "doing right" (see 1 Peter 2:14–15, 20; 3:6, 13, 17; 4:19) and by enduring suffering quietly (see 2:20; 3:14, 17; 4:16, 19; 5:10), Christians will be able "to silence the ignorance of foolish men" (2:12, 15). The household code beginning in 2:18 was modified in light of this premise and employed to address the problem of how Christians should comport themselves in a situation of persecution (Lohse 1954, 74, 80–81; see Schrage 1974, 3–4). Slaves and wives, especially those married to non-Christian husbands, are singled out for instruction because, as Senior notes, they "had to endure the most painful conflict between their Christian freedom and their efforts to live a good life in the world" (Senior 1980, 48). The counsel, however, has wider applications than just to slaves and wives. Christian slaves and wives married to non-Christians become a model of how Christians of all stations are to behave in the face of verbal abuse, scorn, and bitter opposition so that they might win over their pagan adversaries.

The meaning of the domestic code in 1 Peter has been clarified by Elliott, who argues that it has a paradigmatic function (Elliott 1981, 208–233). When compared to other household exhortations in Ephesians, Colossians, and the pastoral epistles, 1 Peter 2:18–25 has noteworthy features that distinguish it. First, the servants are identified as "household servants" (*oiketai,* a word used only three times elsewhere in the New Testament) instead of the more frequent term "slaves" (*douloi),* which appears in the other exhortations to slaves (Eph. 6:5; Col. 3:22; 1 Tim. 6:1; Titus 2:9). Second, in contrast to all other household codes in the New Testament, the servants' duties are mentioned first. Elsewhere, slaves and masters are considered last. Third, no mention whatsoever is made of the masters and their responsibilities: "The focus is directed exclusively to the condition and conduct of household slaves" (Elliott 1981, 206). Fourth, the commands to the servants in verses 18 to 20 are buttressed by a reflection on the suffering of Christ in verses 21 to 25. The exhortation is given a unique and "extensive christological foundation" (Elliott 1981, 206).

The best explanation for these unique features is that 1 Peter 2: 18–25 functions as a paradigm. The household servants are exemplars for all the members of the household of God since "all the members are in a certain sense *oiketai*, like *oikonomoi* (4:10), servants of one another" (Elliott 1981, 207). Their vulnerability typifies the vulnerability of all Christians. Their possible suffering under callous masters squares with the potential suffering of all Christians in a hostile environment (see 1 Peter 1:6; 3:14, 17; 4:1, 13, 16, 19; 5:9–10). What is required of them—fear (2:18), endurance (2:20), a clear conscience (2:19), and doing right (2:20)—is required of all Christians ("fear," 1:17; 2:17; "endurance," 1:6; 5:10; "a clear conscience," 3:16, 21; "doing right," 2:14–15; 3:13, 17). Can it be that slaves alone are called to suffer and follow in the footsteps of Jesus (2:21)? Surely the writer understands this as the calling of all Christians, and because the slaves serve as models for all Christians, this explains why no mention is made of the owners' responsibilities. Elliott concludes, "The focus is reserved for those alone whose condition and calling most clearly represent the situation and vocation of the entire household of God" (Elliott 1981, 207).

As Lillie has observed, "the New Testament uses the humbler rather than the dominating parties in the house-tables as figurative descriptions of true Christian believers" (Lillie 1975, 182). The church is identified as the bride of Christ (1 Cor. 11:3; Eph. 5:23–24; Rev. 21:2, 9; 22:17). Jesus instructed his disciples to turn and become as little children (Matt. 18:1–4). Paul and others identified themselves as slaves of Christ (Rom. 1:1; Gal. 1:10; Phil. 1:1; 2 Tim. 2:24; Titus 1:1; James 1:1; 2 Peter 1:1; Jude 1; Rev. 1:1; and Mark 10:44). The effect of using those who were considered by society to be of the lowest estate as role models for all Christians is to turn any view of gradations of rank or value on its head.

Instructions to the wife. Recognition of the paradigmatic function of the house rules in 1 Peter helps clarify the instructions to wives that follow. The wives were not the focus of attention in 1 Peter 3:1–6 because they were prone to rebelliousness in their newfound freedom in Christ and needed to be bridled with a mandate to be submissive. They were not budding Jezebels (Rev. 2:20). They were addressed because their conversions created potentially grievous discord in their families if the husband remained unconverted. Those counseled were wives married to non-Christians, for their husbands are described as not obeying the Word, and consequently they needed to be won (compare 1 Cor. 9:19–22 for the idea of "winning"). They were not simply unresponsive to the Word; the other occurrences of the word "disobey" in 1 Peter (2:8; 3:20; 4:17) suggest that it refers to active hostility. The husbands were therefore antagonistic to Christianity and certainly not amused when their wives became Christians.

The lot of wives in general was not always blissful in the ancient world, as is reflected in Euripides' *Medea* (244–248):

> We women are of all unhappiest,
> Who, first, must buy, as buys the highest bidder,
> A husband—nay, we do but win for our lives
> A master! Deeper depth of wrong is this.
> Here too is dire risk—will the lord we gain
> Be evil or good? Divorce?—'tis infamy
> To us: we may not even reject a suitor!
>
> Then, coming to new customs, habits new,
> One need be a seer, to know the thing unlearnt
> At home, what manner of man her mate shall be.
> And if we learn our lesson, if our lord
> Dwell with us, plunging not against the yoke,
> Happy our lot is; else—no help but death.
> For the man, when the home-yoke galls his neck,
> Goes forth, to ease a weary sickened heart
> By turning to some friend, some kindred soul:
> We to one heart alone can look for comfort.

The lot of a wife who had, from the husband's perspective, been ensnared by a suspect Oriental superstition could be doubly perilous. Especially was this the case where it was believed that the wife was supposed to adhere to the religious beliefs of her husband. Plutarch, for example, wrote:

> A wife ought not to make friends of her own, but to enjoy her husband's friends in common with him. The gods are the first and most important friends. Wherefore it is becoming for a wife to worship and to know only the gods that her husband believes in, and to shut the front door tight upon all queer rituals and outlandish superstitions. For with no god do stealthy and secret rites performed by a woman find any favor. (*Advice to Bride and Groom* 19.141E)

It was not so delicate a matter when the husband became a Christian, since his wife would normally follow suit (see Acts 16:31–34) and since he had unquestioned freedom of action. For wives it was otherwise. Beare sums up the situation well:

> Many a husband will have felt that his wife was failing in her proper fidelity to him when she became converted to another religion, especially one which compelled her to refuse to worship his gods or to take part in the ordinary religious rites of the household, let alone the public ceremonies. (Beare 1970, 153)

The strain resulting from a mixed marriage can be detected in 1 Corinthians 7:12–16 (compare the later situations of Tertullian, *To His*

Wife, 2.4–7; and Justin, *2 Apology* 2). Some Christians in Corinth apparently felt obliged to separate from or divorce their pagan partner. First Peter recommended neither course. The Christian wife instead was to live out her commitment to Christ within the marriage relationship and in submission to her husband. This meant that she was to be the best wife she could possibly be to her husband. For many it must have been like walking on eggs. She had already breached patriarchal domination by becoming a Christian and disowning the gods of her husband and nation. Like the slave addressed in 1 Peter 2:18–20, she was to accept whatever suffering might come from her situation in the same way Christ did (2:21–25). Living day in and day out in a lion's den with an embittered and all-powerful husband as the lion could easily evoke terror, but the wife was counseled to do right and let nothing terrify her (3:6). It was advice applicable to all Christians: "But even if you do suffer for righteousness' sake, you will be blessed. Have no fear of them, nor be troubled, but in your hearts reverence Christ as Lord" (1 Peter 3:14–15a).

This means that 1 Peter 3:1–6 was not intended to set forth the divinely sanctioned pattern for all marriage relationships. No word at all was addressed to the wife married to a Christian husband. It presented both a stratagem for evangelizing an unbelieving husband and a model of behavior for all Christians—who also were virtually powerless in their world and surrounded by hostile forces (see 3:8–4:6)—to follow. As a stratagem, it was not advice on how the wife might win the affection of her husband, or even advice about marriage at all. Instead, it advised how the wife might win the husband for Christ without a word (3:1–2). It is often pointed out how this corresponds to the experience of Augustine's mother, Monica, who "won" her husband toward the end of his life:

> When she came to marriageable age, she was bestowed upon a husband
> and served him as her lord, and she did all one could to win to Thee,
> speaking to him of Thee by her deportment, whereby Thou madest her
> beautiful and reverently lovable and admirable to her husband. . . .
> Finally, when her husband was now at the very end of his earthly life, she
> won him unto Thee. (Augustine, *Confessions* 9.19, 22)

As a model of Christian conduct, what is required of the wife in 1 Peter 3 is required of *all* members of the household of God. They too are to be submissive (2:13, 5:5–6). The emphasis on the good conduct or behavior *(anastrophē)* of the wife that is to be observed by her non-Christian husband ("when they see your reverent and chaste behavior," 3:2) is no different from the appeal made to all Christians: "Maintain good conduct among the Gentiles, so that in case they speak against you as wrongdoers, they may see your good deeds and glorify

God on the day of visitation" (2:12). The phrase translated "reverent" in 3:2 literally reads "in fear." That does not mean that the wife was to live in fear of her husband (see 3:6) or in reverence of him. "Fear" was used here, as throughout 1 Peter, as an abbreviation, a telegram word, that stood for the fear of God required of all Christians (1:17; 2:17; 3:14–15) as the basis of their conduct in the world. The wives were also encouraged to nurture "a gentle and quiet spirit" (3:4), but it should not be thought that a quiet demeanor was something befitting only wives. "Gentleness" is the same word used in the third beatitude, "Blessed are the meek" (Matt. 5:5), and to describe Jesus (Matt. 11:29; 21:5). It too was supposed to characterize the response of Christians to pagan adversaries: "Always be prepared to make a defense to any one who calls you to account for the hope that is in you, yet do it with gentleness and reverence" (1 Peter 3:15). The admonition to adopt the attitude of quietness needs to be read in the context of hostility experienced by the wife married to the pagan and by the entire community. Quietness reflects the spirit of Jesus, who, when he was reviled, did not revile back (2:23). This was the ideal for all Christians, who were not to return reviling for reviling but to hold their tongues except to bless (3:8–11). The early church encouraged modesty in outward demeanor as a means of commanding respect from outsiders and because it was believed that a quiet, peaceable life would have evangelistic effects in a predominantly pagan society (see 1 Thess. 4:11–12; 2 Thess. 3:12; 1 Tim. 2:1–4). It should not be surprising that this attitude is commended to the wife married to an unbeliever.

A brief word should be said about what 1 Peter 3 has to say about feminine adornment. Those who insist on interpreting the Bible literally should follow the path of early church fathers, who understood verses 3 to 5 (see also 1 Tim. 2:9–10) as a ban on all finery and beautification aids, or "poultices of lust" as Jerome later termed them (see Tertullian, *The Apparel of Women*; Clement of Alexandria, *The Educator*, 3.11.66; Cyprian, *The Dress of Virgins*). The emphasis, however, is on true beauty as something that is spirit deep, not skin deep. Admonitions against outward ornamentation were widespread in the ancient world. According to *1 Enoch* 8.1–2, one of the fallen angels taught mankind the art of making bracelets, decorations, and cosmetics; as a result, adultery soon became widespread (see Isa. 3:18–23). Women were encouraged to cultivate the inner graces if they wished to be genuinely beautiful. Plutarch contended in his *Advice to Bride and Groom:*

> And so a wedded and lawful wife becomes an irresistible thing if she makes everything, dowry, birth, magic charms and even the magic girdle

itself, to be inherent in herself, and by character and virtue succeeds in winning her husband's love. (23.141C)

It is not gold or precious stones or scarlet that makes her such [adorned], but whatever invests her with that something that betokens dignity, good behavior and modesty. (26.141E)

An incident recorded by Livy, probably fictional, is an interesting example of one view of the dangers of ostentatious feminine attire but also reflects a prevalent attitude toward women. The matter concerned a debate in the Roman senate over repeal of the Oppian law (passed in 215 B.C.) that allowed women to possess only half an ounce of gold and banned dyed apparel. Intended to reduce conspicuous consumption in the midst of a war, it had later sparked mutinous demonstrations by annoyed women. Marcus Porcius Cato argued vigorously for keeping the law. "If each of us, citizens, had determined to assert his rights and dignity as a husband with respect to his own spouse, we should have less trouble with the sex as a whole; as it is, our liberty, destroyed at home by female violence, even here in the Forum is crushed and trodden underfoot, and because we have not kept them individually under control, we dread them collectively" (*Histories* 34.2.1–2). Disturbed by the consequences if the pressure from the women should succeed, he continued, "If you suffer them to seize these bonds one by one and wrench themselves free and finally be placed on a parity with their husbands, do you think that you will be able to endure them? The moment they begin to be your equals, they will be your superiors" (24.3.2–3). He was also concerned that repeal of the law would spark a green-eyed competitiveness in dress:

Do you wish, citizens, to start a race like this among your wives, so that the rich shall want to own what no other woman can have and the poor, lest they be despised for their poverty, shall spend beyond their means? Once let these women begin to be ashamed of what they should not be ashamed, and they will not be ashamed of what they ought. She who can buy from her own purse will buy; she who cannot will beg her husband. Poor wretch that husband, both he who yields and he who yields not, since what he will not himself give he will see given by another man. (24. 4.15–17)

First Peter is by no means so cynical, but in keeping with the contemporary appraisal of true beauty, the wife was encouraged to develop a gentle and quiet spirit. By so doing, she would be numbered among the daughters of Sarah. Sarah herself was counted among the four most beautiful women of the Old Testament (along with Rahab, Abigail, and Esther; B. *Meg.* 15b). But it was her character and supposed submission to her husband that were counted as true beauty in 3:5–6.

This picture of Sarah's submissive obedience to her husband is certainly idealized. At times it was Abraham who was obedient to her. His barren wife had, for example, demanded that he cohabit with her slave Hagar so that she might be able to reproduce through her (Gen. 16:2) and later gave him an ultimatum, confirmed by none other than God, to cast out the slave with her son (Gen. 21:10–12). Nor was she always meekly quiet. She lashed out at her husband after Hagar conceived and began to treat her with contempt: "This outrage against me is your fault!" (Gen. 16:5, translation from Speiser 1964, 116). On the only occasion that she called her husband "lord"—just as well translated "husband"—she was laughing derisively on overhearing the news that she and Abraham were to become parents: "My husband is old" (Gen. 18:12). She then lied to God about having laughed (Gen. 18:15). That Sarah was presented as a model for Christian wives married to unbelievers is probably attributable to how she was portrayed in later tradition. According to the rabbis, she was the mother of proselytes. According to Philo (*Allegorical Interpretation*, 3.244–245), she pointed Abraham on the way to virtue (Balch 1981, 105). By imitating Sarah, Peter believed that the Christian wife might also win her husband to virtue and to Christ.

Instructions to the husband. A short concluding word was directed to the Christian husband married to a Christian wife (they are "joint heirs of the grace of life") in 1 Peter 3:7. He was told to live with her, literally "according to knowledge." What is this knowledge? Apparently, it is a distinctively Christian perception that stands over against what was labeled as "the passions of your former ignorance" in 1:14. The Christian husband has come to know God (see Gal. 4:9) and consequently can no longer operate with the value system of his pagan past or surroundings (1 Peter 1:18; 4:2–4). One can draw comparisons with 1 Thessalonians 4:3–5, where Paul asserted it was the will of God "that each one of you *know* how to take a wife for himself in holiness and honor, not in the passion of lust like heathen who do not know God." The Christian husband was expected to relate to his wife in holiness and honor because she is a copartner in the grace God has bestowed on all humanity.

This means that the husband's attitude toward his wife (and women in general) must be influenced by the Christian vision that in Christ there is neither male nor female. A notorious saying attributed to Demosthenes (*Against Neaera* 122) declared, "We keep courtesans for our pleasure, concubines for the regular physical needs of the body, and wives to bear us legitimate children and look after household affairs." The Christian husband, however, was not to regard his wife as a combination brood mare and housemaid. She is not a possession or a toy for one's sexual amusement; she is a person who is precious and consequently to be honored (see 1 Peter 2:7). Beare astutely comments:

> The relationship to God determines the nature of the marriage relationship; through the knowledge of God, the husband learns to set a new value on the wife, not merely as the mother of his children (which in even so exceptional a person as Plato is virtually the only consideration), but as the partner in his eternal hope and in his prayers. (Beare 1970, 157)

The husband and wife were therefore to "cohabit as coheirs" (Elliott 1981, 201). Treating the wife as a co-heir destroys any hierarchical concept of their relationship. To treat her as anything less than an equal directly impinges on the husband's relationship to God. The phrase "lest your prayers be hindered" implies that if the husband should mistreat or debase his wife, he will soon begin to pray like a noisy gong (see 1 Cor. 13:1). The Christian wife may have to endure ill will from her non-Christian husband (1 Peter 3:6), but the Christian husband is never to aggrieve his wife if he wishes to bear the name "Christian."

One last word should be said about the description of the wife as a weaker vessel, sometimes translated "weaker sex." It was not uncommon in Greco-Roman society to describe woman in a derogatory sense as weaker (see Selwyn 1947, 187). For example, in the *Letter of Aristeas* 250, King Ptolemy asked one of the Jewish wise men how he could live amicably with his wife. The answer:

> By recognizing that womankind are by nature headstrong and energetic in the pursuit of their own desires, and subject to sudden changes of opinion through fallacious reasoning, and their nature is essentially weak. It is necessary to deal wisely with them and not to provoke strife.

This is not the connotation of "weaker vessel" in 1 Peter (the husband, it implies, is also a "vessel"; see Acts 9:15; Jer. 18:1–11). In what way, then, did 1 Peter consider the wife to be weaker? It could not refer to a psychological weakness, because she was expected to be able to bear up under intense pressure (3:6). She was not spiritually weaker, since she was designated a co-heir of the grace of life. Perhaps the phrase referred to her physical weakness in comparison to (most) men —she cannot throw a softball as far. It is more meaningful, however, to consider this as a reference to the subjugation of women by the male-dominated culture. Although they were co-heirs in God's kingdom, women were disenfranchised from the male kingdoms of this world. They were vulnerable, powerless, and considered by some to be expendable. This powerlessness, or political "weakness," was not a characteristic inherent in being female but a role prescribed for her by a male-oriented society. She was not weaker because of any personal shortcoming but because she was a woman—a lesser class of persons—

in a man's world. Best suggests that we might have here a practical application of 1 Corinthians 12:22. The wife was not one of the mighty of the world, and therefore the husband was to bestow honor on her (Best 1971, 128). He was not to regard her or treat her as his world did, and Christian marriage was not to be governed by the law of the strongest.

The Pastoral Epistles

The instructions to wives found in the pastoral epistles can be understood only when the problems they were meant to address are clarified. A careful reading reveals that problems concerning marriage have surfaced in the churches.

Marriage and sexual intercourse, even for purposes of procreation, have incurred dishonor among the heretics. First Timothy 4:1–3 was a response to this attitude:

> Now the Spirit expressly says that in later times some will depart from the faith by giving heed to deceitful spirits and doctrines of demons, through the pretensions of liars whose consciences are seared, who forbid marriage and enjoin abstinence from foods.

According to the Gospels, commitment to Christ can cause estrangement from the natural family (see Mark 3:31–35; Matt. 10:37–39), but some early Christians seem to have gone out of their way to create tension. They had set their minds on the things above to the exclusion of nearly all the things below, particularly family responsibilities. Some rejected their family ties and encouraged others to do so as a sign of devotion to Christ. They left houses, wives or husbands, and children, assuming that they were supposed to do this (see Luke 18:29). Marriage was viewed by them as a hindrance that could exclude one from the kingdom (see Luke 14:20). If the various apocryphal acts of the apostles are any indication, this disdain of marriage gained a greater foothold in the second century. One gets the impression from them that the apostles' central message protested against defilement caused by sexual relationships even within marriage, and they created no small outcry from aggrieved husbands and fiancés.

The *Acts of Paul and Thecla* (New Testament Apocrypha) provides a notorious example. According to this work, Paul proclaimed blessed those who keep the flesh chaste for they shall become the temple of God (2.5). He was said to preach that one has no resurrection unless one continues to be chaste and not defile the flesh (2.12). One Thecla, a virgin affianced to Thamyris, was quite captured by this teaching. She wanted to be counted worthy to stand before Paul along with other virgins, and as a consequence she refused to marry. This naturally provoked Thamyris as well as Thecla's mother. Charges were brought against Paul for alienation of affections because of this new doctrine of the Christians (2.14). An attempt, encouraged by her mother, was made to burn Thecla for rebelling against the law of the Iconians. One might think that the canonical advice of Paul, "It is better to marry than to burn" (1 Cor. 7:9, KJV), would apply, but Thecla was miraculously saved by rain and continued to the end of her life preaching the gospel of sexual abstinence. A similar pattern where a woman, incited by the preaching of an apostle, withdraws from a marriage relationship to live an ascetic life is repeated in the *Acts of Thomas* 12–13, the *Acts of Peter* 33–34, and the *Acts of Andrew* (see also Irenaeus, *Against Heresies*, 1.24.2). This negative attitude toward marriage and sexuality must also have infected the church at the time the pastoral epistles were written (see also 1 Cor. 7). When a marriage partner became caught up in this enthusiastic asceticism, serious problems ensued not only for the marriage but also for the Christians' reputation in the community (see Balch 1981, 66–80, for Greco-Roman criticism of Eastern religions).

It can also be detected from 2 Timothy 3:1–9 that the heretics had made particular headway among impressionable women. Verses 6–7 read:

> For among them are those who make their way into households and capture weak women, burdened with sins and swayed by various impulses, who will listen to anybody and can never arrive at a knowledge of the truth.

The instructions to wives in the pastoral epistles must be understood as a response to these problems. Sexuality and marriage were affirmed as creations of God and therefore good. They were not to be rejected but "to be received with thanksgiving by those who believe and *know the truth* (1 Tim. 4:3, emphasis added). Hebrews 13:4, "let marriage be held in honor among all," was a similar response to the negative appraisal of marriage. The difficult passage in 1 Timothy 2:15 should be seen in this light. To say that women will be saved through childbearing was to affirm childbearing. It was not to suggest that the path of salvation was different for men and women. This counsel reappears in 1 Timothy 5:14: "I would have younger widows marry, *bear children,* [and] rule their households." One of the qualifications of the "real" widow was that she had *brought up children* (1 Tim. 5:10). In Titus 2:4–5 the elder women were asked to train younger women "to love their husbands and children, to be sensible, chaste, domestic, kind, and submissive to their husbands." It would seem clear that these instructions were given because there were those who were influencing wives to do otherwise in the name of God. Wives were being dissuaded from living out any marital role, because marriage and bearing and rearing children were seen as impediments to salvation.

An overriding concern in the pastorals is "that the word of God may not be discredited" (Titus 2:5). The Pastor wished to avoid giving the enemy any opportunity to revile the Christian community for outlandish antisocial behavior, particularly when it came to obligations to family and marriage conventions (1 Tim. 5:14). It was a concern of Paul in writing to the Corinthians that "all things should be done decently and in order" (1 Cor. 14:40). Judge points out:

> It could be disastrous if enthusiastic members failed to contain their principles within the privacy of the association, and were led into political indiscretions or offences against the hierarchy of the household. Hence the growing stress on good order and regular leadership within the associations themselves. (Judge 1960, 76)

The stress in the pastoral epistles on the wife's subordination to her husband and her role of domesticity was intended to counter the heretics who encouraged wives to repudiate their marriage ties and roles to pursue some higher calling. It was meant for a particular situation where marriage bonds were being disdained. We do not find in the pastorals a positive theology of marriage relationships but a refutation of developments considered to be dangerous.

1 Corinthians 7

1 Corinthians 7 provides an opportunity to glimpse how Paul viewed the relationship between man and wife operating in the everyday matters of hearth and home. The historical context of Paul's answers to Corinthian queries and confusion will be discussed in chapter 6 (see also D. E. Garland 1983); suffice it to say that the underlying issue was the problem of sexuality and the Christian. In dealing with the problems that were emerging in Corinth between husbands and wives, not once did Paul call for, or even hint of, the wife's submission under the authority of the husband. Quite the contrary. Marriage, as it was portrayed here by Paul, was to operate according to the principle of mutuality and equality. Everything said of the husband was said also of the wife (1 Cor. 7:2,3–4,12–13,14–16,33–34; it is clearly diagrammed by E. Kähler 1960, 17–21). She did not need to be instructed on these matters by the husband (see 1 Cor. 14:35) but was addressed directly as an equally responsible party.

The first section (7:1–5) deals with the sticky subject of conjugal relations between husband and wife. Some couples in Corinth were abstaining from sexual intercourse in a misguided attempt to attain a fancied spiritual perfection. Paul opposed asceticism for marriage partners as deluded. Marriage was to be a fully sexual relationship. The husband and wife owed each other sexual intimacy (7:2–3); it was neither defiling nor optional. The explanation that Paul gave for this opinion was that the wife does not rule (have authority) over her own body, but the husband does. This would have met with husbands' hearty assent in the first-century world where women soon discovered, according to Epictetus, that they had little else to do but to be the bedfellows of men (*Manual* 40; see also B. *Ned.* 20a, *'Erub.* 100a). Paul, however, continued with a statement most atypical in the Greco-Roman world (Cartlidge 1975, 231): the husband does not rule over his own body but the wife does (7:4). The wife's body is not her own but something she freely shares with her husband, and likewise the husband's body is not his own but something he freely shares with his wife. There is no trace of any idea about the husband's rights and the wife's duties (Bailey 1952, 66). In sexual matters, the wife is not expected to submit passively as a docile bed partner. She is an equal partner. *Both* husband *and* wife were to recognize that their spouse has a greater claim on them than they have on themselves. The consequence for Paul as it applied to the Corinthian situation was that one partner may not unilaterally decide to abstain from coitus to pursue some private spiritual discipline, no matter how heavenly minded it might be (7:5).

What is new here, when compared with Judaism, for example, is that withdrawal from each other for spiritual purposes must be a mutual decision. In Judaism, the husband had an inalienable right to absent himself from his wife for study or prayer (see *Testament of Naphtali* 8.8, *Jubilees* 1.8, M. *Ketub.* 5.6, M. *Yoma* 8.1). The wife need not be consulted, only informed. Paul argued, however, that one may abstain only by mutual consent. Regardless of what kind of head the husband may be, he may not head off on spiritual retreat without consulting his wife, who has every right to say no. What is also new from a Jewish perspective is that Paul implied that a wife may also wish to retreat for prayer. She may take the initiative in spiritual matters. This passage is the only one in the New Testament that specifically describes husbands' and wives' making decisions, and the emphasis is on arriving at a solution by mutual agreement and not by husbandly decree.

Another striking passage is found in 7:12–14. Paul contended that Christians yoked to unbelievers need not feel defiled in some way by this union, as if they were joining a member of Christ to a demon, as some may have believed (see 1 Cor. 6:16; 2 Cor. 6:14–7:1). The Christian was never to initiate a divorce simply because the spouse was an unbeliever; and if the unbelieving spouse wished to continue the marriage, the Christian could rest assured that the spouse had been "sanctified" by the Christian wife or husband.

What Paul meant here by "sanctify" is most difficult to unravel. Surely he was not referring to some kind of vicarious sanctification, sanctification by proxy. It was not an argument about sanctification but an argument against divorce. In 1 Corinthians 7:16, Paul recognized that the spouse has not yet been saved and may never be converted: "wife [husband], how do you know whether you will save your husband [wife]?" Neither can it refer to the Christian witness and influence of the believing spouse on the unbelieving, since the perfect tense of the verb is used rather than the present or future. The perfect tense would refer to some action completed in the past with continuing results: the spouse has been sanctified. The answer to what Paul meant by "sanctify" is to be found in the vocabulary of Jewish marriage laws. The verb "sanctify" means "to set apart" or "to consecrate." In the Mishnah, *Qiddushin* (sanctifications, from the verb "to sanctify") is the title of a tractate that discusses betrothals (see B. *Qidd.* 2b). To betroth a wife is to sanctify her; she is set apart from all men by her husband-to-be through money, document, or intercourse (M. *Qidd.* 1.1; see B. *Qidd.* 2b). The husband thereby renders the wife a consecrated object. It is only husbands who can do this. In fact, in all areas of life, women can be sanctified only through the deeds of men (Neusner 1979, 100). What is unique in 1 Corinthians 7:14 is that Paul maintained that the wife also sanctified her husband, set him apart from all men. Both a husband and a wife have the *same* sanctifying power.

The last passage in 1 Corinthians 7 that underscores the mutuality of marriage is found in verses 32 to 34. Paul assumed that the married man is anxious about worldly affairs, or how to please his wife, and the married woman is also anxious about worldly affairs, or how to please her husband. Paul did not scorn this anxiety. He recognized that marriage brings in its wake anxieties and troubles in the flesh (7:28) and would prefer that men and women be free from this to give undivided devotion to the Lord (7:35). One who has a wife and two children to support and care for would not be as free to travel hither and yon across the Mediterranean world as Paul did in his missionary travels. Paul could focus his anxiety on his churches (2 Cor. 11:28); the married man must also be anxious for the welfare of his family. Paul assumed that being married involved being concerned with pleasing the spouse. It would have been taken for granted, of course, that this was the task of a wife; but, according to Paul, the husband has the same goal. He was not to be anxious about how to rule his wife or how to make her submit to his authority, but how to please her. Marriage for Paul entailed mutual dedication.

In 7:25–26, Paul made it clear that he was offering an opinion: "I think." It is the opinion of one who has been counted by the Lord's mercy to be trustworthy, but it is still *his* opinion. He "thinks" that he has the Spirit of God on these matters (7:40). Paul based his opinions not on divine laws of the universe but on what he believed would be to the Corinthians' advantage and would promote for them good order or seemliness (7:35) in their world and situation. Nevertheless, each individual may decide for himself or herself how to live in obedience to God's call when it comes to marriage. Paul would not throw a noose on them (7:35). Each was considered able to make responsible choices. Nor were wives viewed as underlings required to submit to the authority of the husbands. The relationship between husband and wife was to be based on equality and mutuality, not on authority and dominance.

Conclusions

We conclude from our study of the biblical evidence that man and wife were created by God to be equal partners in marriage. A hierarchical relationship in which the husband rules is not the will of God but a distortion of the relationship between man and woman. Although the forced repression of wives into submissive roles in marriage became an almost universal custom and was the normative view in the first century, we find in the New Testament the winds of change. Husbands are to love their wives in the same way Christ demonstrated his love for his people. They are not to put themselves first but their wives first. Wives are to be honored by their husbands as co-heirs of God's grace and therefore equals. Wives and husbands mutually rule over each other's bodies. The principle that is to govern the marriage relationship of those in Christ is therefore to be mutuality and partnership under the lordship of Christ.

3
Marriage Beyond Hierarchy and Equality: Christians in Today's World

We reached the conclusion from our biblical analysis that Christians are to relate to each other in marriage as equals. The relationship is to be based on self-sacrifice rather than self-interest, self-giving love rather than arrogant power, partnership rather than one-sided subordination. This is not an either/or choice for Christians who wish to relate to their spouses according to God's intention.

The model that has been operative for most of Christendom, however, is hierarchical, with the husband as the head—the boss—and the wife as a submissive domestic. Those who argue that the husband-wife relationship is to be hierarchical believe that spiritual equality of males and females before God and superordinate-subordinate relationships with one another are compatible. Husbands are heads, it is claimed, not because they are inherently superior—they exercise their functions with women as spiritual equals—but because they have been called by God to this task (Knight 1977, 59). The primary task of the wife is to accept her place in subordination. If the woman does not submit herself to her husband's leadership, she not only has a problem with her husband but also has sinned against God (Piper 1949).

Proponents of this model foresee serious consequences for ignoring this ordering of life. Piper (1960) has stated that the possibility of a genuine relationship is lost when the partners are equal, since equality brings tension. Clark (1980) calls attempts to minimize the differences between male and female and to disregard the need for hierarchy in marriage one of the most destructive changes in the history of human society. According to him, family life is weakened because the woman has turned her attention from her family's life and her husband's career to her own life and career. Men become irresponsible and impotent, children suffer psychological disorders, and families dissolve. Litfin avows that the universe should be ordered around a series of over/under hierarchical relationships is His idea, a part of His original design. He delegates His authority according to His own pleasure to those whom He places in appropriate positions and it is to Him that His creatures submit when they acknowledge that authority. (Litfin 1979, 267)

To upset this so-called divinely ordained pattern, they warn, is to invite disaster for the family.

Are these forebodings of ill when husbands and wives move toward equal relationships warranted? We have already argued that the hierarchical pattern of marriage was not decreed by God, but does it promote the health and well-being of the family as its supporters argue? To answer this question, we need first to examine the relationship between the hierarchical and partnership models for marriage and actual patterns of marital relating in our own cultural context. We can then turn to an examination of questions of their actual effects in the lives of persons today and thus determine whether the pronouncements of Clark and others are right.

Two Patterns in American Society— Traditional and Companionship

The interpretation of what is the ideal in the Bible has unfortunately been confused with sociological categories in today's society. The male headship/female submission model in traditional American marriage is one where Wife does the cooking, cleaning, and child care using a budget provided by Husband's salary, and Husband provides the economic resources for the family's support and makes the important decisions about family life. Likewise, today's companionship marriages are identified with a biblical model of marital partnership based on equality. In companionship marriage, spouses are roommates who split the chores down the middle, assert themselves in disagreements so that their rights are respected and needs are met, and provide a haven to each other from their careers, where they lead completely separate lives (preferably left at the office).

Authors (e.g., Piper 1960; Knight 1977; Clark 1980) who point to the terrible consequences of equality, the basis of partnership marriage, have wrongly assumed that it is the same thing as contemporary companionship marriage. Companionship marriage, however, is a sociological phenomenon that is a consequence of cultural changes, not an attempt to embrace a biblical vision of marriage. Partnership marriage is not a sociological model for marriage but is instead a biblical ideal. The Bible does not say whether wives should work or stay home, whether husbands should do housework or never put their hands in

54   *Beyond Companionship*

dishwater, or who should discipline children and lead in family worship. It does not say what wives are to consider their roles or what men are to consider theirs except that they are to be worked out in respectful love of one another. Even though partnership marriages are similar to companionship marriages in the lack of prescribed gender roles, companionship marriages are a cultural development, not a biblical ideal.

Defining Traditional and Companionship Marriage Patterns

In 1945 Burgess and Locke, in *The Family—From Institution to Companionship,* concluded from research on marriage and the family in American culture that major changes were materializing: The family was being transformed from the institutional (traditional) form that was based on culturally prescribed sex roles. That model of marriage had been useful in maintaining the order of society in a closed and hierarchical culture. In an open democratic society, however, the importance of social order was being replaced by an emphasis on the quality of relationships between persons. Marriage was therefore going to be defined more by companionship and the assignment of roles through interaction than by prescribed cultural expectations. In subsequent years, every respected sociology of the family textbook discussed institutional versus companionship marriage, with the assumption that companionship marriage was more fitted to our cultural context. It is interesting to note that most recent texts now devote less and less attention to this discussion; the switch to companionship marriage as the ideal has been made. Companionship marriage is valued, if not always practiced. Mace has chosen "traditional" rather than "institutional" as the term to describe the model that is losing out, because it is generally accepted that the "institution" of marriage and the family will remain, though in a different form. "Traditional" will be used here also to refer to marriage based on culturally prescribed sex roles. Mace states that the traditional model is a form "that is passing away": "It was rooted in the traditions of the past, and served well enough in its time; but it is now anachronistic" (Mace 1982a, 15).

Although the traditional marriage form does not hold sway as it did in the past, it nevertheless is still around and is experiencing a resurgence in the 1980s with the attempt by some vocal groups to return to the ways of the past, when men did not do women's work and vice versa. Those who proclaim that the hierarchical marriage model is the biblical way serve as leaders in this movement. Even those who espouse companionship attitudes toward marriage find it difficult to escape traditional ways of doing things that were learned in their formative years in homes structured on the traditional model. Many in so-called companionship marriages are more traditional than they admit.

Traditional marriage. How does the traditional model look in modern American society? In traditional marriages, the husband is more dominant than the wife. It is he who has the last word, although he does not interfere in his wife's own arena of activity and the decisions she makes concerning children and home, unless they are big-ticket items. The husband's position is like the presidency in a democracy; he may delegate certain powers and decision making, but he has the final responsibility (Scanzoni and Scanzoni 1975). He controls the purse strings; the wife may have no idea about the family's finances, debts, and assets.

The roles of husband and wife are based on what is expected of a husband or a wife in the specific cultural group rather than something worked out through negotiation between the individual spouses. Certain tasks are considered "women's work" that men do not do, unless through kindness or necessity (the wife is ill, pregnant, or has increased demands because of her employment outside the home) they stoop to help out. The wife's role is to care for the home and children. The husband's primary role is that of breadwinner. If possible, the wife does not work outside the home, since this would reflect negatively on her husband and would undermine her primary work as wife and mother. If she does work outside the home, it is usually out of financial necessity and is considered a stopgap measure rather than a career.

The differences in the roles of husband and wife result in different assumptions spouses make as they structure their lives and juggle responsibilities. The wife operates out of a basic philosophy that "if the family does well, I do too," whereas the husband reasons, "if I do well, the family does too" (Scanzoni 1978). The woman is therefore primarily invested in her home and family; the man, in his career and self-development.

Leisure activities tend to be with same-sex friends rather than with each other. Women talk with women; men participate in or watch sports together. Social gatherings find the men congregated separately from the women. Because of their different interests, a husband and wife may have little to talk about together. Peplau observes that

> traditional men typically believe that men should conceal their tender feelings; masculinity is defined in part by being "tough" and presenting a strong impression to others. Traditional men may not learn how to disclose feelings nor believe that they should. For both men and women, relations with same-sex friends and relatives may be a more important source of companionship than marriage. (Peplau 1983, 249)

Traditional marriages exist in all social classes and take many different forms. Turner (1970) identified three such forms based on the role of the wife, because her role is traditionally pivotal for home and family. In the homemaker role, the wife is an expert in home management and child rearing, spheres in which she influences her husband as well. In the role of companion, the wife is concerned with providing a haven for her husband from the workaday world and focuses on her personal attractiveness and grace and her skills as a hostess. In the role of humanist, the wife is active in her church and community as a volunteer. Often, a wife in a traditional marriage will perform all three roles to a greater or lesser extent.

Although this pattern of marriage seems compatible with the hierarchical pattern that some discern from scripture, they differ. In a hierarchical interpretation, ultimate authority and power lie with God. God bestows authority on the husband, who in turn delegates some to the wife. In the sociological pattern of traditional marriage, God may or may not be a part of the picture in the minds of the couple. Patterns of relating develop simply because this is the way things are done; role assignments are "right" because they are culturally prescribed, not necessarily because they are believed to be God-ordained. For this reason, as the culture changes, gradual changes occur as well in the marital pattern.

This gradual change is apparent in traditional patterns of marriage in our culture that reflect customs separated from their significance in the past. For example, a young man may ask his girlfriend's father for permission to marry her, although the father's permission has little weight now in the daughter's right to marry if she is of age. The father still "gives the bride away" at the wedding ceremony as if she were chattel, although *patria potestas* has long since disappeared. The custom of women working primarily as homemakers is rapidly changing also; in our society, women employed outside the home outnumber full-time homemakers (Fullerton 1980). This is, in part, a response to such cultural changes as smaller families, the emphasis on consumerism, the economic pressures of inflation and high costs of educating children, the development of a fleet of laborsaving devices and convenience foods, as well as a reflection of the change in male-female relationships. Nevertheless, most still believe that the husband's career is primary and the wife's career is secondary to the needs of the family and the husband's career decisions.

In actuality, many American couples are somewhere between a hierarchical pattern of relating and a companionship pattern, struggling with learned patterns of behavior and attitudes that do not always fit together. To speak of traditional marriage patterns, therefore, is to speak of a whole continuum of relationships that are, in reality, united only by an emphasis on order and defined expectations, with the man retaining at least most of the authority and responsibility. Peplau dubs the modifications of traditional marriage patterns "modern marriage"

(Peplau 1983). In modern marriage, the male is still dominant but not as strongly; roles are still specialized but not in all areas; and more responsibility is shared. Togetherness and companionship are often important.

Both traditional marriage and modern marriage as we have described them are working models of marriage seemingly congruent with the hierarchical model for marriage as interpreted from scripture. They are not, however, the only patterns of relating that can be derived from this scripturally based model. A pattern where fathers arrange marriages and pass control of their daughters over to the complete authority of their husbands, where wives are cloistered in their homes and allowed to leave the domicile only with permission and then only when prudently veiled, also is congruent with this hierarchical ideal.

Companionship marriage. Unlike traditional patterns that are consciously modeled on hierarchical principles purportedly derived from scripture, companionship marriage patterns in our culture do not pretend to correspond to a model of partnership derived from the scripture. Companionship marriage is an outgrowth of modern humanism and the belief in the potential of persons for growth. It reflects changes in secular society, not an attempt to live out biblical principles. Nevertheless, the changes that have led to companionship marriage have provided a supportive cultural context for Christians who want to have marriages based on equality and partnership.

Companionship marriage and egalitarian marriage are terms used interchangeably to refer to marriage based on equality of the partners; spouses are companions to each other and share both power and responsibility. Gender-based role specialization is absent both inside and outside the marriage (Peplau 1983). Young and Willmott (1973) call this phenomenon "symmetrical" marriage, because partners match each other rather than complement each other. Division of labor is accomplished according to the situation and the spouses' needs and abilities rather than according to gender. How this works itself out varies with each couple. Both may be employed or only one; they may share a job or both have part-time careers. They may do housekeeping chores together, take turns, or divide tasks according to skill and interest. No matter who does what, the critical issues are that partners consider themselves equals, that specific expectations are worked out together rather than assumed because of gender, and that both grow as individuals, whatever that growth may mean for each.

Because each couple must work out its own pattern, this model requires a great deal of interpersonal skill in expressing needs and wishes, in understanding the partner, and in negotiating differences. Mace defines three essential elements for a successful companionship marriage: commitment to growth, an effectively functioning communication system, and the ability to make creative use of conflict (Mace 1982a). This last element receives the most emphasis, because "the closer couples try to move to each other, the more conflict they tend to develop" (Mace 1982a, 30). Issues that are not issues in traditional marriages have to be dealt with, such as: Who gets up with the baby at 2 A.M.? Who stays home from work to greet the plumber? Who addresses the Christmas cards? And so on. Mace defines this model of marriage as a two-vote system. Marriages with only one vote are largely conflict free; but in a two-vote system, the possibility of endless discussion and disagreement always lurks (Mace 1982a).

It is virtually impossible, however, to keep things in perfect balance, to keep things "equal." A favorite *Sesame Street* episode of ours has Bert eyeing Ernie's piece of pie. Bert complains that his piece is smaller than Ernie's, so Ernie eats part of his to make them equal. Then Bert's is larger, so Ernie takes a bite of Bert's to even things up. On it goes, until two empty plates and Bert's empty stomach remain. It is hard enough to cut equivalent pieces of pie, but to divide a constantly changing list of household responsibilities and such amorphous concepts as power or dominance, or even time, into equal units is virtually impossible (Bernard 1982).

For this reason, although many couples are egalitarian in attitude, truly egalitarian relationships are rarely achieved. In fact, relationships that are devoid of gender-based stereotypes appear to be extremely difficult to establish. In a study of dual-career marriages, for example, Poloma and Garland found that only one couple of the fifty-three they interviewed in which both spouses were employed was actually egalitarian. In all the others, the wife still carried the responsibility for domestic tasks and the husband's job was seen as more important (Poloma and Garland 1971). Cultural variations in companionship marriage have also been discovered in research, suggesting that the egalitarian ideal is more apparent in some groups than in others. In the United States, role relationships in black families on the whole are far more egalitarian and less gender-related than in white families, and rigid gender-based role prescriptions are most common among middle-class whites, even those who would most emphasize companionship in their marriage (Willie and Greenblatt 1978).

The goal of the companionship model is the individual growth and self-actualization of the partners and the growth of the relationship. The question that comes to mind is, "Growth toward what?" The assumption is that the purpose of growth in the marriage is to achieve deeper intimacy with each other—the process is the goal. Wife and husband are to develop their gifts as individuals in the larger world outside the marriage and then use this greater maturity to deepen the intimacy and sharing of the marriage. The marriage has no major function except to meet the spouses' interpersonal needs and to enable the individuals to accomplish their own tasks and personal goals. Other functions of marriage, even procreation, are less significant than the emotional nurture of the partners.

The major obstacle to the success of companionship marriage, therefore, is often identified as a lack of interpersonal skill (Mace 1982a). It is through our interpersonal relating, after all, that intimacy develops. As important as interpersonal skills are, however, they do not guarantee "success" in marriage. Skillful communication cannot give meaning to life or provide fulfillment. It is here that companionship marriage and partnership marriage are most clearly different. The goal of marriage based on partnership is not the relationship in and of itself, but pursuit of the purposes of the marriage as the couple has identified them in the will of God. Partnership marriage does not focus on itself, an earthly institution, but strives to transcend itself by focusing on a joint task.

In the companionship model, authority and responsibility are to be divided; in partnership they may take many different shapes depending on the context and tasks of the couple. Structure, decision-making processes, and prominence of careers cannot be prescribed by the partnership model. It proposes no particular way of doing things but instead focuses on a vision and a purpose that go beyond the marriage itself. The companionship pattern and the ideal of partnership are not comparable, since they operate at different levels. Companionship marriage is like Robert's Rules of Order; the concern is how to do things so that each is treated fairly and equitably. It coordinates the partners' activity but says nothing about the purpose of the activity. The purpose of relating is central to partnership marriage, not the details of process beyond the assumption of equality. It transcends rules and patterns of working together, yet it guides behavior and interpersonal relationships through the vision it gives to all of life. In summary, companionship marriage addresses power distribution (see Scanzoni 1979); partnership marriage is concerned with the relationship's purpose. Companionship marriage is primarily a focus on structure and process; partnership marriage is primarily a focus on content and intention.

The Effects of Hierarchical and Companionship Marriage Patterns

Although the hierarchical model derived from scripture and traditional marriage in our own culture are not equivalents, traditional marriage does reflect a hierarchical arrangement of roles and can thus suggest implications for the hierarchical model in our cultural context. We have argued that the partnership model derived from scripture and our own culture's companionship marriage cannot be considered equivalents. Nevertheless, the emphasis on equality in companionship marriage forms the foundation for partnership marriage as well. From this perspective, an examination of companionship marriage can also suggest the effects that partnership marriage might have. The accusations by proponents of the hierarchical view that this emphasis on equality undermines the health and well-being of the family deserve an answer. What are the effects of traditional and companionship patterns of marital relating? We approach this material with the qualification that research findings concerning patterns of marriage cannot directly confirm or refute the view that one model or the other is "better," because they can only examine current sociological patterns, not ideological models. Yet we find in this research help in clarifying the impact of models in the actual lives of persons.

Advantages of traditional marriage. The major argument from a pragmatic perspective in favor of a traditional model is the relative ease of establishing this kind of marriage. Specifically, there are four features of traditional marriage that make it "easier" than companionship marriage.

Traditional marriage is more predictable. When the roles of spouses are defined by tradition, persons are clearer about what they are getting into when they marry. Apart from personal quirks and individual abilities that influence the quality of performance on particular assigned roles, one wife or husband is pretty much like another—at least compared to those in a companionship marriage. One knows what to expect. Small differences in expectations may need to be ironed out, but if a man and woman have grown up in the same cultural group, these will probably be minor rather than major differences. Great-grandma may have had a choice between Farmer Simmons and Farmer Gray; but apart from minor differences, such as whether she would live north or south of town, the constraints of her life—what her day-in day-out living would entail—would be similar. In short, marriage was not a life-style choice but a choice of a partner within a prescribed life-style.

By contrast, just about anything goes in a companionship marriage. The choice between Mr. Simmons and Mr. Gray involves a joint decision about life-style. Mr. Simmons may want to write novels and live in the Rocky Mountains with a career-oriented wife to support him; Mr. Gray may not know what he wants or where he might wander, but he wants a partner with whom to share decisions and the future. One may want no children; the other, five. The differences can multiply indefinitely. But these differences are not a matter of choosing one life-style over another—a red sports car instead of a beige station wagon. It is expected that both partners' dreams and values will be integrated and that in some way a relationship will evolve which includes and enhances both—a tall order!

Traditional marriage is less overtly conflictual. It follows that every decision has to be made together in a companionship marriage; by definition, nothing is "given" except the commitment to each other to work things through. The potential for conflict is therefore enormous. This is true not only for newlyweds but also for those who begin their marriage in a traditional pattern and, after struggling to meet the needs of both partners, attempt to move toward a companionship life-style together. Charlotte Holt Clinebell tells about her struggle:

> In some ways it's a difficult and painful thing to equalize a relationship which has been chiefly Parent-Child or sun-satellite for many years. When I first started not being home for lunch every day, Howard felt deprived. And I found it difficult to recognize that it was as much my responsibility as his to keep gas in the car. Those are just the little things, the tip of the iceberg. Many things are harder than the old way because we have to plan and negotiate our differences and argue at times about whose responsibility is what. But the gains are big. (Clinebell 1973, 36–37)

Despite the orderliness of the traditional pattern, however, the difference from the companionship model is not so much that less conflict arises as in how the conflict is handled. Wives in traditional marriages tend to be significantly more depressed and to suffer more from other mental health disorders than men, working married women, and unmarried women (Bernard 1982). These symptoms seem directly related to internalized conflict. Bernard concludes in her review of the research on women in marriage that a traditional life-style demands that wives be housewives and that "being a housewife makes women sick" (Bernard 1982, 48).

Interpersonal conflict may not be obvious to the observer in a traditional relationship, but it is present. Often, the power struggles in a traditional marriage take place in nonverbal ways. Anyone who grew up with traditionally oriented parents can usually attest to the fact that wives are not necessarily powerless just because they are not the family heads. The use of tears, silence, headaches, and "forgetting" the underwear needs washing or Hubby does not like fried liver are effective methods of expressing anger and of balancing power differentials. The definition of power is the ability to have intended effects on the behavior of another (Scanzoni 1979). To have power (or powerlessness) prescribed as a legitimate part of one's role is not the same thing as exercising or not exercising power in given situations. This means also that while a relationship may appear static, a constant change occurs in the actual power dynamics. The Greek folk saying that the husband is the head but the wife is the neck and decides which way the head will turn is sometimes the case in so-called traditional marriages. Even in the Roman family, where a wife had little legitimate power, Cato recognized her ability to use indirect methods when he expressed his fear of what would happen if women were allowed to have jewelry (see chapter 2; see also Juvenal, *Satires* 6). The quiet of a traditional marriage, then, should not be mistaken for harmony.

Dating and marriage patterns encourage traditional marriage. An egalitarian—equal—relationship is most difficult to achieve not only because it is hard to divvy up everything equally but also because mating patterns in our culture are based on pairing unequals. Men want to date women who are younger, less educated, less bright, and shorter than they are. Women want to date men who are older, better educated, smarter, and taller. Both want an attractive partner, but this is about the only characteristic not based on the man's being "more than" the woman. Bernard labels this the "marriage gradient:" "The girl wants to be able to 'look up' to her husband, and he, of course, wants her to" (Bernard 1982, 33). When this is the basis for initial attraction, establishing equity is even more difficult. It is hard enough for persons who perceive themselves to be equal in most respects.

Socialization patterns encourage traditional marriage. How many times do we find ourselves acting just like our same-sex parent quite unintentionally because he or she has been our primary gender model and object of identification? Most of us who are approaching middle age cut our teeth in traditional homes, did our homework watching George Burns and Gracie Allen, *Father Knows Best*, and *I Love Lucy*, and learned that men are the ones who have the answers and women are dingbats. Most women took a course or two in home economics in junior high or high school, while most of the boys took "shop." Women learned to cook and sew and take care of a house, and it is simply easier to let the one with more skill in these areas do these tasks. It is easier not to change.

Unfortunately, this ease often means that women keep adding on responsibilities that in the short run seem easier for her to do but in the long run lead to an overwhelming work load. Consistently, research points out that in dual-career marriages, despite the fact that both are employed, the wife carries most of the responsibility for the maintenance of hearth and home, including caring for children and aging parents. Women have 50 percent less leisure time than their husbands when both are working (Szalai 1973). Condran and Bode report that whether or not the wife works does not strongly affect the actual division of household labor. They conclude: "Attitudes and sympathies may have changed, but husbands still don't wash the dishes very often" (Condran and Bode 1982, 425; see also Yogev 1981). In another study, these findings were corroborated. Husbands were found to spend about 10 hours per week on household tasks whether or not the wife works outside the home, while housewives spend about 30 hours and working wives 20 hours on housework (Ferber 1982). The result of the pileup of responsibilities is that the woman finds herself expected by her family and herself to be Super Woman, a role described best by Ellen Goodman:

> Super Woman gets up in the morning and wakes her 2.6 children. She then goes downstairs and feeds them a Grade A nutritional breakfast and then goes upstairs and gets dressed in her Anne Klein suit and goes off to her $35,000-a-year job doing work which is creative and socially useful. Then she comes home after work and spends a meaningful hour with her children because, after all, it's not the quantity of time—it's the quality of time. Following that she goes into the kitchen and creates a Julia Child 60-minute gourmet recipe, having a wonderful family discussion about the checks and balances of the U.S. government system. The children go upstairs to bed and she and her husband spend another hour in their own meaningful relationship at which point they go upstairs and she is multi-orgasmic until midnight. (Goodman 1979)

Unfortunately, some evenings Super Woman must forego some of those meaningful discussions while she changes sheets, feeds the washing machine, and scrubs the kitchen floor. If she budgets her time well, however, she can do it all without dropping a stitch and without making her husband uncomfortable with her flurry of activity or forgetting to say thank you because he pitches in on occasion. At least, that is how it works in fantasyland. Perhaps the only thing as frustrating as trying to live out this myth is being the husband of a woman trying to live it out.

Advantages of companionship marriage. When the choice is between a traditional model and a companionship model in which the wife pursues her own development but retains traditional role assignments, the traditional model looks easier for everyone—easier, perhaps, but not as satisfying. Let us now turn to the advantages of companionship marriage.

Companionship marriage is more satisfying. Research has consistently pointed out that couples in companionship relationships are more satisfied with their marriages than those in traditional relationships. As early as 1952, Lu found that couples in egalitarian relationships reported greater adjustment (i.e., happiness or satisfaction) than those in which either partner was dominant. Since that time, others have consistently found that couples are simply more satisfied when their relationship is egalitarian rather than hierarchical (see Bean, Curtis, and Marcum 1977; Blood and Wolfe 1960; Centers, Raven, and Rodrigues 1971; Locke and Karlsson 1952; Michel 1967; Pond, Rule, and Hamilton 1963).

Companionship marriages are more stable. Contrary to popular belief, companionship marriages are actually more stable (less likely to end in divorce) than traditional marriages. In interviewing both married and divorced women, Scanzoni (1968) found that divorced women reported their former marriages to be more authoritarian—hierarchical —than married women. The married women reported more joint decision making in their marriages—the companionship model. In their interviews with low-income persons, Osmond and Martin (1978) also found that the companionship model described the marriages of 72 percent of married persons; only 29 percent were in traditional relationships. Yet of the divorced and separated persons, 73 percent described their former marriage as traditional rather than companionship in pattern. Even though traditional marriage forms were the norm in the past when marriages were more stable than today, we cannot attribute this stability to a hierarchical structure for marital roles. Other factors, such as societal pressure, more dependent children, and women's economic dependence and lack of alternatives, kept the marriages together. With the elimination of these factors, hierarchical marriage appears to be even less stable than companionship marriage is.

Companionship marriages are less likely to be violent. Violence is more likely to occur in homes where the husband has all the power and makes all the decisions than it is in homes where spouses share decision making. Walker (1979) found that spouse abusers and their abused partners typically believe in and live out a traditional model of marriage. In their revealing research, Straus, Gelles, and Steinmetz found that fewer than 3 percent of wives in egalitarian marriages had been beaten by their husbands in the previous year. In traditional marriages where the husband is dominant, 10.7 percent of wives had been beaten —a rate of violence more than 300 percent higher than for egalitarian marriages (Straus, Gelles, and Steinmetz 1980). One explanation for this sobering statistic is that men in hierarchical relationships have their identity as men tied to the submission of their wives. When a wife is not submissive, or at least when he perceives her not to be, he has the need to "show her who's the boss around here." He must not only restore the order of the marital relationship but also restore his damaged male identity. His identity is linked to the amount of power he wields over others.

Companionship marriages are more flexible in response to crisis. We have already mentioned the mounting pressure with little relief experienced by women living in traditional marriages and working outside the home. Because roles are gender-defined rather than interpersonally defined, no mechanism makes change possible when change is necessary, other than the gradual cultural changes that occur over generations. After all, gender is not changeable; interpersonal relationships are. This does not pose a problem as long as everything stays the same, but that is not exactly a description of our world! When a wife who heretofore has been at home goes to work, a dramatic change must take place in how the household is managed. In a traditional marriage, the only response possible is her absorption of the new demands through a delicate juggling act. The husband may "help out," but the responsibility for the home remains hers.

Other crises experienced by the couple may create even greater demands and add stress to the marriage: a seriously ill child, the demands of aging parents, the illness or unemployment of a spouse, and so on. Companionship partners tackle the crisis by struggling through changes in their patterns of doing things—not a simple matter but not necessarily relationship-threatening either. For the traditional marriage, such a change in patterns is a challenge to the very contract on which the marriage is formulated.

One major characteristic that distinguishes a functional from a dysfunctional family in coping with stress is the degree to which family roles are flexible or rigid (McCubbin and Figley 1983). In their seminal research with healthy families, Lewis and his colleagues found a continuum of structure that correlates with the level of functioning of a family. The most severely dysfunctional families tend to be chaotic and lack structure; families operating with some level of difficulty are rigid in their structure, and the healthiest families have a highly flexible structure (Lewis and others 1976; Lewis and Looney 1983). If we were to locate traditional and companionship patterns on this continuum, it is apparent that traditional patterns with their rigidity correspond to families with some level of difficulty, and companionship patterns with their flexibility correspond to optimally functional marriages. Supporting this theory, Larson (1984) found that of families suffering through the crisis of unemployment, those in traditional marriages were having far more difficulties with communication, harmony, and overall marital satisfaction than those in egalitarian (companionship) marriages. This study corroborates earlier research findings:

> The lower scores on these marriage and family life variables can most likely be attributed to the rigid nature of traditional marital role expectations. This rigidity inhibits a couple's adaptation to new roles as unemployment places pressure on established marital roles. (Larson 1984, 510)

Half the spouses are healthier in companionship marriage; the other half are less lonely. Companionship marriage is what its name says—companionship. Bernard (1982) has well documented the suffering imposed on women by traditional marriage, in which they "dwindle" into wives. Their God-given gifts are ignored as they are pressed into prescribed expectations. Meanwhile, husbands are left with awesome responsibilities for the fate of the family without a companion with which to share them for fear of neglecting his duty. Husband and wife share their meals, toothpaste, and bed, but not work, dreams, or souls.

In conclusion, at every point the research indicates that equality is a more functional base for marriage than hierarchy. Those who argue that egalitarian role relationships lead to a myriad of social ills have no support for their position.

From Companionship to Partnership

Despite the advantages of companionship marriage, it is not the vision of partnership described in the Bible. We have stated that this vision transcends any particular cultural pattern in a given time and context. How do we bring our interpretation of the Bible into making decisions about everyday life that must be made in our marriages? In our culture, someone must wash dishes, someone must go to work and bring home a paycheck, and someone must diaper the baby. Characteristics of our own cultural context influence the living out of the vision of partnership marriage for our own time and place. Partnership can only develop from a base of equality between persons. Until the advent of companionship marriage, this was difficult for Christians because of the constraints of gender-based hierarchical roles for spouses. Partnership is not possible when one partner has experienced submission as a given and not as a choice. It is for this reason that the companionship pattern is often linked with a partnership model.

Companionship marriage is structured by negotiated role assignments based on fairness: "If you'll do this, I'll do that." This bargaining approach to marriage is fostered by the prominence of social exchange theory in describing (though not necessarily prescribing) marital relating (Nye 1979) and by *quid pro quo* as a basis of some intervention strategies for marital difficulties (e.g., Lederer and Jackson 1968). Clinebell's book title *Meet Me in the Middle* summarizes this kind of thinking; it is a fifty-fifty approach. Although it does not achieve partnership, it does provide an alternative to hierarchical relating from which partnership can develop. Only from equality can persons move beyond the issues of order and fairness to a different level of relating based on partnership. As the antithesis of hierarchical relating, it enables spouses to wrestle with issues of authority and responsibility and then move on.

Equality must be the basis from which partnership can grow. It should not be disdained, but neither should it be mistaken as the goal. Many wives agonize over how they can be submissive when they are so angry about the injustice of a sexist society and the unchallenged sexism in their own marriages. A Christian wife finds herself trying to act on her faith by being lovingly submissive and serving—doing the dishes or laundry or whatever else has been the expectation—but she wants to do these tasks as an act of love, not simply because it is her job. All the while, however, she is seething inside, or depressed, because her service is taken for granted, as something expected of her as a wife. Occasionally she may erupt, angry at her partner for what appears to be his complacency in the face of her self-giving service. She may then regard her anger as a further sign of how far she is from achieving the will of God, which deepens her frustration as she attempts once again to be more loving. It is only when the couple can break out of the old role expectations that she can choose submission. One cannot *choose* to submit when no other choice is available.

Martha and Matt had been married for five years and both had been pursuing their own careers when they had their first child. Martha chose to work only part-time while their son was an infant. Their daughter was born two years later. During the years they were both working, Matt and Martha had fairly evenly divided the housework and other home responsibilities, although Martha did most of the cooking. After the birth of the children, Martha began taking on more of the housework responsibilities since she was there to do it. During the five years that she worked part-time, this pattern worked well; but Martha began to feel rising resentment. Jobs they had once shared had become her responsibility; even parenting the children seemed to be more her responsibility than Matt's. He was always eager to help out, and she appreciated his pitching in on the dishes or giving the children baths or reading stories. Why was she always saying thank you when he did things he ought to be doing anyway? She was firm in her desire to be Christlike in her relationship with her family; she wanted to be loving and to place the needs of her husband and family foremost, as she believed was important. Nevertheless, her husband undervalued her efforts as the mere fulfillment of her responsibilities rather than as the sacrifice of her own interests and time as she saw them, and she found herself often controlling rage by slamming pots and pans around and even by exclaiming to Matt on more than one exasperating evening, "I am your wife, not your servant!"

It was only as they sorted through their expectations that Matt and Martha began to understand what was happening to them. Martha could not change her feelings about caring for her family simply by chiding herself that she needed to do what she was doing in love. Nor could Matt communicate his appreciation for her by "helping out." It took a major reordering of responsibilities to establish a mutually felt equality from which they could serve each other and work together in their mutual parenting task. They had to work out in their own lives the understanding that love means acceptance of the other—and one's self—as an equal, with neither partner being more important. At times that meant challenging gender-role stereotypes which did not reflect their individuality.

What characterized the process of change for this young couple was not necessarily a division of chores on a more equitable basis so that all was equal, or even a modification of this ideal. Instead, it was the recognition that they were not simply roommates who loved each other while each pursued independent goals and dreams. They committed themselves to a joint task—parenting—and worked toward a relationship that furthered their work on that task and other tasks together. They became partners; mutual respect and equality were implicit in their decisions and in the approaches to change that they chose.

The basis of partnership marriage is the mutual respect, equality, and intimacy found in companionship marriage, but it involves still more. It is a partnership in a joint calling from God. Like the hierarchical model and our culture's traditional marriage, the model of the partnership and the companionship pattern have similar characteristics, but they are not equivalent. Although the companionship pattern is a good base for partnership, it focuses on the power distribution and dynamics of relating rather than the purposefulness of the marital relationship. The similarities and differences between these models from scriptural and cultural patterns can be found in Table 1.

Nevertheless, companionship marriage is a cultural pattern that may lead couples toward a pattern of marriage that accords with the vision of partnership in the Bible. It provides a starting point and makes partnership a possibility. In the end it is hoped that Christians in our culture will be able to put away egalitarian thinking, as they are now putting away hierarchical thinking, and become more concerned with their calling and task from God than with the current and necessary focus on power and equality. When we reach that point, we can put away the scales that measure how much power and responsibility each has and how fair and equal marriage roles are. The ultimate goal is not order, or equality, but fulfilling the purpose of marriage intended by God for each couple. Hierarchical and companionship patterns are concerned with the structure (roles and power relationship) and the processes (intimacy and conflict management) of marriage. The ideal of partnership addresses the overarching purposefulness of the marriage and thus transcends concerns about roles even while assuming equality.

In many ways, moving from companionship to partnership is like the moral growth of a child. For preschoolers, right is whatever Mommy and Daddy say. Parents are an unquestioned authority, although not always obeyed. Here we recognize a parallel with the traditional pattern of marriage that does not question the authority and supremacy of the husband, even though these may be subtly modified or undermined.

During the elementary school years, fairness becomes the child's criterion for "right." If another child got two pieces of candy, I should too. How many times does the parent of an eight-year-old hear, "But that's not fair!" Most companionship marriages—or hierarchical marriages becoming companionship-oriented—begin here with a sense of the injustice of traditional gender roles. The objective is to even things up. Many of us still solve things that way. We worry about whether we are being treated fairly or not. This concern for fairness is actually a process of defining one's self through which the child learns that both self and others are persons with worth. The child obtains "identity." A similar process occurs in marriage. The companionship marriage has in view fairness, equity, and identity—the goal is self-actualization.

From the development of self-identity and worth the child is able to move beyond making sure that he or she gets his or her just due into maturity. Maturity comes when persons are ready to use themselves in some purpose larger than themselves—a career, a social change effort, the care of others. It is only as one has experienced justice and has learned to deal justly with others as persons as valuable as one's self that one can give one's self over to a cause. Similarly, it is only when a couple has experienced justice and equality in relating with each other that these issues can be transcended by giving themselves over to goals larger than treating each other equally and furthering each other's personal growth. Companionship can then become partnership, because role structures do not matter. Wife may cook and husband may mow the lawn, but these activities have an entirely different meaning than they do in the hierarchical relationship.

In fact, when we move from both traditional and companionship

Table 1. Comparison of Biblical Models and Cultural Patterns

	Biblical Models		Cultural Patterns	
	Hierarchical	Mutual Submission	Traditional	Companionship
Motto	"Wives, be subject" (Eph. 5:22)	"Be subject to one another out of reverence for Christ" (Eph. 5:21)	"The man wears the pants in this family"	"Love one another, but make not a bond of love" (Gibran's *The Prophet*)
Goal	Order	The meaning and purpose of the relationship in God's will	Order	Individual autonomy and self-actualization
Structure	Gender roles, particularly woman's, clearly assigned	[not specified]	Gender roles, particularly woman's, clearly assigned	Flexible, negotiated roles, to meet individual needs and desires
Authority	God-man-woman	Each, who then gives it up for the other, and both under the authority of God	Husband	Shared
Decision making	Issues settled by husband with reference to legalistic principles and rules	Mutual, with their joint calling as the context	Husband decides or delegates to wife	Each asserts own needs and desires, then works toward consensus or compromise

	Biblical Models		Cultural Patterns	
	Hierarchical	Mutual Submission	Traditional	Companionship
Preparation	Training by elders in gender roles	Experience of the love of Christ and Christian life-style (as well as interpersonal skills)	Training by parents and society in appropriate gender roles	Interpersonal skills of communication and conflict management
Personal energy requirements	Relationship functions on automatic pilot—runs smoothly in highly specified patterns	Requires submission of all of self	Automatic pilot	Requires much energy and interpersonal discussion
Response to changing context over time	Static—change is slow and creates crisis	Constantly changing to meet the demands of their work together	Static—change is slow and creates crisis	Constantly changing to meet changing needs of the individuals
Emotional tone	Respect	Sacrificial love	Secure in one's place	Free yet interdependent
Career prominence	Husband's work outside the family, wife's within	[not specified]	Husband's career is predominant, wife is primarily homemaker with employment secondary if at all	Variety of options, basing decisions on needs, abilities, and desires of each person
Focus	Structure—husband as head, wife submissive	Goal—the meaning and purpose of this marriage	Structure	Process—whatever individual growth requires

patterns toward the vision of partnership marriage, we may find that marriage includes both aspects of equal sharing and aspects in which one or the other partner takes the lead. In a partnership marriage, spouses submit themselves to a purpose beyond having their own needs met. It is not the structure of the relationship that is important, it is what gives the couple meaning and purpose.

For example, two studies report that in examining the pattern of relationship, marital satisfaction, and amount of stress experienced by partners, whether the wife works or not is not so important as whether her working is part of the couple's vision of what is important (Scanzoni and Fox 1980; Fendrich 1984). Similarly, Lewis and others (1976) found that it was not a family's role structure that was so important to its well-being as it was the family's flexibility in meeting changing demands and goals.

Theorists of human relationships have identified two basic patterns of interaction, based on equality and difference (Watzlawick, Beavin, and Jackson 1967). Equality is the basis for symmetrical relating; partners focus on their alikeness and emphasize sharing. On the other hand, difference is the basis for complementary relationships; one partner is superior or "primary" and the other is secondary or "one-down." Complementary relationships are characterized by one partner's caring for or being responsible for the other. We identify symmetrical partners as "two peas in a pod"; complementary partners are Jack Sprat and his fat wife ("opposites attract"). The results of each kind of relating are quite different. Symmetrical relating often results in conflict and change; complementary relating results in less intense interaction and stability.

Traditional marriage emphasizes complementary relating and companionship marriage emphasizes symmetrical relating. It is apparent, however, that neither pattern alone is ideal. As couples move beyond both, they can choose to combine the best of each pattern into a model of relating unique to their own needs and goals. Areas of their relationship exist in which one partner exercises primary responsibility and "cares for" the spouse (complementary relating) and areas in which they are equal companions, working together and tackling differences (symmetrical relating). Relationships that become stuck in a consistently symmetrical pattern risk flying apart when changes occur too rapidly or when conflict is too intense. Relationships that are stuck in a consistently complementary pattern are at best often boring and distant and at worst may disintegrate when the same patterns of relating do not adapt to the changing needs of the partners and their tasks.

In embracing both models of relating, the vision of partnership marriage uses the two patterns as means of achieving the purposes of the marital relationship, rather than making them the definition of the relationship. We all need and want to be cared for at times—when we are ill, disappointed, tired, or even jubilant (it is fun to have someone else prepare a celebrative event for us when we have something we wish to celebrate). Similarly, there is a special joy that comes from caring for our partner—surprising them with breakfast in bed or listening with concern to their troubles. This kind of complementary relating —caring for and being cared for—is helpful and useful. It is also reassuring to know that our partner will take care of certain responsibilities, whether it is getting the car serviced when necessary or paying the bills, without our having to worry about it. Complementary roles such as these save much needless hassle and provide stability and continuity. On the other hand, it is reassuring to know that any of these established patterns can change when it is necessary; we also relate symmetrically. When one of us feels pulled into new career directions, we will make the decision together. When new responsibilities call for attention, such as an aging parent who needs personal care, we will tackle the responsibility together. Many tasks are shared; many issues take our combined gifts and efforts.

Counselors often are faced with couples who are "stuck" in one pattern or another. The change strategy is therefore to introduce into the relationship the alternative pattern of relating to give the relationship more balance. Two simple examples will help illustrate these strategies. These are offered as illustrations of symmetrical and complementary relationship patterns and are not intended as models of effective marriage counseling.

Example 1: A symmetrical relationship with complementary change. James and Carol sought help because they seemed to quarrel about everything, especially who was carrying the bigger load. What really disturbed them, however, was their constant disagreement over how to discipline the children and what the rules were to be. They felt they had to agree on everything, to present the kids with a united front, but instead always seemed to clash. The first change effort by the counselor was to tell James that for three days he was to make all the rules for the kids and be responsible for the discipline. Carol was to support him whether she agreed with him or not. (The counselor discussed with both of them their ideas about parenting so that there was assurance that their expectations were reasonable and their discipline not extreme or violent). For the next three days, Carol was to take over and James was to support her. The children were to be informed of the plan, and they would go from there. They were not asked to do this indefinitely, but this plan gave them a week to relate in a complementary pattern rather than their overused symmetrical style. They could experiment with a pattern of relating different from their former attempts to achieve total accord on every issue.

Example 2: A complementary relationship with symmetrical change. By contrast, Laura and Jim had been married for twenty-five years. Now that the children were grown, they seemed to have little to talk about with each other. They consulted a counselor not because they were particularly unhappy so much as because they were hopeful that they might build more closeness into their relationship. They each worked at their own jobs and met their home responsibilities without conflict but without much enthusiasm. The counselor told them that on the next Friday night, they were to decide what kind of dinner they would like to prepare together. They were to shop for the ingredients, cook the meal, and clean up together. It was to be something neither had prepared before, so that neither would operate as "expert." Again, the counselor's assignment was made not because it was "right" but because it related to the larger goals of the couple. It was not expected that they would conduct this ritual every Friday night; but it gave them an experience of symmetrical relating, of sharing a task rather than dividing it and each doing one part in parallel fashion.

The use of complementary and symmetrical patterns also can be seen in how the actions and teachings of Jesus and Paul were designed to intervene in marriage and other relationships between men and women in the early church. Jesus addressed a world stuck in a pattern of complementary—hierarchical—relationships, with the same person (woman) always on the bottom. Into this pattern he introduced symmetry-equality. Marriage partners cannot, however, move easily from a rigid hierarchical pattern to equality without experiencing stress and the potentially serious disruption of their lives.

An analogy from a twentieth-century January in Minnesota will serve to illustrate. You do not get into your car on a minus-10-degree snowy winter morning, turn on the motor, and within seconds rev it up to 70 miles an hour (or even 55!) without risking throwing a rod or crashing into something or someone on slick roads. Some members of the early church were throwing some rods and hitting some bridge abutments in their move from static hierarchical marriage to the dynamic equality that Jesus taught. Paul feared they were destroying the very institution of marriage that was to portray ideal male-female relatedness. Because you go slowly until the motor is a little warmer does not mean that you do not want to reach your destination—that is the very reason for slowing down! So at times Paul and others used expedient role specifications in male-female relationships to provide some stability in a time of sudden and overwhelming change. Paul and later authors introduced "complementary" relationships, particularly in worship, not as the goal or the ideal for how men and women were to relate for all time, but with the intention of giving balance and allowing for the integration of change.

Marriage between Christians is to be more than a way to order our lives, more than companionship between persons who have agreed to be intimate with each other over a lifetime. It is to be a partnership in a joint task that is larger than either partner can accomplish alone. It is a partnership that is ordered around the meaning and purpose of our relatedness. That does not mean that our lives do not need order—they do—or that intimacy is not important—it is. Both of these are essential to partnership. But in and of themselves they do not comprise the vision of marriage that is to be partnership with each other and with God. Neither order nor intimacy is the goal that should determine what a marriage is to be like. Mace quotes a radio talk of Lord Beveridge:

> Our fathers had a saying about marriage, that if two people ride on a horse, one of the two must ride behind. Today marriage is more like two people riding abreast on the same horse, doing a rather difficult balancing feat and each holding one rein. It's more companionable than the old way, but it's more complicated, and must at times be rather confusing to the horse. (Quoted in Mace 1973, 60)

In a partnership marriage, the focus has shifted; it is no longer how are we going to organize ourselves to ride this horse, but where are we going? The destination then helps determine the means for getting there. What is our role in the will of God; what is our work together? Does it lead over hurdles, or is it a long journey over desert? Deciding which it is will help determine whether we sit the old way or take turns sitting in front, whether we try Lord Beveridge's delicate balancing or walk and let the horse carry provisions for our trek. Too many are letting how they ride the horse determine where they are going, rather than allowing where they are going to determine the use of the horse! In short, the pattern of a couple's relationship needs to reflect the meaning of their life together and its purpose in the will of God. The scripture does not lay out specific role expectations or provide a how-to-do-it marriage manual. What is clear is that God does not order relationship roles by gender. In that spirit, couples may—must—choose to order their lives to fit their context and the task to which they have been called.

4

Marriage with a Purpose: Beyond Ourselves

Two characteristics of humanity are said to distinguish us from the rest of creation—how we raise our young and how we manipulate and transform our environment through the use of our heads and our hands (Bronfenbrenner and Crouter 1982). These characteristic human activities have long been associated with family (raising our young) and work (transforming our environment), but assigning these two activities to separate spheres with little overlap is a relatively recent phenomenon. A look at this separation is important for an understanding of the current role of marriage in the lives of individuals.

An Overview of Family and Work

Until the nineteenth century, work and home life were one; the family functioned as a center for economic production as well as the primary source for meeting the interpersonal needs of its members. For most people, work and home, family and work colleagues, religious expression, and the ebb and flow of daily life were intertwined in the same world of existence—the family household. In this traditional world women were subordinate, but they were colleagues in the economic support of the family rather than dependents. One need only think of colonial and frontier history, when the wife spun the thread, wove the cloth, made clothes from the homespun, churned the butter, canned and preserved the produce, butchered the livestock, cared for the dairy cattle and chickens, made the candles, prepared medicinal concoctions for the sick and cared for them, taught the children their lessons by the hearth, made soap, and so on. In 1890, the sewing machine and the eggbeater were the only mechanical aids in most homes (Smuts 1959). When the wife was needed in the fields, she worked beside her husband harvesting or planting. The work of husband and wife, though defined by different tasks, was integrated and interdependent.

In a variety of cultures and in both rural settings and in trades and small businesses, the roles of women have characteristically been much broader than the current domestic role of housewife. In Proverbs, the model Hebrew wife was not only a good mother and housekeeper but an economic contributor as well, a manager of domestic industry. A good wife considers a field and buys it, plants a vineyard and sells her merchandise profitably (Prov. 31:16–18) and thereby leaves her husband free to sit and converse wisely among the elders of the land (Prov. 31:23; see Jer. 31:22). It was not until the turn of this century that housekeeping was considered a full-time occupation for women (Melville 1980).

In the nineteenth century, work became separated from the home. Men went away to factories, carrying lunch pails, not just to nearby fields or to the front-room shop. Soon this division became not only reality but the model, the way things are supposed to be (Lasch 1980). Home became idealized as a haven from the work world. The family had been stripped of its productive functions. If the wife was still productive, it was as an employee selling her labor. Her work had no relationship to that of her husband except that earnings were pooled. Certainly the wife's labor in the home—preparing meals, cleaning, sewing—was helpful, but it did not contribute substantially to the economic well-being of the family and was thus, in a wage-oriented world, of lesser importance. For the most part, the mutual interdependence of spouses in work was lost. This was not true for everyone; many rural families and small businesses retained the old interdependence. The ideal, however, had been changed.

For those who associate meaning and purpose in living with productiveness, an American value, this division left only childbearing and child rearing tasks as the primary source of meaning for the marriage and the family. Yet time committed to this task was also diminishing. According to census data, the average parents today spend only 18 percent of their married lives rearing young children; a century ago they spent 54 percent of their lives with young children (Bane 1976). Children are now more of an interruption in the ongoing march of years than they are a primary definition of the function of the marital relationship.

The Sociological Functions of Marriage Today

In premodern times the family functioned in six major roles for which it now has minimal—if any—responsibility. These roles were:

economic (producing goods and services for family members and for sale), protective (protecting members from outside threats such as enemies, illness, and isolation), religious (educating and providing avenues for religious development and expression), recreative (providing opportunities for rest, creative expression outside of normal responsibilities, and play), educational (teaching skills, knowledge, and values necessary for functioning in society), and status placement (providing a niche in the social order by identifying the individual as a member of this specific family—one of the Garlands, or Jed's boy). (See Ogburn and Tibbitts 1934 for further discussion of the functions and roles of the family). As we have seen, the economic function has been transferred to the factory and office. The protective function is no longer served by the rifle over the door and Mom's poultices; we now have police and armies, physicians and insurance. The religious function is, at least in most families, no longer met by family worship and disciplined religious instruction of children; we rely on churches and church schools for this purpose. The recreational function is no longer served by taffy pulls and family sings; we have a burgeoning sports and entertainment industry to satiate every desire. Finally, the family is no longer responsible for status placement. This function now rests with the individual; who you are is based not on family name so much as on individual accomplishments.

Marriage and the family now have only two major functions not served by other societal institutions. The first of these is a vestige of the economic function reversed—the consumer function. Instead of being the main unit of production, the family is now considered to be the main unit of consumption (Duberman 1977). For the most part, spouses pool their income and draw from the common pot for making purchases. Big-ticket items—cars, refrigerators, houses—are bought to serve the family unit. Spouses have to integrate and coordinate their spending, if not their work, in order to function effectively. Duberman, in fact, goes so far as to suggest that this will be the *only* function of the family in the future (Duberman 1977).

With productiveness removed from the family and consumerism a primary family activity, what sense of purpose many couples feel comes from their joint consumption—taking the boat out on weekends, buying and furnishing a house, traveling or entertaining. Such experiences may be meaningful and important and may transcend consumerism as an experience of sharing and togetherness. For most, however, these experiences are relatively isolated and segregated from day-in day-out living. Instead of providing a guiding purpose for all of a person's activities, they further segregate the meaningful moment from the relatively meaningless round of daily activities. Monday through Friday are endured because they bring the promise of the weekend and its pleasurable and perhaps meaningful activities. Spouses remain isolated from each other in their work activities and share primarily in periodic leisure pursuits. Being play partners for each other is hardly a task that can command a lifetime commitment and the will to overcome whatever obstacles are encountered in marriage.

The other remaining function of marriage and the family is affective: the family provides a setting in which the individual can express and meet needs, where acceptance and belonging are available for each member just for being a member. The family is still the one group that is supposed to support a member no matter what happens. It is the affective function that is paramount in establishing, maintaining, and dissolving marriages. As important as consumerism has become, few couples stay together for the sake of the house, let alone the refrigerator. A graphic example of the extent to which the affective function has become the primary function of marriage is Miller's list of the duties of a spouse (Miller 1983, 158):

1. To provide the partner with sexual pleasure
2. To provide the partner with encouragement to express aggression appropriately
3. To allay the partner's old anxieties
4. To avoid mobilizing new anxieties

Others would broaden this list to include providing a sense of belonging, listening empathically and communicating acceptance and understanding, sharing one's self with the spouse, and developing intimacy. In short, the function of marriage is to meet interpersonal needs.

An interesting way of following the changing functions of marriage and the family over time is to trace the development and changes in the structure of physical living and working space for the family. Until the eighteenth century, privacy was not a guideline for building houses. People ate, slept, worked, played, bathed, and entertained visitors in the same general-purpose rooms. Work, caring for children, discussing matters of import, family spats, even sexual relations took place in the shared space without today's walls of privacy. By the eighteenth century, however, the boundaries between family and neighbors became more sharply drawn and family relationships became more significant and exclusive (Melville 1980).

The evolution in family relationships is still apparent in continuing changes in architecture. During the first half of this century, most middle-class American houses were built with front porches. It was here that, weather permitting, the family spent its time together during an afternoon rest or during the evening hours before bedtime. A fond memory is playing in the front yard with other neighbor children amid the murmur of parents' voices as they sipped iced tea brought from the supper table and talked together on the porch until long after dark. Family time was public behavior; other neighbors also spent a good bit of time on their porches and could see and hear much of one another's goings-on. Friends called and joked back and forth from one porch or yard to another or sauntered over to "visit" for a while.

In recent decades, however, new architectural conventions have reflected changing social ideals (Melville 1980). In middle-class America, the public front porch has given way to the private enclosed patio or deck and the climate-controlled "family room." The front yard is now a carefully manicured "face." Laborsaving devices and convenience products have taken the productiveness out of the home, while architecture and social convention have placed the affective function within it, with buffers to keep interference out.

Duberman argues that the affective function has not stopped evolving with its investment in the family, and this is reflected in the home, the family's ideal physical environment. Not only have the family and its needs been moved inside its walls but the members are more and more walled off from one another by our individualistic ideals, as well as by our architecture. Rooms have become specialized, with primary regard for the privacy of persons from one another. In the ideal home, parents have a good bit of privacy even from the children, with their own bath and sitting area and often their own phone line and television. Children may have a "playroom" separate from the rest of the family's living spaces. The parents may even have privacy from each other, with separate closets and dressing areas, even recreation spaces (the spare bedroom for Mom's crafts or office, the basement for Dad's woodworking or study).

Duberman suggests that the affective function of marriage and the family is being infringed on by our culture's love of individualism. She writes:

> A new ideology is growing in this country and it exalts the individual. It impels us to reach more into ourselves and to rely on ourselves. It urges us to withdraw from dependence on others, to avoid entanglements, and to keep our relationships temporary and tentative. Individualism, reliance on oneself, is becoming the supreme ethic. Our struggle is to free ourselves from involvement with all others, including the family, and to recognize that others do not really understand who we are, what we want, why we do as we do, or what we hope to become. (Duberman 1977, 22)

One indicator of growing individualism in marriage is our acceptance of divorce as a natural step if self-actualization and fulfillment are not forthcoming in a marriage. The assumption is that if my partner does not meet my needs, I must be responsible enough for myself to find fulfillment elsewhere. Individualism therefore heightens the demands placed on marriage and in turn decreases its stability. This does not mean that divorce is undertaken lightly or with less stress but that it is culturally prescribed when a marriage does not measure up to these standards.

Another indicator of the effect of individualism on marriage is the rising acceptance of professional counseling as useful and functional for all persons at various times in their lives, not just for the severely disturbed. At least in more affluent groups, primary relationships, family and friends, and even spouses are not expected to deal with problems that can be helped by professional counseling. If I cannot take care of them myself, I need professional help to learn how. One woman tells of her experience after her baby was stillborn. When she was still grieving after one month, her husband sent her to a psychiatrist. Reflecting on this, she said, "He and my friends wanted to be rid of my grieving" (Stringham, Riley, and Ross 1982). Similarly, some of the mushrooming self-help literature that addresses particular problems or challenges of life unintentionally supports the assumption that it is the individual's responsibility to meet his or her own needs and difficulties.

Most of us like having the option to be able to take individual action, and there is value in people's taking responsibility for themselves and getting help when they need it. Nevertheless, the emphasis on individualism affects marriage negatively; it removes some of the significant functions of marriage, and it weakens the ties and support of family and friends. What is often not recognized is that in the so-called "good old days" when divorce was almost unheard of, marriages were stable because they were multifunctional. Marriage was necessary for economic, religious, and social well-being. Affection and intimacy were not the glue that held husband and wife together; they were held together by external forces, and many interpersonal needs were met by kinfolk. Now marriage is held together almost exclusively by the internal interpersonal relationship. Few of us want to go back to a subsistence existence or to a one-room cabin in order to return some of the lost functions to the family. Unless we bomb ourselves back to the Stone Age, this is an irreversible change, and for most of us it is desirable; we prefer staying together as a couple because we want to rather than because there are no other choices.

Does this mean, then, that we must accept greater and greater instability in marital relationships as a result of these irreversible changes? Can anyone reasonably expect to make a lifetime commitment and stick with it? Joint consumerism is hardly a sufficient basis for Christian marriage. Jesus contended that a person's life does not consist of the abundance of possessions (Luke 12:15) and warned against laying up treasures for oneself while not being "rich toward God" (Luke 12:21).

Likewise, marriage does not consist of the abundance of possessions, and one that is held together only by the function of consumerism will pass like a summer cloud. Mammon (material wealth) always fails (Luke 16:9)—in this life and in the life to come. In the same way, married partners devoted only to nurturing themselves on separate paths of individual growth are poor risks for marital survival. Is there a stronger basis of marital commitment?

The Task Function of Marriage

For Christians, an answer to this question can be found in the somewhat puzzling paradigm of mutual submission on which our model of marriage as a partnership is based. A caricature of mutual submission is the picture of a man and a woman standing before a doorway, each forever bowing and saying to the other, "After you, dear." "No, dear, after you." No doubt, concern for each other's needs and support and care for each other are part of the meaning of mutual submission. Marriage extends far beyond this, however. It is not only concerned with the well-being of the other but also with the calling and task of the marital relationship. Spouses become partners in a calling or a task that transcends the relationship itself. If the union of Christ and the church is to be compared to the union of husband and wife, as it is in Ephesians 5, it would follow that the marriage relationship has a transcendent purpose in God's scheme of things. According to McLain and Weigert, transcendence is "the quality of experiences that take on meaning of greater strength and scope than that which is available in the everyday lifeworld" (McLain and Weigert 1979, 189). It is not only a good in this transient life but, according to Leonard, "reaches beyond itself toward participation in the creative/redemptive work of God" (Leonard 1984, 9).

Premises Concerning the Task and Purpose of Marriage

We would suggest five premises that can help clarify the concept of task in partnership marriage. First, *marriage is a unity,* an "organism" with a task and a purpose of its own beyond the mere summation of the tasks and purposes of the individual spouses. In recent years, family theorists have embraced systemic definitions of the family in which the family is defined as larger than the sum of the individuals that form it. Minuchin (1984) has dubbed the family a "multibodied organism." The same concept is vividly expressed in the biblical concept of "one flesh." The image of God is the relationship between persons, the two becoming one (Gen. 1:27). Human life from its very beginning is described as the relationship between man and woman. To be human is to be a partner, and from the very beginning we were given a task. Immediately after creation, "God blessed them and God said to them, 'Be fruitful and multiply, and fill the earth and subdue it' " (Gen. 1:28). As Newbigin states, "Human life from its beginning is a life of shared relationship in the context of a task—a task which is continuous with God's creative work in the natural world" (Newbigin 1978, 77).

In the New Testament, the marriage of Prisca (diminutive, Priscilla) and Aquila characterized this kind of marriage. Prisca was certainly not the junior partner in this relationship. Of the six times this couple is mentioned (Acts 18:2, 18, 26; Rom. 16:3–5a; 1 Cor. 16:19; 2 Tim. 4:19), her name appears first in four of them. Once, Paul included greetings to the Corinthian church from both of them (1 Cor. 16:19). This is noteworthy; it was not customary to include the wife's name in sending greetings inasmuch as the husband's name alone would normally suffice (Fiorenza 1984, 178). Yet Prisca's name stands with her husband's and indicates her importance both to Paul and to the community. Paul had come to know this couple in Corinth after they, along with other Jews, had been banished from Rome by the Emperor Claudius. Paul stayed with them and worked with them in their common trade as "tentmakers" or leather workers (Acts 18:3). When they later moved to Ephesus, Prisca and Aquila heard the eloquent Apollos preaching in the synagogues, and they *together* took him and expounded the way of God more accurately for him (Acts 18:26). The text indicates that Prisca was equally involved in instructing Apollos, a male, and one with a thorough knowledge of scripture (Acts 18:24), in theology.

From these brief references to this couple, it is clear that their relationship was based on equality; they were "partners" together as well as "fellow workers" of Paul (Rom. 16:3). More importantly, their marriage had a purpose beyond itself. Together, they dedicated themselves to a greater calling than making tents or making themselves happy. They opened the doors of their home to the Christian family, taking in Paul (Acts 18:3) and later hosting a house church in Ephesus that became a missionary center (1 Cor. 16:19) and perhaps also one in Rome (Rom. 16:5). Paul said that all the churches of the Gentiles gave thanks for them and their work, and he especially, since they risked their necks for his life (Rom. 16:4). What incident Paul had in mind is impossible to know (perhaps Acts 19:23). His catalog of travails in 2 Corinthians 11:23 suggests that there were many times when his own neck was in peril and needed saving. Prisca and Aquila, then, functioned as partners together; their marriage was more than mutual need-meeting. No doubt they had individual gifts, but the linking of their names together in the New Testament indicates the importance of their partnership in ministry beyond their individual contributions.

Their marriage had a purpose beyond the promotion of Prisca's and Aquila's individual growth; they worked together as a team, as partners in a joint task that transcended their relationship.

A second premise for understanding partnership marriage is that *the task or purpose of each marriage is unique* and cannot be imposed by a standard definition of the function of marriage. No one can define the purpose for a couple's marriage, just as no one can define the purpose of life for another individual. Finding one's task, the purpose and meaningfulness of marriage, is not like choosing a career or planning a project together; it is an individual and lifelong endeavor just as it is for the individual Christian.

Some couples experience purpose thrust upon them; others may go through a process of searching together. Some find their tasks in the opportunities for service together in family and community life. It may be as varied as mutual involvement in service to church (see Rom. 12:6–13) or issues of social concern, or spending a lifetime together serving as missionaries with a different people in a faraway place. It may be caring for one's own children together, or widening one's family circle to include persons who lack a family. It may be vocation or avocation, family-focused or focused on neighborhood or world community. It is in the process of mutually submitting themselves to God's will that the couple defines that which is meaningful and purposeful for their relationship.

Most couples do not go through a conscious process of determining what their mutual task is or even identifying specifically what it is that gives meaning to their life together. It is most often identified in retrospect or by the ways others know them. This leads to the third premise, *the task or purpose of a marriage is often not explicitly defined but can be found in the structure of relationship rules and values that define a couple's life together.* The concept of a marriage's task or purpose is foreign to most couples. That does not mean, however, that an implicit purpose around which their relationship centers does not exist. How do they spend their resources of energy, time, and material goods? What is it that beckons them to struggle on when they are weary or their relationship is at an ebb? What are the effects of their relationship for themselves and for others? Answering such questions as these may identify the relative emptiness of some marriages, but for others it may provide impetus to greater commitment to that purpose which before was only unconsciously felt.

Fourth, just as it does for the individual, *the task or purpose of a marriage varies over time.* The best example of this is the task of parenting, which may be all-consuming for parents of preschoolers but—as the children grow to young adulthood—diminishes as the steering purpose of their life together. Tasks therefore develop new dimensions or may end, and the couple must then search for a new task or purpose. Such changes result both in upheaval and in the excitement of new possibilities.

In another respect, the content of a couple's task varies not only during their lifetime together but also from day to day and hour to hour. What matters is not the meaning of their relationship in general but the specific meaning of their life together at a given moment. Frankl has suggested that to ask what is the meaning in life is like asking a chess champion, "Tell me, Master, what is the best move in the world?":

> There simply is no such thing as the best or even a good move apart from a particular situation in a game and the particular personality of one's opponent. The same holds for human existence. One should not search for an abstract meaning of life. Everyone has his own specific vocation or mission in life; everyone must carry out a concrete assignment that demands fulfillment. . . . Thus, everyone's task is as unique as is his specific opportunity to implement it." (Frankl 1959, 171–172)

We are suggesting that this is true not only for the individual but also for marriage. As each situation in life offers the couple challenges, they respond in their life together and, in the process, create meaning and purpose for their marriage.

Finally, *a significant source of meaning in marriage comes from the partners' roles as co-creators.* Whether they bring children into the world or are a creative influence on the lives of others, spouses create. Without creating, love remains an abstract concept, a gust of emotion. It is only in the process of co-creation that partners grow spiritually and are strengthened in their own calling as well as in their relationship. The process of marriage is therefore a process of creation. Almost every couple is creative in three ways.

First, *couples create a shared physical environment.* They build their nest together and may conceive and give birth to children.

Second, *couples create an emotional world* of ideas and patterns of relating. They develop relationship norms and processes of communication that are a reality, whether blessing or burden, for their children and others who share their world. For example, children learn the meaning of marriage and the role of a spouse primarily from the model parents provide. Adults evaluate their own relationships by observing the marital experiences of others they know—how they work out differences, communicate respect and appreciation, set priorities, and so on. In addition to the influence on others, a couple's relationship world nourishes or dampens the dreams and possibilities of the individual partners and makes possible collaboration in present and future activities not possible for either alone.

Third, *couples create yesterday together.* The couple shares a past, and that past, including even their individual pasts that were not initially shared experiences, is rewoven as it is discussed. From their two separate memories one cloth is woven. McLain and Weigert (1979) call this process "biographical fusion." We have all listened to a couple telling the story of some past event and, in the telling of it, correcting each other and making it a common tale. This story belongs not to the past but to the present, for it communicates to themselves and to others who they are, what they are like, what their weaknesses and strengths are, what is important to them, and what is not important enough to be remembered. These stories are passed on to children and give subtle shape to their lives, providing more significant roots than a genealogical tree that only lists names on a paper. The past lives on in the future not only through stories of the past but also through their rehearsal and the reaffirmation of values the couple wishes to shape their future. By sharing their definition of the past and its meaning, marital partners have a basis for collaboration in the future, for working through conflict, and for sifting out the chaff from the wheat in their lives (Elder 1981). Their future together is based on a mutual foundation. It gives direction to their task together.

Implications

Partnership marriage is marriage based on submission of partners to each other in the calling and task of their relationship. This calling, the purpose of their relationship, transcends their relationship through mutual creative involvement in the past as well as in the present and future according to their understanding of God's intention for their lives and the world. This model of marriage assumes that a couple's work together, their mutual calling, is intrinsic to their fulfillment as partners. It contrasts with the popular view that partners must first find meaning and fulfillment in shared intimacy before they can share themselves with others. We call this popular view "fountain marriage."

Fountain Marriage

The fountain model of marriage is the one often espoused when any attention is given to the calling of a couple beyond their interpersonal relating. In this pattern of marriage, the love of a husband and wife "overflows" into shared love for a child or a task. Implicit in this model is the belief that the relationship between husband and wife must first be filled to overflowing, so that some "leftover" love will flow into other tasks and demands. One can conceive of a three-tiered fountain. The top and smallest level signifies the marriage. As it is filled to the brim, some of the water (love, concern, involvement) flows to the next lower level, the children and other family members. This spills over into the lowest and largest level—church and community—that is never full enough to overflow.

One piece of a fountain is not visible, the pipe and pump that recirculates the water to the top level from the bottom. This represents the input to the marriage that comes from involvement in the other levels of life. It is recognized that a marriage receives some sustenance through these outside involvements. Nevertheless, the water pumped back to the marriage is far less than that expended in other involvements; some is lost to evaporation and to people dipping from the fountain. In some marriages there is little or no water to be pumped; all the resources are expended in the first level in taking care of the socioemotional needs of the spouses so that none overflows to the other two levels. If there is some overflow into the family level, children and parents in the second level soak up any remaining resources.

The fountain model of marriage is an application at the interpersonal level of Maslow's theory concerning the needs of the individual. According to Maslow, concern for others can develop only after one's own needs are met. Physiological needs such as food and rest must be cared for before a person develops concern for much else. When these needs are met, needs for safety and security then rise to the surface of concern. When security and safety needs are met, needs for love, belonging, and then esteem emerge. Finally, when all these levels of need are met, the need for self-actualization, the need to dedicate one's self to some task or vocation that transcends the self, is recognized. All one's basic needs must be met first, however, before one can focus on self-actualization, before turning from what one needs to survive to what is of ultimate value (see Maslow 1968). Even the ideal of self-actualization still focuses on the subjective experiences and fulfillment of the individual, however, rather than on the meaning that transcends the individual. Wallach and Wallach conclude:

> The idea that what matters is within oneself fails to encourage any efforts to further that which is valued, but instead encourages focusing on one's own subjective experiences. Maslow himself was concerned about this possibly leading to an ever-escalating search for triggers to wonderful experiences, with the rest of the world all but forgotten. However, although he clearly did not intend to encourage such an attitude, his doctrine seems inevitably to do so. (Wallach and Wallach 1983 161)

In the fountain model of marriage, Maslow's theory has been applied to marital relationships; it is assumed that the spouses' needs—for trust and stability, communication and sexual expression, and intimacy and interpersonal sharing—must be met first. When these needs are cared for, the marriage can become purposeful beyond its own parameters.

Basic needs of trust, security, intimacy, and love must first be met before partners can begin to move beyond themselves. Unfortunately, this emphasis on individual need-meeting cannot result in a fulfilling relationship, because it is sterile. Something has to matter beyond our own development for us to experience our own life as meaningful. Wallach and Wallach conclude that what matters is for couples to be committed to shared values and working together toward the same ends. The emphasis on fulfillment and on what individuals want and feel runs counter to what we know gives meaning to their lives (see Wallach and Wallach 1983).

Both the theory that self-transcendence is dependent on the meeting of all the levels of need that are more "primary" and the fountain model of marriage that is derived from this theory break down under the actual experience of some persons and marital partners. Frankl's observations of concentration camp experiences, for example, tell against the belief that one's primary needs must be met before one can focus outside one's own needs. In fact, he turns Maslow's theory upside down, pointing out the possibilities for self-transcendence and meaning in life in the most deprived of circumstances (see Frankl 1959). Couples, too, can experience this transcendence, often in difficult circumstances in which all their interpersonal needs are not met. Yet their marriage is fulfilling—"meaningful"—because of a joint effort for some purpose. They live to further something they value. Meeting each other's needs in marriage is important, but it is not the goal of the marriage. For example, in the crisis of a child's serious illness or the dramatic alteration of life-style brought on by changing careers, a couple can glimpse the purpose and meaning of their life together. Together they are able to endure and accomplish what neither could do alone. This meaning is not dependent on their momentary happiness or destroyed by stress and interpersonal friction.

Achtemeier points to Jeremiah as a figure who discovered that we are not to get our needs met first and then proceed to the task before us; rather, we find our needs met, our meaning and purposefulness, in the task itself. Jeremiah complained that his work for God was causing him great suffering. God's response was that he would be renewed and strengthened, saved and delivered, *when he returned to his work, through his work* (Jer. 15: 19–21). It was a matter not of being restored and then going out to the task but of finding his salvation, his life, his purpose and fulfillment, in the task before him (Achtemeier 1976, 147).

Jesus based discipleship on the paradox, "Whoever would save his life will lose it, and whoever loses his life for my sake will find it" (Matt. 16:25; see Matt. 10:39; Mark 8:35; Luke 9:24; 17:33; John 12:25). A life wholly absorbed in its own selfish ends is self-defeating. Fulfillment occurs only when one empties oneself of self-concern and becomes devoted to higher claims (see 2 Cor. 5:15). We contend that the same is true of a marriage relationship. A marriage relationship that is devoted only to the self-fulfillment of the individual partners—much less to consumerism—is destined to be emotionally brackish and spiritually barren. Fulfillment comes only when the couple is able together to turn outward in self-giving. This does not mean that we can ignore nurturing our care for each other. Taking time alone together to rekindle love and intimacy is important, but it cannot be the sole foundation of marriage.

Children and the Task of Marriage

The most universal extension of marriage beyond the needs of individual spouses has been the begetting and nurture of children. Social science research, however, has not supported the premise that children bring purpose and meaning to marriage; in fact, caring for children appears to be a physical and psychological drain that can be detrimental to intimacy and self-actualization in today's marital relationships. Most research has indicated that marital quality—"satisfaction" and "happiness"—decline with the arrival of children, and that this effect lasts as long as there are small children in the home. Decline in marital quality is most marked for mothers rather than fathers (see Luckey 1970; Feldman 1971; Ryder 1973; Russell 1974; Rollins and Galligan 1978; Belsky, Spanier, and Rovine 1983). Children add stress to a couple's resources of time, energy, and money (see LaRossa 1983; Miller and Myers-Walls 1983; Myers-Walls 1984). The only study that refutes this conclusion suggests that the stress of parenting creates difficulty only in the sexual relationship of the couple, with all other changes being less problematic (Harriman 1983). How can we square the finding that children are often a drain on the marital relationship with the belief that parenting children is one way to fulfill the need for purpose and task in marriage?

It is interesting that Glenn and McLanahan, while adding their own research to the large body of evidence that children adversely affect marital quality, conclude that "the negative effects may predominate only in societies in which values are unusually individualistic" (Glenn and McLanahan 1982, 71). Some indirect evidence indicates that this is so in our own cultural setting. Religious couples have been found to want more children than nonreligious couples, even when social class and income are controlled (Mosher and Hendershot 1984). Researchers conclude that the trend for nonreligious couples to desire fewer children indicates their concern only for the present. When spouses consider the goal of self-actualization as primary, they do not want to make the necessary sacrifice in time, money, and energy that the rearing of children requires in our culture.

A second point needs to be considered regarding the question of how children can be considered a source of fulfillment in marriage in the face of research findings. Although it takes two persons to conceive a child, it does not necessarily take two to raise that child. In fact, caring for children is traditionally the task of mothers, with periodic involvement of fathers. One need only look at theories of child development and child psychopathology to find evidence that, in our society, mothers are seen as crucial for the development of a child, whereas fathers are considered only peripheral. For example, the authors of a recent volume that reviews the research on the role of parents' work on the development of their children repeatedly point out in dismay that the variables of the employment of fathers have been almost totally disregarded by research, whereas the employment of mothers has been considered a critical variable in children's development (Kamerman and Hayes 1982). Parents work in two separate worlds, and the task of nurturing and rearing children has for the most part belonged almost exclusively to the mother, whether she has employment outside the home or not.

This has not always been the case. When work was not segregated from the home, men were involved in the care and rearing of children. Children helped in the toil of the fields or the family's business; time spent together was not leisure but integral to the support of the family. When men left the fields and the family shop for the factory, however, the children were left behind. The career patterns of husband and wife diverged, husband in the world of work and wife in the world of nurturing children and maintaining the home, church, and community. Children who had been useful members of the family with their own contributions to its maintenance became "dependents." It is no wonder, then, that as children became the more exclusive responsibility of the mother, they also became, like work, an interference in spousal relations rather than a pivotal source of mutual involvement.

The interference children create in a marital relationship has been addressed in two ways. First, interference is eliminated by reinvesting fathers in the care and nurture of their children so that parenting again becomes a mutual involvement. Increasingly, the significance of fathers' involving themselves in the routines of child care is being recognized as important for the child, the father, and the marital relationship (e.g., Fein 1980). The subtle changes in parenting roles herald the sharing of responsibilities in the day-in day-out tasks of parenting. More and more fathers are changing diapers, fixing snacks, playing Chutes and Ladders, and giving baths.

A second way of addressing the issue of children's interference in marriage is to divest the marriage of children. This approach not only includes the choice not to have children or to limit the number of children but also underlies the advice that parents need to protect their relationship from the interference of children. Spouses need time alone together, to share thoughts and feelings, to relate sexually with each other, and in general to rekindle their relationship. Unfortunately, the idea that more is better is an axiom of our society and results in the conviction that the more time spouses can be alone together, the better for the marriage—and, by extension, the better for the children. Yet time together with children can also offer fulfillment and strength to the marriage in which there is a mutual involvement in the tasks—and joys —of child rearing.

The operating principle for many spouses is to protect their time together as a couple so as to nurture a fulfilling relationship. The concern is for quantity of time. The prevalent attitude about time spent on parent-child relating, on the other hand, is that the quality of time is more important than the quantity. Parent-child time is treated like orange juice concentrate. The amount of water (time) extracted from the concentrate is not as important as ensuring that all those good vitamins and pulp are preserved (the "quality" of parent-child relationship). Parents, however, become concerned over what constitutes quality time. It appears to mean the interaction of child with parents without distractions of work, chores, or other people. Quality time with our spouse also means being alone together without the distractions of work and children. The result is that now not only is work separated from family but different family relationships are separated from one another. It is unfortunate that we have understood marital intimacy as a process that occurs only in isolation and that must be prepared for and nurtured as an end in itself. Intimacy, like happiness, is a side effect of mutual involvement in pursuing another goal; it eludes us when it becomes the primary focus.

The nagging, unspoken concern for spouses is that they do not spend enough time either together or with their children. This worry appears rooted in the emphasis on quality time together, in spite of the fact that shortened workdays and laborsaving devices are increasing the time available for families. For example, when the famous Middletown survey of 1924 was repeated in 1978, it was found that parents spend much more time with their children now (in 1978) than they did in 1924 (Caplow and Chadwick 1979), even though the employment of mothers increased drastically during this interim. Perhaps our worry about how much time is enough is not so much related to actual clock hours of time for children and parents to be together as it is to the nature of that time together. Quality time, given our culture's investment of the affective function in marriage and the family, means sharing our thoughts and feelings and talking about ourselves. It is you-me time, experiencing being together in the here and now. In our view, it is a lack of transcendent meaning for the marriage that fuels the continuing unrest with time spent together when all the evidence suggests that there is more time than ever for couples to be together without interference from work or children. Because this time together has been separated from work and children, from that which goes beyond the relationship, no amount of you-me time can satisfy the search for meaning and fulfillment in marriage.

Children either force us to move beyond our marriage into service together, or they become yet another wedge of time sliced from our resources for meeting our own and each other's needs. That is why the birth of children is such a critical juncture for a marriage, since most couples have not considered marriage to be anything other than the meeting of each other's needs. Like it or not, the arrival of children means that our life together never quite belongs to us again, and in an age of self-actualization and "doing my own thing," most of us are not prepared to like it. Herein lies the explanation of the research findings relating the arrival and rearing of children with the plummeting satisfaction spouses feel with their marriage. Paradoxically, however, it is through the giving up of our focus on self and finding meaning for the marriage beyond exclusive intimacy that marital fulfillment and happiness can occur.

Spouse Careers and the Purpose of Marriage

Another aspect of life that affects the purpose and meaning of marriage for couples is their occupation or profession. We have already discussed the separation of work and family. Unlike the rearing of children, it is not usually assumed that a connection exists between the world of work and the purpose of marriage. The spouse is peripheral, not integral, to what most of us do with the majority of our day. At home, discussion of our work world is optional. Many spouses simply do not converse about the activities of their work with each other because they value home as a refuge, a shelter from the demands of the workday. That means they do not share a major portion of their lives —their energy, interests, and commitments—with their spouses. At times this can lead to jealousy and resentment that a major portion of our partner's commitment and time is dedicated to an arena that excludes us, reminiscent of the jealousy fathers felt in the last generation over the exclusive and all-absorbing commitment of mother to child.

The meaning of our work has a great deal to do with its relationship to our understanding of Christian calling and partnership marriage. A short discussion of the meaning of work is therefore in order. Work is designated a "career" when it contributes to society and individual fulfillment. It is designated an "occupation" when it is merely seen as a means to earn money, a job. In some respects this differentiation comes from the characteristics of the work. It is much harder to feel fulfillment working in a factory stuffing coupons into cereal boxes than it is guiding young minds as a teacher. In a large manufacturing setting, even the trades and skilled crafts seem to have lost the capability for meaning. The work is separated from the service, and the craftspersons seldom serve customers with faces and lives in which their craft has a function. Wallach and Wallach write:

> A retired tailor of 80 is proud of the role played by the neighborhood tailor working in America, believing that such tailors made it possible for poor people to wear coats. No matter how inexpensively it must be done, he points out, the tailor must remember that how well he cuts and sews the garment will mean the difference between whether a poor person can keep warm or not: "A coat is not a piece of cloth only. The tailor is connected to the one who wears it and he should not forget it." (Wallach and Wallach 1983, 3)

For many, particularly those in occupations rather than professions, the connection between their work and the lives of people affected by their work has been forgotten or lost in the bigness of production and enterprise. The work has no intrinsic value except as a means to a paycheck. The result is that our days become segmented; a major portion of our energy is given to making money to support the other portion, our personal and family life where we are supposed to find fulfillment. Work becomes separated from marriage and family, from fulfillment and transcendence. Can the work life of the individual become a significant aspect of the partnership marriage? Just as with bearing and nurturing children, not all partnership marriages will find their meaning and purpose in the world of work, but for many couples this indeed can become a focus of their calling together.

Some couples have sought the meaning of their marriage in sharing their work with each other. Women have frequently lived through the careers of their husbands, thus meeting some of this need for a mutual task. Because her involvement has been more peripheral than his, however, this approach to work lacks the mutuality to make it a satisfactory solution to the dilemma of defining meaning and purpose for the marriage. The wife who has supported her husband's career by entertaining colleagues, listening and supporting him in the ups and downs of his pursuits, even providing secretarial services for him, cannot usually carry on their joint work when he dies. It was *his* work, even though she may have spent most of her time clearing other responsibilities out of the way so that he could pursue it. If this was their only task together, the purpose found in the marriage ends with his burial. This is not the case, however, when both have worked together with comparable contributions to the work and with respect for each other. If one is left, critical changes take place, but the remaining partner can go on to continue what they had begun together.

Fromm's statement that "no man must be the means for the ends of another" (Fromm 1956, 12) is applicable here. One spouse may not use the partner to further his or her own career or any other aspect of what is perceived to be self-actualization. Yet, if self-actualization is the goal of marriage, the use of the other partner as a means to individual goals is almost inevitable. Only when they have a sense of partnership in some task, some purpose that transcends the marriage and themselves, do they avoid using each other to further their own self-centered ends.

We do not want to confuse the employment status of partners with the purpose of their lives together. The key is partnership in the task before them as a couple, not necessarily who is salaried and who is volunteering services or has a lesser employment position—or whether either is employed at all in the area of their work together. Often partners who have identified their calling with their careers do indeed have parallel employment patterns—a physician and nurse, co-pastors, two teachers. Although research on dual-career marriages has recently proliferated, the effects of spouses sharing or integrating careers have not yet been explored. This work pattern includes job sharing by a few pioneers, as well as those in similar and complementary roles—two lawyers, marriage counselors, and so forth.

Concerned about the possibility of competitiveness between spouses, Sanders and Suls (1982) set up a laboratory experiment to study the effects of competition between marital partners. They found that competition interferes with intimacy. This is not particularly surprising, but the conclusions drawn from this experiment point to the biases inherent in our culture about spouses working together. They write: "One plausible strategy . . . might be to pursue independent goals so that it is very difficult to directly compare performance" and "It would be expected that the more satisfactory the marriage the less overlap there would be between the partners' ego-defining pursuits" (Sanders and Suls 1982). But this experiment was a laboratory game in which competition was *built in* and cannot be equated with the sharing of a goal and task by a couple in their life together. The research did not test whether a relationship exists between shared goals and competition. Although the researchers do not conclude this, others may use this kind of research to suggest that parallel or interdependent careers pose a dangerous threat to marital intimacy, and we had better keep work and family separate. Why assume that shared goals must lead to competition?

All dual-career marriages in our culture potentially create relationship stress, with the increased demands of two careers, along with maintaining a household, multiplied again if there are children. There are also risks and potential problems when spouses share mutual work-related goals or pursue parallel rather than unrelated career patterns, such as the narrowing of interests and susceptibility to added stress created by professional changes that affect both. Nevertheless, shared or complementary careers have the potential for giving added meaning and purpose to the marriage. Husband and wife are reunited as co-workers rather than as spare-time sharers, although the reunion takes place in a separate workplace instead of the home and family fields. The separation of work from relationship no longer separates spouses from each other—they are again teammates, not just playmates. There is a time to work together and a time to play together.

This is not to suggest that both spouses need to be employed to have a fruitful, purposeful marriage, or even that the purpose of marriage is necessarily to be found in the work involvements of spouses. We are merely suggesting that work is a major investment of a person's life, and this is one area that can be fruitful for spouses who are exploring the meaning and purpose of their life together. Janet and Robert Aldridge tell the story of their personal pilgrimage in defining the meaning of their marriage (Wallis 1983). As Janet and Robert came increasingly to identify their task as a couple with the search for world peace, his employment as a nuclear engineer developing nuclear weapons became incompatible with the meaning they wanted their lives to have. Together they committed themselves to the purposes of peace. That meant resigning from a lucrative job and beginning a new life and occupations that support their goals and calling as a couple and as parents of ten children.

Even when individual careers are not central to a couple's purposes, the employment of spouses needs to be congruent with what is meaningful for partners in the tasks they have undertaken. For the Aldridges, that meant sacrifice and wrenching change. Even the structure of the work, whatever its content, is significant. Whether that structure is two careers, one career, two part-time jobs, or full careers plus moonlighting, it needs to be relative to the calling of the marriage. For example, research indicates that it is not whether the wife is employed or not that is significant to the marital satisfaction spouses experience but the degree to which her working fits the couple's expectations and what is important to them (see Houseknecht and Macke 1981; Hiller and Philliber 1982; Fendrich 1984; Thomas, Albrecht, and White 1984). Women and men who both want to work, and do, and women and men who want the wife not to be working, and she does not, are more satisfied than spouses who want the wife to be at home but she has to work for financial reasons or who want the wife to work but she is unemployed. In other words, whether the wife works or not is not as important as whether the partners' work patterns enable them to pursue what is mutually important to them.

According to value orientation theory, American culture is primarily a "doing" culture. A "doing" culture is one oriented to competitiveness, the striving for upward mobility in jobs and social contacts, and to how the world views our accomplishments. It is a characteristic of our culture that the meaning and purpose of life are tied to employment. The first question usually asked of a stranger is, "What do you do?" Two other cultural orientations describe other cultures than mainstream American society. A "being" orientation involves spontaneous expression of feelings and thoughts in any given situation. The "being-in-becoming" orientation shares with "being" a concern with what the person is rather than what he or she can accomplish. It stresses, however, the development of different aspects of the person, developing interests and gifts rather than finishing a job in a particular time frame (McGoldrick, Pearce, and Giordano 1982).

Our culture values "doing," but when it comes to marriage, "being" or "being-in-becoming" are valued. The model of partnership marriage in some respects is a reuniting of the values of "doing" and "being." It is concerned primarily not with doing for accomplishment's sake, or with spontaneity, or with development of the self, but it involves all three. The purpose or meaningfulness of the relationship appears to be a "doing" orientation, yet it is a doing with a difference. It is concerned not with the appearance of accomplishments but with doing as an expression of the meaning and purpose of the marital relationship. Work cannot be work for its own sake or for the delayed gratification promised by the salary it earns; it is no longer to be divorced from the rest of life but is to be reintegrated with what is meaningful and purposeful in the family. It is no longer doing in order to *become* (future), but doing because of who we *are* (present)—ministers called by God to a task.

Conclusion

Being fruitful and multiplying is the way the purposefulness of marriage is described in Genesis. When parenting or another task is mutual, a couple shares the depths of despair but also the heights of joy in service to others. These are not merely shared as each reports his or her experiences in a separate arena to each other and receives empathy and support, they are *experienced together.* Empathy and support happen not only in talking about their experience but also in the actions of each in response to the other in the shared work. Our shared experience, not just our discussion of individual experience, unites us.

Whitaker and Keith have used tennis as an analogy. The relationship that focuses on exclusive intimacy is like playing singles tennis together: the ball of communication is batted back and forth, as the players respond to each other, each focusing exclusively on the other. As marriage deepens, however, the image of playing doubles becomes more appropriate. As they put it:

> One learns how to invest the whole self and how to use restraint. There is a thrill in moving to the net together, it is a pleasure to back up the partner when he or she has the initiative and there are opportunities to take risks on your own, to let yourself get out of position knowing that you are backed up by a partner. Victory celebrations are fuller and losses are better endured. (Whitaker and Keith 1977, 70)

Spouses are partners in their task together and together reap the mutuality of working together, the risk of relying on the other, and the sense of working together as one. Telling a spouse about the game does not hold a candle to playing it together when it comes to intimacy, sharing, and, most of all, giving meaning and purpose to the relationship.

A Cautionary Note. The focus of partnership marriage is on the purpose and calling of the relationship, the task of husband and wife to make their relationship meaningful in the context of God's will. This chapter and previous ones have been strongly weighted toward the purposefulness and task side of marriage to balance what we see as the overemphasis in our society on the you-me relationship and issues of intimacy in marriage. These are important, and we do not want to slight them; they are the focus of the next two chapters. Behind our emphasis on task and purpose is the concern that when we lose the perspective given by the purposefulness of marriage, we risk turning marriage into a self-centered system that mirrors the individualistic, self-actualizing goals of our society.

For example, literature for a couples communication program states that a "relationship comes alive only when you and your partner get involved with each other. This happens when you focus on yourself, your partner, and especially on the two of you together" (Miller, Nunnally, and Wackman 1979, 15). This statement is part of the introduction to one of the most useful approaches to helping couples communicate more intimately and effectively with each other; the emphasis on the importance of marriage and family is critical. But it can be misconstrued to mean that this is the totality of relationship. Believing that the essence of marriage is primarily "being" with one another—spontaneously expressing thoughts and feelings—can cause us to neglect searching for and defining the purposes of our marriage in the day-in day-out living together in our home, community, and world.

5
Using Conflict and Anger
for Strengthening Marriage

To paraphrase an ancient Greek comic poet, "They all say that whoever marries has storms, and knowing this they marry anyway" (*Greek Anthology* 10.116). No matter what form marriage has taken across the years, conflict is sure to arise. Perhaps it all began when Adam attempted to wash his hands of any responsibility for violating God's command by claiming it was all the fault of "the woman whom thou gavest to be with me" (Gen. 3:12). What Eve said to this later when they were alone is not recorded, but one might surmise what it was from firsthand experience in marital spats.

Most significant marital conflict is generated by the most insignificant details of family living: "You never wipe off the kitchen counter when you're through fixing a snack"; "Why can't you put your dirty clothes in the hamper"; "Why do you always have to be cleaning; I want my things left where I put them." On and on it can go (fill in your own favorite squabble). Plutarch was on target when he contended: "It is the petty, continual, daily clashes between man and wife, unnoticed by the great majority, that disrupt and mar married life" (Plutarch, *Advice to Bride and Groom* 22.141B). In modern American life, Murray Straus found that people argue most about housekeeping issues. In a national random sample, one out of three American couples stated that they always disagree about cooking and cleaning. Thirty percent also stated that they disagreed all the time about sexual matters; 25 percent disagreed about social activities; 20 percent about money. These are issues that couples said they *always* disagreed about; they do not include those issues that couples said they only disagreed about *sometimes* in the course of their daily life together (Straus, Gelles, and Steinmetz 1980). The saying, "It will all come out in the wash," has a different meaning and particular significance when it comes to marriage, for however we handle the issue of who does the wash and all the other "small" tasks in our life together establishes the climate for day-in day-out living and loving together.

Why do seemingly insignificant issues play such a critical role in marriage? One reason is that, though they may be small, they are pervasive. They are like tiny pebbles, otherwise unnoticeable until they get inside your shoe. These small issues tend to get "inside our shoes," where they annoy out of all proportion to their size. Husbands and wives share living, eating, and sleeping space; it is this extensive sharing that is the ground for both intimacy and irritation. Mace has pointed out that differences between people become disagreements when space is limited (Mace 1982b). For example, the different opinions about sleeping with windows open or closed have no importance to work colleagues—unless they share a bedroom. For spouses, however, differences over opening bedroom windows, acceptable kitchen tidiness, and where to keep scissors and tape, as well as similarities such as wanting to shower at the same time, virtually ensure frustration and conflict.

A second reason minor issues become major irritants is that they are indirectly related to power over one's own life. Who does what chores, for example, directly affects a very precious commodity in our society —time. Edmiston points out: "Whoever does the dishes . . . and the laundry . . . and the thousand little services [families] require . . . is to a large extent prevented from doing anything else" (Edmiston 1977, 615). Time is not the only aspect of our life that is affected by these things; the quality of our sleep (windows open or not), our private rituals (bathing without someone impatient for us to hurry up), and other preferred patterns of living (reading the paper without finding articles torn out) are all directly related to feeling that we have some control over our daily lives.

Third, a trifling matter can become momentous when we interpret it as meaning that our partner does not understand us, does not appreciate us, or does not love us because the partner appears insensitive to our preferences or plans. For example, the partner may foul our shared living space by strewing newspapers about or ignore our need for a good night's sleep by reading with the light on until midnight or thwart our anticipated pleasure in having a late-evening snack by eating the last piece of cake without our knowledge. We do not think of these "minor" aspects of life as being major, and indeed they are not essential aspects of our personhood, but they can cause a great deal of disturbance. Why didn't my loved one love me (substitute also "respect me," "appreciate me") enough to save me from this particular aggravation? Small issues, then, become metaphors for the mutual concern and understanding of each other in the entire relationship.

In marriage, conflict with our partner most often is rooted in our differences. It could be said that the differences that attract also beget grounds for attack. There are a myriad of theories of attraction and mate selection based on differences between partners; for our purposes it is important to recognize that differences are sources both of satisfaction and of frustration. Marriage to one's clone might be quiet, but it would also be boring. Difference and conflict serve an important function in marriage; they challenge the partners to change and to grow. Joan fell in love with Tom in part because he was so carefree and spontaneous; she felt a freedom with him that she had not felt before, because she always tended to make detailed plans and to focus on responsibilities rather than possibilities. An ongoing argument since their marriage is that Joan likes to know where they stand financially and to operate with a budget; Tom likes to buy what they need or want at the time and to deal with the finances when the money runs out. If they are successful in dealing with their differences, Tom and Joan will learn from each other and over time will find themselves changed from the way they were before they committed themselves to a joint life and a joint checking account. Joan will perhaps become more spontaneous and allow herself not always to be in charge. Tom may learn to recognize and provide for the long-term needs and commitments of both of them as well as for his immediate concerns and interests.

Differences, then, are something to be appreciated. In the words of W. H. Auden, "the awareness of sameness is friendship; the awareness of difference is love." Our differences serve to pull us together as well as to keep us apart. Coming to terms with being both separate yet connected, both different yet the same, is a critical underlying function of marital conflict. Love pulls partners together; conflict reminds them of their differences. It draws attention to the importance of maintaining an individual identity after being joined together in marriage. Of course, conflict also draws attention to the need for changes in the relationship to accommodate those differences.

Guernsey (1984) speaks of distinguishing between "unity" and "uniformity." "Unity" refers to our commitment to one another to accept our differences and foibles and to overcome them together. Uniformity is important only to Fisher-Price families, those who need to be interchangeable in all the little settings of the toy world; it is not a part of vital, creative marriage. At least one research study indicates that a relatively high level of conflict exists in marriage compared with other interpersonal relationships, and that those relationships producing the greatest satisfaction also produce the greatest conflict. Conflict is not only necessary in marriage but is also compatible with marital satisfaction (Argyle and Furnham 1983).

Despite the fact that conflict is fundamental to the growth of the marriage and the seed from which love grows, conflict can be a pitfall for a couple. Partners may work through conflict and find themselves closer and the relationship more functional, or they may experience alienation and the decay of some aspects of relating as they restore a false peace.

In summary, conflict is to be seen as an inevitable and functional part of married life. However, conflict can mean many things, from quiet discussion over dinner about where we would like to go on vacation next summer to tearful, dish-throwing accusations of betrayal. Conflict is not simply a matter of interpersonal difference; it most often implies the communication of feelings about those differences—namely, anger.

Anger

One of the chief fomentors of conflict in marriage is the anger of one or both spouses. We need to address the genesis and communication of anger before examining the processes of conflict in marriage. Figure 2 is a simplistic representation of how anger begins and is communicated.

Physiological Arousal

Anger has its roots in physiological arousal. As a result of some threat, the individual experiences such physical changes as increased heart rate, tightening of muscles, and changes in the breathing and digestive systems. In marriage, the perceived threat may be to self-esteem ("Why is he embarrassing me by telling that story in front of our friends?"), to preferred patterns of living, as we have discussed, or to the commitment of the relationship ("She is flirting with that man"). It is obvious that physiological arousal is not a beginning point but rather a response to the ongoing cycle of events in the relationship. The linear process depicted in Figure 2 is therefore one element in the larger system of marital interaction.

The threats mentioned concern behaviors of the spouse that directly threaten the partner in some respect. Physiological arousal that leads to anger in a marriage may be caused by stimuli outside the marriage. In addition to differences between the spouses, two other sources of anger within marriage are deflected anger and the rehearsal of anger.

Deflected anger. Perhaps one of the most frustrating forms of marital conflict is begun by deflected anger. The physical arousal associated with anger is generated by another relationship or by another source, but it is transferred to the marital relationship. In the ensuing exchange

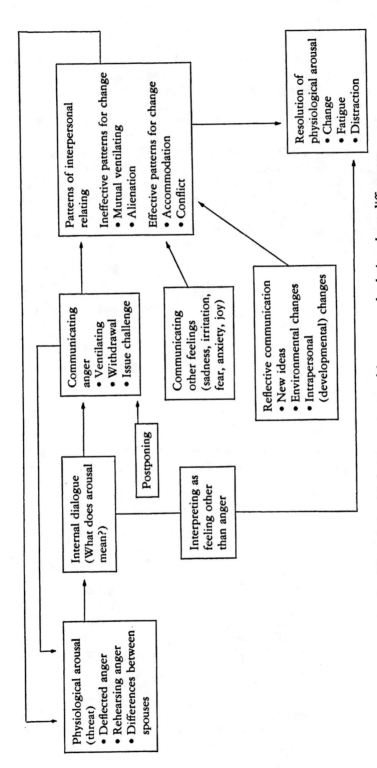

Figure 2. The relationship between anger and interpersonal relating about differences

between the partners, the intensity of the anger that erupts does not seem to fit either of their interpretations of the issue in the marital relationship.

Mark's mother calls him at the office, interrupting an important meeting, to tell him how upset his father has been that he has not come by to visit or to help them put up storm windows for the winter. Mark listens impatiently, frustrated because he is missing what is going on in the meeting and because his mother does not seem to understand the pressure he has been under. He also feels guilty because he wants to put his family first, and work responsibilities have interfered. He thinks to himself that he simply cannot stretch far enough to meet all the demands. When he arrives home later in the day, his eight-year-old daughter greets him with a tearful reproach: "You didn't come to my school program today." Only then does Mark remember the school note that had come two weeks ago and the excitement of his daughter that had been building for days. He had planned to go, but today it had completely slipped his mind. His wife gives him a disgusted look and then asks if he remembered to pick up charcoal on his way home. He angrily replies, "No! I'll go get it after I have had a chance to sit down for a moment to glance at the paper. Now leave me alone!" Her response—"I wish you would remember to do the things that you say you will do; we really need to get the charcoal started now if we're going to eat at a decent hour"—is met with an outburst of rage: "You expect me to do everything! You never give me credit for the things I *do* remember—only the things I forget! I'm sick and tired of being badgered all the time!" Normally mild-mannered Mark has exploded into a raging fury. His wife is not sure where all of this rancor came from, but she feels righteously indignant. All she did was ask him to pick up charcoal; he had agreed to do this and she was counting on it. "I am the one who has the right to be angry," says she to herself. In the battle that follows, both feel unfairly blamed and misunderstood.

Mark's conflict was with everyone and no one—his mother, his daughter, his wife, and, above all, himself. However, his wife received the brunt of his anger. Anger communicates one's interpretation of one's physiological state. That does not mean that the physiological state was necessarily caused by—or even related to—the issue at hand. Mark had felt the rising tension all day—knots in his stomach, an "Excedrin headache," and muscle tension that caused him to jump at small things. Physiological changes became anger in the process of internal dialogue, as he berated himself for forgetting the storm windows and his daughter's program, and in interpersonal communication, as he lashed out at his wife.

The more separated the source of provocation is from the expression of anger, the more difficult it is to engage in conflict that is productive.

Much anger does not stem from the specific incident where it is expressed, but rather from the buildup of tension and frustration that comes from living. Anytime we are cold or hot, hungry, tired, exercising, bombarded by noise, crowded into an elevator or at a sale, or interrupted when we are under pressure to finish some task, we are more likely to become angry (Tavris 1982). Our adrenaline is already up before the incident that sparks the tinder already laid. In the lifestyles of most of us, we experience a constant level of physiological arousal or agitation. The slightest frustration or increase in demands on us may push us over the edge into feelings of anger. One source of anger in marriage, then, is the buildup of physiological arousal related to frustrations that have little or no direct relationship to the marriage, but that find expression there because some incident in the marriage becomes the scapegoat for all the rest.

Another aspect of deflected anger is the phenomenon of blame-placing. Someone has said that a major reason for getting married is that it gives a person someone to blame for everything that goes wrong. Mark's anger could have a taken different shape. When reproached by his daughter for missing her performance, he could have demanded indignantly of his wife, "Why didn't you remind me about the program? I left that note from school out on the kitchen cabinet so I would get the date right. What did you do with it? You probably threw it away. I don't understand why you can't just leave things alone!" With whom is Mike angry? We might be tempted to say that he is really angry at himself and is taking out his anger on his wife. In actuality, the anger—the communication—is aimed at her. He is angry at her. By focusing on her, he has turned the issue into an interpersonal conflict, and he does not have to face up to his own responsibility in the matter. Instead of being "slow to anger" and examining the sources of his frustration and deciding what to do with it, he lashes out, creating an unncessary breach in the marital relationship and losing out on a chance for self-examination.

It is easy to channel frustration building from other sources into the marital relationship because there is often a trace of responsibility on the part of the spouse for which he or she can be blamed. Mark's wife did not remind him and indeed may have thrown away the school notice. This could be just enough for Mark to blame her and launch the couple into a quarrel. No matter how creatively they may change their strategy for handling important notes, Mark's difficulties with demands from aging parents, a high-pressure job, and his young daughter are ignored. Even the small issue of what to do with school notices may not be resolved, since Mark is not asking for a new system for handling important notes so much as he is trying to get himself off the hook by showing that his wife is more to blame than he is.

It should be noted, too, that deflected anger does not have to be aroused by other persons; physical objects that do not perform as they are "supposed" to can also generate physiological arousal that may be deflected at the spouse. A car that will not start, a malfunctioning water heater, a broken zipper, or a map that does not give all the street names in a strange city can incite a marital battle.

To summarize, some anger directed at the partner stems from frustrations—physiological arousal—that have built up from other areas of life. The wise advice in James to be quick to hear, slow to speak, and thereby slow to anger (James 1:19) enables us to reflect on and determine the source of the frustration and irritation before it provokes inappropriate anger.

Rehearsing anger from other sources. Often a spouse comes to his or her partner with a problem not directly concerned with the marriage to discuss the issue and get the partner's reaction to plans for addressing the problem. For example, how different it might have been had Mark come into the house and said to his wife, "I am so angry and upset. I disappointed Amy by not showing up for her program. I really intended to go, but I didn't write it down in my calendar. I left the note out, but that's been two weeks ago and it is no longer there. On top of that, Mom called me in the middle of an important meeting today, all in a flap because I haven't been over to help Dad with the storm windows. I can't seem to pull everything together." His wife could have responded, "Think about it on your way to pick up the charcoal." She might also have said something like, "You sound miserable, and I know Amy was terribly disappointed. But your mother seems to be pushing awfully hard; I don't see why the storm windows are so urgent." Whether they come up with any solutions or not, Mark feels the support of his wife rather than that he has alienated and angered yet another person. Their discussion of his feelings and the situation does not reduce what he is feeling; it gives shape to it. First, he begins to separate the issues rather than lumping his mother and his daughter together as two more pulls on him. He may also be able to focus his anger at his mother into a plan for telling her not to call him at work except for an emergency. Tavris says, "Talking out an emotion doesn't reduce it, *it rehearses it*" (Tavris 1982, 132).

Feelings are the meanings we give to the physiological arousal we experience. What we feel depends on how we interpret what we are experiencing in a particular context. Are we excited, angry, hurt, embarrassed? Only as we try to make sense out of our racing heart and flushed face do we *feel* angry or hurt or sad. Talking about it with someone else, such as our spouse, can help us define what we are feeling. As we talk through what has happened to us, we rehearse our experience and give ourselves reasons and labels for what we are feeling. Rehearsing anger, then, is in essence externalizing the "internal dialogue" that defines what one is feeling as anger.

Unfortunately, spouses are not always up to the task of helping each other with problems generated in other relationships. A spouse may respond to our hurt or frustration with anger at its source and make demands that a specific suggestion be followed. "Mark, I cannot believe your mother. I can understand your forgetting Amy's program and why you feel so badly about that, but I do not see why storm windows are such a big deal. For her to call you in the middle of a workday! She thinks she owns you. How can she treat you like that? You do so much for them, but it's never enough. If you don't call and give her a piece of your mind, I will!"

Mark will then be likely to rise to the defense of his mother, and again he will be angry with his wife (and she with him), this time over the role of his parents in their lives. This is perhaps an issue that needs to be addressed, but it does not deal with Mark's initial concern. He is left with his original problem and now finds himself angry with his wife as well.

Why does this kind of conflict happen? First, we love our mates and want to protect them from hurt, disappointment, and frustration. When someone or something hurts them, we feel threatened and become aroused ourselves. Often the channel for dealing with that arousal is with the spouse rather than with the actual source of difficulty. What is meant by us to be a caring response frequently becomes a challenge: "If you don't call your mother, I will." As spouses discuss the problematic situation, both experience the increase in adrenaline and other physiological changes associated with arousal. Physiologically, the fire is laid and the kindling is added; all it takes is a match to set the conflict ablaze. In marital discussions, plenty of matches are usually lying about —small grievances or aggravations. Mark's wife could have responded by attacking Mark instead of his mother: "You never remember anything; you just get more and more irresponsible. I know how your mother feels; I always have to stay on your back to get things done."

It is therefore an easy step from rehearsing the outside issue to expressing anger at another. The spouse is a readily available target, whereas the original participant in the conflict (in this case, Mark's mother) is not present. One may also feel considerably more comfortable being angry with the spouse than with the original participant; it may seem much safer and less threatening to argue with each other than to try to change the relationship with a parent or other person outside the marriage.

Differences between spouses. Since the ingredients of a marriage are two different people, the third category of sources of conflict consists of those that arise from differences. Peterson (1983) has identified three kinds of differences that create interpersonal conflict in marriage. The first are those related to *specific behavior*. One spouse complains about something the other does—he leaves the toilet seat up; she sets glasses on the furniture and leaves water rings. Second are differences related to the norms governing *classes of behavior*. Norms are the expectations for the way things ought to be done. A typical argument might center on household chores—they have divided them equally, but she does not think he does his share with any consistency or thoroughness. Or one spouse may view the expectations of the other as illegitimate —she is angry that he expects her to stay home from work for a full week with the six-year-old who has chicken pox when she considers her job just as important as his. The third category of differences are those related to *personal dispositions*. He may be a morning person who jumps cheerily out of bed whistling and ready to talk, cuddle, or take a jog together; she does not want even to look at another person until she has had her coffee and has been up for at least two hours.

One's latest marital squabbles probably will not fit neatly into any one of these categories. Marital conflict is rarely simple or caused by just one issue; it is more often a combination of things. A couple discovers that their daughter has chicken pox at seven o'clock in the morning when their dispositions match the least and the wife is staring at the dishes that her husband left in the sink from the night before. Tavris aptly describes marital conflict as the "marital onion":

> Efforts to dig up the "root" of anger in marriage aren't using the right metaphor; marital anger is more like the concentric layers of an onion. (The tearful aspect of both onions and anger is pertinent.) Most attempts to diagnose the cause of marital anger concentrate on one layer only: background differences, or the clash of personalities, or immediate issues of disagreement. But for most of us the layers overlap intricately. (Tavris 1982, 204)

Internal Dialogue

It should be clear by this point that it is not a particular event per se that provokes anger but rather the person's interpretations and beliefs about what that event means. A person need not be controlled by emotions but can actively control and change them through the interpretation given to life events (Meichenbaum and Turk, 1976). The physiological arousal that comes with increased adrenaline and noradrenaline levels in our system does not by itself cause us to feel anger, depression, rage, or any other feeling (Tavris 1982). It is *how we understand our situation*, how we interpret the meaning of events, that turns the anxiety over a spouse who is unexpectedly late into either fear that harm has come or anger that we have been betrayed or forgotten. There has to be a connection between physiological arousal and its psychological meaning before we "feel" emotions.

To illustrate, Alan calls Susan in the middle of the afternoon to tell her that he has received an unexpected promotion. When she hears his voice on the phone, she immediately becomes tense and her heart begins to beat faster because he does not usually call during the middle of the day. She wonders, "What is up?" In a split second she may rehearse in her mind several possibilities—threats—such as that something terrible has happened or that he is going to have to work late when she has already invited friends for dinner. After hearing his news, she thinks to herself, He is going to be gone even more and work longer hours with more pressure. How can he be so excited? Can't he imagine how I feel about this? She has attached an interpretation to her physiological state—what little time they have together is being threatened. On the other hand, she might have interpreted his news to mean that, since he is moving a step up in his career, he may have more independence and be able to set his own schedule, enabling them to have more time together. Her excitement then becomes joy and anticipation, not anger.

Communicating Anger

Susan wails, "But Alan, I hardly see you now! I hate that company, and I hate what you are letting it do to us!" It is her interpretation of the news that she communicates to Alan—her anger. Until the emotional state is communicated to the self in internal dialogue and then, most often, to another, it is only physiological excitement. It is through the process of communication that it takes the shape of anger, joy, or sorrow.

This definition of anger is quite different from those who would say that anger is itself the physiological state and requires expression before the interpersonal issues can be addressed. They advise that one first get the anger out of the way and then handle the conflict situation rationally. This approach suggests that the anger and the issue are separable, that experiences and our subjective interpretation and response to them can be pulled apart and addressed individually. This is impossible; we can respond to each other only through our subjective interpretations of our experiences together. We may try to get the anger out of the way first by either "clearing the air" through ventilation or by "calming down," distracting ourselves with something else, only to find that when we return to discuss the issue "rationally" the anger resurfaces. The issue, after all, is that event that either triggered or has been identified with the physiological arousal, and nothing has yet occurred to change the connections between the arousal, the internal dialogue, and the anger. We only know the event through our experience of it. The issue and the feelings about it are integrally related and cannot be separated. Anger is *not* the intrapersonal state of physiological excitement but the communication of our interpretation of environmental happenings in which we find ourselves responding physiologically. The admonition to be slow to anger in James 1:19 assumes that anger is not physiological arousal (over which we have no control) or something that someone else does to us, but something we do. We do not have control over physiological arousal, but we can choose to have control over our interpretation and use of it.

Anger serves the important function in marriage of pointing out when the expectations of one or both partners are not being met. Tavris observes, "Most angry episodes are social events: they assume meanings only in terms of the social contract between participants" (Tavris 1982, 18). The contract referred to is not the formal marriage contract but the implicit contracts of everyday living that are defined by "oughts" that may or may not be verbalized. Spouses ought never to leave the car almost empty of gasoline, they ought to be available to each other sexually, they ought to kiss each other good-bye when parting and hug one another spontaneously, and so on. Both partners have their lists. When these "oughts" are transgressed, the partner feels threatened—this marriage is not turning out as it is supposed to, and my partner does not love (appreciate, respect, cherish) me as I want or expect. These "oughts" also operate with other persons and with inanimate objects—drivers ought not to cut in front of me; the television ought to work when I want to watch my favorite program, Granddad ought not to tell the children ghost stories that give them nightmares.

Anger is to marriage, then, what a warning light on a car dashboard is for the driver; it is a quick way of signaling that a problem exists. Like a thermometer reading that indicates a fever, anger indicates a dysfunction somewhere. When a thermometer registers a four-year-old's temperature as 102 degrees, the mother does not throw it away thinking it must be wrong. She takes the child to the doctor in the hope of finding out what is the matter and how to treat it. Too often, when spouses become angry, they ignore the warning light instead of recognizing that something is amiss that requires attention. It may be like the chicken pox, a miserable problem that has to be lived with for a while, but time-limited (for example, anger over the distance between husband and wife while she finishes her master's thesis). Or it may be chronic, such as dissatisfaction with the way differences are handled, that calls for a change in the marital relationship. Finally, it may be a signal that the marriage has become the arena for fighting over issues that belong elsewhere.

Anger, therefore, is useful as a signal that something is amiss. It need not be bad, nor is it necessarily sinful, so long as it is expressed in the service of the relationship. It can be distorted and misused, however, and may overshadow and damage the very relationship it is intended to protect.

What to Do with Anger in Marriage

Most of us have our preferred ways of expressing anger to our spouses. Some of us yell, some slam doors, some become sullen, some state our feelings and needs. Although skills of communication are beyond the scope of this book, we will discuss briefly ways of expressing anger in marriage.

Communicating anger is a decision. Do I want to vindicate myself and show my spouse to be inconsiderate, inept, or in other ways less than what I am? Or do I want to express anger in such a way that the spouse is not diminished and the relationship between us is strengthened? Most of us do not consciously think through our choice, but the choice is made nevertheless. Anger can be communicated through ventilating feelings, withdrawing, or issuing a challenge. A partner can also choose to postpone angry communication for a later time.

Ventilating Anger

In ventilating anger, the focus is on self-expression, with less or no focus on resolving the issue that initially was interpreted as justifying the anger. Ventilation may include a verbal barrage, a quiet but devastating remark, hostile humor (Lester 1983), or acting out. Acting out includes a host of ways to ventilate anger, from flirting with someone else or "accidentally" spilling ink on the partner's favorite sweater to physical abuse. "Let it all hang out" has for twenty years been our justification for uncensored expression of whatever feeling flits or stomps through our system.

A myriad of different psychotherapeutic schools promote releasing pent-up hostility, dredging up long-buried anger, and giving free rein to our feelings. Some have even encouraged spouses to flail one another with foam rubber bats. Tavris's book *Anger: The Misunderstood Emotion* is a serious critique of these approaches to anger. She reports research indicating that ranting and raving, stomping and snorting do not get rid of anger; they just increase it. Since anger is an interpretation that we give to a state of physiological arousal, it makes sense that any expression that prolongs physiological arousal will increase or strengthen our interpretation of anger. Shouting, throwing things, and even "talking it all out" tend to prolong physiological arousal. Straus's research on family violence found that couples who yell at each other do not then feel less angry but instead more angry (Straus, Gelles, and Steinmetz 1980). Tavris says, "This is why a minor annoyance, when expressed in hostile language or behavior, can flare into a major argument. Letting off steam can make the atmosphere very hot and humid" (Tavris 1982, 128–129). It can lead to violence between persons over what initially was a "minor" issue.

It is not the expression of anger that is problematic so much as the feeding of anger, treating the anger as the focus, "getting *it* out of my system," rather than recognizing that *it* is only an indicator of an interpersonal conflict. Attention needs to be directed to the issue, not the indicator. Responding to underwear left by the partner on the bathroom floor with "You are the biggest slob who ever walked the earth!" will probably not result in a calm discussion to resolve the issue of where to put dirty clothes and who is supposed to do it. Instead, the personal attack and self-defense become the center of attention. This results in catharsis rather than relationship change. Ventilation does not solve anything and often makes resolution even more difficult.

It is anger communicated through ventilation that is most discussed by the biblical authors. The ventilator is the fool spoken of in the Wisdom Literature who, being quick to anger, suffers consequences that are unintended and sometimes irreparably harmful (Prov. 14:17, 29; Eccl. 7:9). In the Bible, anger is recognized as a natural human emotion from the time of Cain, but it is not treated with complaisance because of the harm it can cause when ventilated rather than used in the service of the relationship. Often, ventilation took the form of physical assault or verbal hostility. Cain's anger over the rejection of his own offering and the acceptance of Abel's led to his murder of his brother (Gen. 4:4–8). Jacob cursed the anger of his sons, Simeon and Levi, that wrought the treacherous attack on Shechem and brought dishonor to the family name (Gen. 34:18–31; 49:5–7). Moses' fit of anger resulted in his slaying an Egyptian and his subsequent flight into the wilderness (Ex. 2:11–15). David frequently had to dodge projectiles suddenly hurled at him by the fuming and fretting Saul. Absalom's anger at the rape of his sister, Tamar, led to his carefully plotted murder of his guilty half-brother, Amnon, two years later and his subsequent exile (2 Sam. 13). The anger of the synagogue crowd in Nazareth over Jesus' sermon (Luke 4:28) boiled over at the cross when people could finally get a secure hold on him. Paul continued this animosity, "breathing threats and murder" against Christians (Acts 9:1) to his everlasting regret (1 Cor. 15:9). It is because anger is the first step toward murder that Jesus equates the two in Matthew 5:22 (see *Didache* 3.2). Murder begins with the murderous look and the contemptuous slur, both ventilated anger. When one treats others as inconsequential nothings, one has in effect already rubbed them out.

The *Testament of Daniel* 2.2 (Pseudepigrapha) reflects the negative appraisal of anger to be found in Judaism; anger is there described as a blindness that does not allow one to see the face of another with truth. Not only can anger cut us off from others; it can blind us when we need to see most clearly—a relationship with one we love may be at stake. An explosion of anger can destroy us and wipe out all those around us from the fallout (see Hos. 4:2–3). For this reason, James contends that anger does not work the righteousness of God (see James 1:19–20).

In Ephesians 4:26, Psalm 4:4 is quoted: "Be angry, but sin not." This is not to be taken as permission to be angry as long as we can be angry without sinning. The psalm is cited as a well-known proverb, and the double imperative reflects a Hebrew idiom, a concessive imperative, that is best translated, "If you are angry, do not let anger lead you into sin" (NEB; see Barth 1974, 513). It does not grant permission to be angry. The fact that five verses later the readers are enjoined to put away all bitterness, temper, and anger, along with all malice (Eph. 4:31; Col. 3:8) makes clear that anger was not stamped with approval (see 2 Cor. 12:20; Gal. 5:20; Col. 3:8; 1 Tim. 2:8, Titus 1:7). The saying in Ephesians 4:26 warns that anger is an ally of the devil and seeks to check smoldering anger by placing a time limit on it: "Do not let the sun go down on your anger" (see also Plutarch, *On Brotherly Love*, 488C). Since the new day began at sunset for the Jews, this was an injunction to rid oneself of the anger immediately. Otherwise, the danger is ever present that the devil will take possession of one's heart (Eph. 4:27), and the anger will be ventilated inappropriately. The power of unchecked anger easily leads to destruction rather than restoration of a relationship. God similarly warned Cain that, because of his anger, sin was crouching at the door (Gen. 4:7).

Withdrawal. Unfortunately, some people fear the effects of ventilation so much that they choose strategies for communicating anger that can be equally damaging. They simply withdraw from the partner. This is often the result of suppressing angry communication. It is like trying to tell yourself to ignore the fact that you have a temperature of 102 degrees. That does not make the fever go away. By ignoring the fever, the illness goes untreated and may worsen, and the ill person becomes susceptible to other problems that may develop because of impaired functioning (decisions may be unwise; attention may be limited, leading to greater chances of accidents).

Likewise, when anger is ignored, the problem goes unaddressed. The communication of anger becomes less direct and less intentional

—the scowling face, the simmering resentment, the slammed door, the turned back in bed. It still communicates, although the original issue that caused the anger cycle may be unclear to the other partner since it is only anger that is communicated, not what the issue is that generated the anger. As frustration builds, suppressed anger communicated by withdrawal may contribute to ventilation by the other partner. The spouse who first became angry and withdrew continues in internal dialogue; instead of telling my partner how I feel, I tell myself. In my mind I go over and over the injustice, the hurt, the unfairness of whatever it is. In effect, a feedback loop has been established between the physiological arousal and the withdrawal. The more I reflect on the injustice that has been endured, the greater the physiological arousal that feeds the righteous indignation ("the more I thought about it, the madder I got"). It may also lead to ventilating the anger, and perhaps to a pattern of alternating ventilation and withdrawal.

It should be noted here that withdrawal is not the same thing as interpreting the physiological arousal as a feeling other than anger. Withdrawal is angry communication. It is my perception that some aspect of our contract with each other has been broken and I have been treated unjustly, and I communicate my perception of this issue to you nonverbally.

The problem with both ventilation and withdrawal is that the focus is on the anger, not the issue. Anger is either communicated for its own sake or suppressed because it is seen as intrinsically bad. This offers little chance for creative change. Jesus did not rampage through the Temple in order to "get his anger out of his system." Nor did he warn others to be careful with anger because it is intrinsically bad. The communication of anger is a powerful resource for change. Change sometimes follows the quiet voice of reason; other situations call for the intensity Jesus demonstrated in the Temple.

Issue challenge. Issue challenge is the spouse's use of anger to confront the partner with the need for some kind of change. This requires defining the issue in such a way that it can be the focus for change. "You are a slob" is not a helpful issue definition; it is ventilation. Not only does it put the spouse on the defensive and less willing to consider changes, it does not indicate what kind of change is needed. "I really get angry when I find your books and papers all over the dining table. I wish you would find someplace else to keep your stuff that isn't right in the middle of everything," is a confrontation that is less likely to be met with defensiveness and more likely to lead to constructive change. In their research on marital conflict, Raush and his colleagues found that conflict is much easier to resolve when issues of conflict are specific, substantive, and defined at the situational level. They conclude, "Issue-oriented conflicts are much less heated than relationship-oriented conflicts, and couples who redefine a confrontation about their relationship in terms of a specific focus have an easier time resolving it" (Raush and others 1974, 199–200). By contrast, when spouses ventilate, blaming each other for the problem and attributing the problem to general personality characteristics (you're sloppy, inconsiderate, cruel) rather than specific issues (your clothes are all over the bedroom; you left the car without gas again; you left the dog out in the rain), conflict escalates and can destroy intimacy and personal esteem as well as decreasing the chances of resolving the initial problem (Gottman 1979; Madden and Janoff-Bulman 1979).

Ephesians 4:25–32 provides some guidelines for avoiding these destructive patterns of communicating anger. It admonishes us to speak the truth to our neighbor, who also includes our spouse, who sleeps next to us. We are to live honestly together. That means dealing with the differences when they grate so that they do not lead to destructive anger that saps the emotional energy of the relationship. This requires handling our anger—and all our talk—so that it "may impart grace" (v. 29). Ventilation or withdrawal does not do this. Anger is therefore not to be communicated for its own sake but for a specific end—namely, "edifying," or building up the other (v. 29). That means that anger should be communicated at a time and place in which it can be helpful rather than harmful—"as fits the occasion" (v. 29). We are not to give our negative emotions a life of their own. They are to be used as needed and when fitting, and then so that they do not overshadow our kindness and forgiveness (v. 32).

Postponing Anger

Anger can also be put off; that is, its expression can be postponed. One may decide that the anger does need to be expressed but yet recognize that now is not the time. Other things may demand our own and our partner's attention, or perhaps one or both spouses need time to think about the situation before trying to resolve it. This is different from interpreting the arousal as a feeling other than anger. The anger will be communicated, only at a later time. Both postponement and examining our interpretation of the issues take into consideration other demands that are more important than attention to the feelings of the partners. It is important to take care of things that come between us, but it is not always the most important thing. By delaying angry communication, we can give ourselves time to reexamine our interpretation of the situation to see if another interpretation would be more helpful. We can also choose a strategy for communicating anger that has the most likelihood of creatively addressing the issue. In other words, through postponement we allow ourselves more time for internal dialogue before communicating with our partner.

Interpreting as a Feeling Other than Anger

Anger is an interpretation of our physiological state and events in our life, and interpretations can be changed. When Sharon finds her husband's jogging clothes and a wet towel on the bedroom floor, she may feel a rush of anger. If, however, she remembers that her husband has a very important presentation to make this morning and was running late, her interpretations of the event may change. "He had his mind on other things. If it happens again tomorrow, though, I'll definitely tell him what I think!" The feeling of anger is gone. More accurately, the physiological arousal is reinterpreted as frustration or irritation. She does not take this as an indication of her husband's selfish expectation that her job is to run around picking up after him. Rather, she sees this as a reflection of the fact that he is under a lot of pressure and did not intend to make things harder for her. She also intuits that this is not a good time to bring up the problem of his untidiness or to open up conflict. Her initial arousal is resolved; she has distracted herself from it with her concern for her husband's situation. No need for change was perceived.

We do not need to give voice to all our internal dialogue. This does not mean that we ignore it or brood about it or express it indirectly. Bochner (1979) speaks of the "inherent dialectic" in interpersonal communication. He writes, "Individuals in intimate relationships seek an equilibrium point between the need to be open in their relationships and the need to protect the mate or family member from the consequences of such openness" (Fitzpatrick, Fallis, and Vance 1982). A balance ought to exist between being quiet and being open. As Tavris notes:

> For most of us, most of the time, there isn't a single diagnosis; there are many, intersecting, with one or another being more important this week and not so important next week. For most of us, most of the time, differences aren't "settled," once and for all; they just lurk there, waiting for the chance to wreak mischief and misunderstanding. Couples who are not defeated by rage and the conflicts that cause it know two things: when to keep quiet about trivial angers, for the sake of civility, and how to argue about important ones, for the sake of personal autonomy and change. (Tavris 1982, 222–223)

It is often the case that when arousal is reinterpreted, it will quickly be forgotten. If it is not, a partner usually has had time to think through the situation and decide how to communicate in a way that will be effective for bringing about needed change rather than simply venting the spleen.

Conflict

Conflict is not the inevitable result of angry communication in marriage. In a sense, angry communication is to the marital partnership what physiological arousal is to the individual—a signal that needs to be heeded but that may be interpreted and responded to in various ways. Only one of these is conflict. The method of angry communication—ventilating feelings, withdrawal, or issue challenge—is influential in the marital system's response to the anger, but it is not completely determinative. The response of one partner to the other's communication of anger and the reaction of the angry spouse to that response also influence the pattern of interaction that results. An example may make this clearer.

Linda is angry with Joe for opening the bedroom window in 20-degree weather. She may express anger through ventilation, snarling sarcastically, "I'm surprised we don't both have pneumonia. I should have married Craig; at least I'd be living in Florida where I wouldn't freeze to death at night." Although she has expressed anger, she has not directly requested change, finding satisfaction in giving Joe a piece of her mind. While Joe has received her indirect message that she doesn't like the window open, his feeling response to her crack about a former relationship may command more of his attention than any inclination to show concern for his wife by shutting the window. Out of spite he might open the window wider, which would provoke Linda even more. A pattern of *mutual ventilation* often results in increasing physiological arousal and more intense ventilation—verbal hostility and physical acting out. No change was requested, and no change will be forthcoming until one or both change their strategy of communication (for example, Linda may withdraw by refusing to talk further or leave to sleep on the couch), or the arousal is resolved through fatigue.

Joe may also respond to Linda's anger by withdrawing. Refusing to respond to her sarcasm, he may simply get in bed, turn his back, and go to sleep, leaving her fuming and frustrated. Both will experience greater emotional distance from each other. This *alienation,* in which partners avoid each other and communicate anger through withdrawal (silence or reduced and constrained verbal communication and physical avoidance), is often punctuated with ventilation. This pattern may continue for some time, until the partners distract themselves from the painful interaction and call a truce, or until alienation becomes a permanent pattern of relating.

Joe, on the other hand, may confront Linda's remarks about wishing she were in Florida by straightforwardly identifying the issue. "I take it that you don't like sleeping with the window open." If Linda responds more positively, and if it is not a major issue for Joe—perhaps he opened the window because he assumed that Linda liked it that way —the result will be *accommodation*. In an accommodation pattern, the request for change is met with compliance. Joe shuts the window. .

If Joe does care, however, the result may be *conflict*. According to Peterson, conflict is an interpersonal process occurring whenever one person's actions interfere with the actions of the other: "Everything from direct physical obstruction to nonverbal innuendos that affect the cognitive and emotional states of partners may qualify as interference" (Peterson 1983, 366). Conflict may be either constructive or destructive. *Destructive conflict* expands and escalates so that it moves beyond the initial issue, which becomes lost in the process and remains unresolved. Instead of defining the issue, conflict degenerates into mutual ventilation. When Linda says to Joe, "I should have married Craig; at least I'd be in sunny Florida now," he may not catch or may choose to ignore that her barbed comment has to do simply with the bedroom window. "Yeah, you sure should have. Why don't you just go see what he would say to that now?" She may counter, "You think nobody would be interested in me just because I've gained a few pounds. You don't have to say it; I know what you're thinking. Well, maybe I'll surprise you someday." Somehow, the problem of the open window has been forgotten. The issue is left unresolved to cause conflict another night, and both partners feel wounded and alienated. Conflict has degenerated into ventilation and then alienation.

Constructive conflict, on the other hand, is characterized by a concentration on the specific issue, use of problem-solving strategies, and a minimum of threat and defensiveness (Raush and others 1974). Joe may focus the issue by responding to Linda's taunt about Florida, "Are you asking me to close the window?" She may then reply, "Yes, I've been cold at night. Can't you close it, at least most of the way?" He answers, "Well, I like it open, but if you can't sleep. . . . What if I just leave it open a crack?" She agrees to compromise. "All right, we can try it. And let's switch sides so you are closer to the window." Deutsch has suggested that the features of constructive conflict are similar to the processes involved in creative thinking (Deutsch 1969). When issues are considered solvable, the search for alternative solutions expands on the original suggestions. The partners concentrate on developing creative strategies for cooperation rather than on one triumphing over the other through argument or persuasion.

To put the difference between conflict and anger another way, conflict is an interpersonal process; anger is *communication* about an *intra*-personal (internal and individual) process that has *inter*personal ramifications. The model presented here is simplistic and incomplete. It should be clear, however, that both effective or ineffective patterns of personal relating can be the result of any of the methods of communicating anger used by a spouse (see Figure 2). Although mutual ventilating often results when one partner ventilates feelings, and conflict or accommodation results from issue challenge, this is not always the case. It may actually take ventilation on the part of one spouse to move the relationship into a needed conflict if the partner is particularly deaf to criticism and slow to consider change. It is for this reason that no valuation was placed on the strategies for communicating anger, even though ventilating feelings and withdrawal are at best dangerous. On the other hand, from the perspective of the marital system, accommodation and conflict can unequivocably be called more effective patterns of interaction than mutual ventilating and alienation.

Other Sources of Marital Conflict

Reflective communication. Anger is not the only origin of marital conflict. Partners struggle with conflict whenever they reconcile differing needs, values, and intentions. These differences may or may not be accompanied by anger. As diagrammed in Figure 2, couples often need to accommodate new ideas, environmental changes, or individual changes (e.g., developmental changes resulting from aging processes, changing priorities, etc.) in relating to each other. For example, new ideas may include one partner's reading an article on marital communication and asking the spouse to try out some of the suggestions, or a partner's suggesting a different way of approaching child discipline. Changes in the environment include such things as a sister's phoning to say that she is coming for a three-week visit with her four preschoolers, or the city's putting a four-lane highway in front of the family home. Intrapersonal changes that affect the marital environment include the wife's finding out that she is pregnant or the husband's discovering that he has a heart condition. Dealing with the conflict such changes generate is critical for the personal growth of the spouses and the strength of the marriage.

Unfortunately, when issues do not generate anger we often ignore them. Our longings, our secret dreams, even our daily little gripes go undiscussed because we know to discuss them may lead to conflict and angry communication. By avoiding them we may also miss what may be significant possibilities for marital growth and service.

Other feelings involved in interpersonal relating. It should be noted that other kinds of communicated feelings can also lead to the four patterns of interpersonal relating described (mutual ventilating, alienation, accommodation, and conflict). For example, joy is a feeling we often communicate to our partners. Usually it is expressed in ventilation. Alice has just completed a difficult project she has been working on; she calls Tony and exuberantly shares her relief and pleasure, and they plan a celebration dinner together. She has "ventilated" her joy, and the celebration can be considered "mutual ventilation." Communication may contain primarily information rather than feelings, yet information always contains an element of difference, since it is the "newness" or "difference" of a message that defines it as information. It suggests a new idea that is different from other ideas or a change in the accustomed environment. Because information always involves "difference" in some way, it always includes a feeling interpretation about that difference and generates a feeling response in the receiver. In other words, the separation between communicating information and feelings is really a false dichotomy.

Even the shouted message, "Pick up some milk on your way home!" as a spouse is leaving the house, contains a feeling message, whether overtly identified or not. The "difference" that is being communicated is probably as simple as the fact that the partner just reached for some milk for cereal and realized (new information) that there is only a little left. The feeling component of the message may include, "I'm glad we're partners and I can count on you," or, if the tone is different, "I'm angry at always having to remind you. You forgot yesterday; don't forget today. I wish you were more responsible." The communication of information, therefore, may result in conflict, either immediately or after spouses mull over the message and their feeling response to it.

The Other Side of Anger

The marital partnership is more than a summation of the communication strategies of the individual partners; it is the interaction between them. Each has some influence, but that influence is not total. The other side of angry confrontation is listening and understanding. Speaking the truth can edify only if someone is listening.

Speaking and listening have become the basis for many of the approaches to learning communication and conflict resolution skills, and with good reason (see, for example, Miller, Nunnally, and Wackman 1979; Guerney 1977). In conflict situations particularly, we sometimes try to give the appearance of listening to our partner when we are only rehearsing in our head how we will rebut as soon as our partner stops to catch a breath. Our focus is on ourselves and our own position, not on our partner. The proverb "A fool takes no pleasure in understanding, but only in expressing an opinion" (Prov. 18:2) is apt. The folly is that as long as we concentrate only on our own thoughts and feelings and not on understanding our partner, the chance for resolution is slim and the chances for conflict escalation, blaming, and alienation are high. Listening and communicating understanding are not easy. They require mastery of interpersonal skills that are particularly difficult in the midst of conflict.

Our discussion of angry communication and resolving conflict is predicated on the basic tenet of chapter 4, mutual submission. If one partner—the husband—is to make all the decisions, little need for discussion exists except for him to gather information for more enlightened decision making. If partners are equals who are trying to work out what is "fair," the concern might be more for developing individual assertiveness and sharpening debating skills. Some approaches to family life education based on social exchange theory actually advocate that persons consciously engage in a process of self-centered bargaining with each other. In our opinion, these are not adequate models for Christians handling conflict.

The only passage in scripture that specifically addresses resolution of conflict in marriage is found in 1 Corinthians 7:4–5. Paul advised couples to reach a decision—in this case whether or not to withdraw from sexual relations for a period of prayer—by mutual agreement. One spouse is not to take control of decision making or attempt to outargue the other. It is through submitting ourselves (our thoughts, feelings, needs, and desires) to each other and together considering our task and purpose together that we are to come to a decision. It may be that one gives in and agrees with the other, or that we compromise by coming up with a solution different from either of our first wishes, or that we agree to coexist without changing anything but our perception of the problem. What is important is that the way is cleared for continued work together. Perhaps no other resource is more important in this process than partners' forgiveness of each other.

Forgiveness

Forgiveness is a means by which one person short-circuits the cycle of retaliation, reprisals, and punishment by refusing to return hurt for hurt. It is the decision not to meet ventilation with ventilation or to strike back at the one who offends us, but instead to halt the process of slap for slap, insult for insult, wrong for wrong (see Matt. 5:38–39, 1 Peter 3:9–12; Rom. 12:17–21). The one who decides to do this changes the focus of the difficulty from hurt and anger and satisfying some abstract notion of justice to the question of the future together. The forgiver recognizes that retaliation does not lead to reconciliation and masters the feelings of hurt, anger, or alienation to see what can be done to solve the problem. The feelings are not ignored but placed in the service of removing the barriers that have disrupted fellowship in order to begin the healing process that will restore the relationship. The one who forgives says, in effect, "I am hurt and angry, but it will not help either of us for me to ventilate my feelings or to try to get even. I want to see what we can do to make things right between us. Let's learn from what has happened and move on into the future together. Let's not stay here any longer." Forgiveness costs emotional energy, but it frees one from spinning his or her tires in the muck of anger and hurt that can come in every marriage.

Forgiveness enables us to keep our eyes on our mutual task, our work together in God's kingdom, and keep all else in perspective. To be able to forgive requires commitment to the other. Being willing to forgive means that we are not preoccupied with getting our just due. Put in the language of social exchange theory, "commitment indicates to the exchange partner that the marketing of resources is no longer necessary and that the partner can be assured that the current exchange will continue regardless of market conditions" (McDonald 1981, 834).

Although forgiveness is a process of moving beyond the cycle of retaliation, it does not mean forgetting what has happened. Jesus' parable of the unforgiving servant (Matt. 18:21–35) indicates that forgiving does not mean forgetting. In the parable, a king forgave an enormous debt when the servant pleaded with him, but the same servant turned a deaf ear to the pleas of a fellow servant who owed him a comparatively paltry sum. Instead, he hauled him by the neck to the debtor's prison. When word of this reached the king, he was more than a little miffed:

> Then his lord summoned him and said to him, "You wicked servant! I forgave you all that debt because you besought me; and should not you have had mercy on your fellow servant, as I had mercy on you?" (Matt. 18:32–33)

When the king forgave the servant, he expected that a change would take place within the servant, who should also exude mercy. The servant, however, misinterpreted this forgiveness as a sign of his special favor with the king. Instead of extending this same kind of forgiveness to others, he thought that he could throw his weight around and began to take advantage of his supposed privileged position by bullying his fellow servant. The king, to the surprise of the servant, had not forgotten what he had done for him or its cost. Forgiving the servant did not mean forgetting what needed forgiveness. As Smedes perceptively notes:

> If you forget, you will not forgive at all. You can never forgive people for things you have forgotten about. You need to forgive precisely be-

cause you have not forgotten what someone did; your memory keeps the pain alive long after the actual hurt has stopped. (Smedes 1984, 38–39)

In a marriage relationship, we free our partners from making restitution for their behavior when we forgive, but we also expect them to take responsibility to behave differently in the future. Forgiveness does not come with no strings attached (see Matt. 6:12, 14–15). The forgiveness of the king in the parable required something of the servant: "Was it not necessary for you to be merciful as well?" Forgiveness is not a passive swallowing of hurt but a means of reconciling two persons, an expectancy of willingness on the part of the forgiven to change—to recognize the wrongdoing and turn away from it.

Fairness concentrates on the past, forgiveness on the future. The past is not forgotten, however; it is remembered so that change will occur. Smedes argues for what he calls "redemptive remembering":

> There is a healing way to remember the wrongs of our irreversible past, a way that can bring hope for the future along with our sorrow for the past. Redemptive remembering keeps a clear picture of the past, but it adds a new setting and shifts its focus. (Smedes 1984, 136)

In the exodus, the people of Israel were told by Moses never to forget what they had seen and experienced. They were to remember their own sin, God's forgiveness, and the miracle of renewal. The prodigal son presumably never forgot the pigsty, and his father never forgot the emotional cost that his son's rash behavior exacted. By showering the returning son with overwhelming tokens of his forgiveness, however, the father demonstrated his hope that the prodigal son would become the reformed son. The parable is silent on this, but it may be assumed that the long-lost son did not spend the rest of his time celebrating his return but began to fulfill his filial duties and within a few days grabbed a hoe to help out with the farm work. The one who has offended and is forgiven, if truly repentant, has a desire to compensate in some way (see, for example, Zacchaeus), not to earn the forgiveness but to help to restore the relationship that has gone awry (Moule 1982, 252–255). Smede writes:

> Redemptive remembering drives us to a better future, it does not nail us to a worse past. When Israel remembered its own past bondage, the memory incited them to seek justice in the present. You were once strangers in a strange land; remember now to be hospitable to the stranger in your land. You were exploited by unjust masters; remember not to exploit your own poor people. You were slaves once; remember to set your own slaves free. Good hopes for a better life were filaments in the light ignited by the redemptive memory of Jewish suffering. (Smedes 1984, 137)

What does this mean for marital partners? It certainly does not mean that the past offense, the extramarital affair or the betrayed secret, is continually kept in mind or stored up as ammunition for the next conflict. Instead, forgiveness is a process of remembering our growth through the challenges, the hurts, and the anger that we have weathered together and that may have left scars but that ultimately strengthened our commitment to each other. Remembering is a celebration of our commitment, our mutual struggle to grow and to love each other in spite of our past failings. It remembers not only my forgiveness but also your repentance.

If forgiveness is not forgetting, it is also not quick absolution or a chance to avoid responsibility for what has happened between us. Often forgiveness is used as a cheap way to restore the status quo, to avoid looking at what has happened and what it means in our relationship. By using forgiveness in this way, we do not have to face the conflict that underlies your action and my hurt. If I say, "Forget it; I forgive you," perhaps everything will be back to normal and we will not have to think about it.

Jan and Kyle have worked out a careful budget so that they will be able to have the money they need to send Jan back to school for her master's degree. For the third month in a row, however, Kyle spends more than was allotted for some clothes he wants that were "on sale." When Jan looks at the depleted checkbook, she feels dismay and hurt by what she interprets as Kyle's selfishness and lack of support. When she confronts him with this, he responds, "But they were on sale and I needed them! I know you want to go to school, and I'm sorry." Jan's response is a long-suffering "Okay, I understand. Don't worry about it." Through this process of cheap forgiveness, they avoid reexamining their priorities. Jan is left feeling that her needs and dreams are not important to Kyle; and Kyle's betrayal of their agreement is left unchallenged, probably to happen again. Nothing in the relationship changes, and only a false harmony is maintained.

The problem with the process of forgiveness is that it often needs to be mutual. Both have often caused the hurt. If we really commit ourselves to looking at what has happened together and at what needs to change so that our future will be different, it may mean that both of us will need to make changes. Often it is easier to say "I forgive you" than to struggle together to understand how change needs to take place. Kyle is not the only one who needs to examine his betrayal of their mutual goals. Jan, too, needs to face her lack of responsibility in confronting him with the importance of school to her and with the need to review their goals to determine if there is genuine agreement.

Forgiveness does not say "If you will change your behavior, I will

forgive you" or "I'll forget it if you promise never to do it again."
Instead, we suggest that it means rolling up one's sleeves and tackling
the hurt *together*. Determining who caused the conflict and hurt—which
focuses on the past—is not as important as deciding how we can get
back on course or chart a new one. What is important is not attaching
blame to one or the other for what has happened, but how we can learn
from this and rebuild our partnership.

Forgiveness also does not excuse or tolerate. Excusing is just the
opposite of forgiving, since it assumes that the partner was not really
responsible for what happened. We can forgive only if we think the
other is responsible for the hurt (Smede 1984). Excusing simply looks
over the wrongs as unavoidable occurrences. This is what the wife did
who tripped over the jogging clothes on the floor. Her anger was
appeased when she remembered that her husband was particularly
preoccupied today. It was not premeditated sloppiness. This was not
forgiveness, because she did not hold him responsible this morning.
Forgiveness implies that some change is needed; she decided that no
change was needed—unless it happened again. Excusing can be quite
useful in marriage, but it is not to be confused with forgiveness. Forgiveness recognizes responsibility for wrongs and the capability and
need for change.

Forgiveness, however, does not restore the relationship, since it takes
two to relate. As evidenced by his spontaneous and undignified sprint
to hug his long-lost son, the father of the prodigal had already forgiven
him for his actions long before he ever returned home and got out his
confession. The relationship, however, could not be restored until the
son returned home. God forgives us, but that does not put us in the
right relationship with God unless we respond and turn from our old
ways. It is the same for interpersonal relationships. Forgiveness is only
a part of the process of reconciliation; the other side is repentance.
Forgiveness alone is not enough; we can forgive someone who does not
repent, but this does not restore the relationship. We need to forgive
whether repentance is there or not, but that alone does not build the
relationship as mutual examination and forgiveness and repentance do.

6

Sexuality and Intimacy

Perhaps in no other area has the message of the Bible been more misrepresented than in conventional descriptions of its estimate of sexuality in the lives of men and women. Most social scientists today regard the stance of Christianity toward sexuality to be at best unsympathetic and at worst a major contributor to the problems some people experience in sexual functioning. We have the legacy of the church fathers to thank for the fact that sin is popularly equated with "sex." They are easy targets for modern authors who wish to pillory their crotchety abhorrence of sexuality. Tannahill, in her popular history of sex, writes:

> It was Augustine who epitomized a general feeling among the Church Fathers that the act of intercourse was fundamentally disgusting. Arnobius called it filthy and degrading, Methodius unseemly, Jerome unclean, Tertullian shameful, Ambrose a defilement. In fact there was an unstated consensus that God ought to have invented a better way of dealing with the problem of procreation. Augustine . . . set his mind to the problem and concluded that the fault lay not with God but with Adam and Eve. (Tannahill 1980, 141)

As a result of these prevailing ideas, the church has rarely, if ever, celebrated human sexuality. Sexual intercourse is still viewed by some as an unwelcome necessity for reproducing the species and certainly sinful if it is engaged in for any other purpose, such as pleasure. The social scientists and helping professionals are therefore not unjustified in regarding Christian values as antagonistic toward sexuality since so many theologians have voiced antisexual sentiments. The attempted repression of sexuality by the church in the name of piety has had injurious effects on the lives of many who have vainly attempted to deny or thwart their sexual feelings.

In contrast to the emphasis of the church on the moral issues of sexuality, social scientists have sought to uncover the actual sexual behavior of persons. Research on sexuality (which in our culture now packs more punch than theological pronouncements) has dispelled myths and cleared the air regarding sexual practices that people engaged in but felt guilty about (for example, Kinsey, Pomeroy, and Martin 1948; Kinsey and others 1953; Masters and Johnson 1966). Unfortunately, this "white-coat" approach has riveted attention on the physiology and practices of sexual behavior to the neglect of the meaning and value of the behavior for persons. Our culture's fascination with experimental research and its reaction against a heritage of repressive attitudes has resulted in a widespread view that optimal sexuality has to do with physiological functioning in which values may be an undesirable encumbrance.

When sexual behavior is separated from values, however, it loses any meaning beyond the release of sexual tension. If we wish to appreciate our sexuality, we must do more than study charts of male and female anatomy, graphs of human sexual response, and research about the sexual practices and satisfaction of couples. These are not unimportant, but they cannot alone define sexuality because as objective measures they do not probe the *meaning* of sexuality for persons. Meaning is subjective; it is how people construe for themselves the implicit and explicit purposes of their behavior. This chapter will focus on the values and meaning of sexuality for Christians in marriage. We will also refer to the physiological and interpersonal dynamics of sexuality as they illustrate and provide the context for understanding how to live out God's intention for us as sexual creatures.

First, however, clarification is needed on the appraisal of sexuality in the Bible. Is it viewed as an inherently dangerous siren that lures us to destruction and must therefore be thwarted unless we want to burn in hell as well as burn with passion? Or is this approach the legacy of early church monks whose inclinations toward morbid asceticism led them to suborn the Bible to support their own opinions of the matter? It is our view that the latter is correct, and we will turn our attention to Paul, who has earned the undeserved reputation of being anti-sex and anti-marriage.

Was Paul Anti-Sex?

Paul is accused by many of being one of the main culprits in steering the church toward an ascetic view of sexuality. Such statements as, "It is well for a man not to touch a woman," "Because of the temptation to immorality, each man should have his own wife and each woman her own husband," "It is better to marry than to be aflame with passion," and "Let those who have wives live as though they had none," found in 1 Corinthians 7 and taken out of context, seem hardly to be grateful praise for sex or marriage. What are we to make of this? Did Paul consider marriage to be simply a prophylactic against fornication, a necessary evil owing to the weakness of the flesh (Lietzmann and Kümmel 1949, 29), "a venereal safety valve" (Phipps 1982, 129), or "lawful concubinage" (Leenhardt 1946, 22)? The statement "to avoid fornication, let every man have his own wife" would appear to be "hardly a smashing blow in favor of marital bliss" (Cartlidge 1975, 224). Did Paul believe that sexual activity resulted in some kind of spiritual pollution, as is implied by the description in Revelation 14:4 of the hundred and forty thousand as those "who have not defiled themselves with women"? Does his statement "the unmarried woman or girl is anxious about the affairs of the Lord, how to be holy in body and spirit" (1 Cor. 7:34) imply that the married woman was somehow not holy in body and spirit because of her sexual contact with her husband? These questions can be answered only by investigating the historical context of 1 Corinthians 7, where these statements appear.

In 1 Corinthians 7, Paul was not presenting a compendium of his views on marriage and sexuality. He was reacting to specific difficulties concerning marriage and countering aberrant views of sexuality that had evolved in the church in Corinth. As interpreters, however, we face the obstacle of trying to discover what these difficulties and views were when we can only listen to one side of the conversation and must reason from Paul's responses what it was that prompted them. But this must be done if Paul is to be correctly understood.

In 7:1, Paul alerted his readers that he was now going to speak to the issues raised in their letter to him: "Now concerning the matters about which you wrote. . . ." The phrase "now concerning" *(peri de)* appears elsewhere in the letter to introduce a topic from the Corinthians' list of concerns where they either had asked for Paul's specific response or had made statements that evoked his response (see 7:25; 8:1; 12:1; 16:1, 12). This confirms that Paul was reacting in chapter 7 to something that had been raised by the Corinthians and not providing a summary of his views on sex and marriage.

Both the translation and the punctuation of 1 Corinthians 7:1 require attention. First, the *New International Version* and *Today's English Version* are quite off the mark when they render it "It is good for a man not to marry" or "A man does well not to marry." This is a misguided attempt to bring 7:1 in line with 7:8–9, (NEB) "Better be married than burn" (see Hurd 1965, 61–74, 154–159; Fee 1980, 307–314). The verb in Greek means "to touch" and was used as a euphemism for sexual intercourse (see Gen. 20:4, 6; Prov. 6:29; and other sexual euphemisms in 1 Cor. 7:2–5: "have," "what is due," "refuse one another"). Verse 1 should be translated accordingly: "It is good for a

man not to have sexual relations with a woman." Second, the punctuation found in most translations—Now concerning what you wrote. It
is good for a man not to touch a woman—leads the reader to believe
that Paul was offering the Corinthians his own opinion. There is increasing agreement among interpreters that Paul was instead quoting
from the Corinthians' letter or employing a slogan of a Corinthian
faction that he wished to refute. Paul quoted other Corinthian slogans
elsewhere in this letter for the same purpose (see 6:12; 8:1,4; 10:23;
and possibly 1:12; 2:14; 8:8; 11:2; 14:34–35; 15:12), and they are
frequently placed in quotation marks in modern translations. If Paul
were citing an opinion held by some Christians in Corinth, verse 1
should be punctuated: Now concerning what you wrote: "It is good for
a man not to touch a woman."

This is a reasonable conclusion for three reasons. First, Paul tended
in the letter to cite Corinthian catchphrases in order to reinterpret
them. Second, in every other place where the introductory phrase
"now concerning" appears in the letter, the subject matter is specifically
mentioned. Since he implied that he was going to respond to issues
raised in the letter from the Corinthians, it would seem more likely that
he would give them some clue as to precisely what in their letter he was
responding to than that he would begin immediately to advance his
own opinions without any introduction of the topic. Finally, verse 1
cannot reflect Paul's opinion regarding sexuality since in verses 2 to 5
he argued that sexual relations within marriage are not optional and
better avoided but are required. Because he argued this so vigorously,
and later wrote that marriage was not a sin (7:8–9, 36), it can mean only
that someone in Corinth was saying just the opposite—sexual abstinence is best even for married couples. We therefore conclude that in
7:1 Paul quoted from the Corinthian letter to provide a subject heading
for the new section, and this quotation does not reflect Paul's own
opinion on the matter. On the contrary, it was something he wished to
refute.

We have seen in chapter 2, in our discussion of the pastoral epistles,
that the early church was plagued by those who reasoned that sexual
activity somehow sullied one's spiritual nature (see Col. 2:21; 1 Tim.
4:1–3; Heb. 13:4). It is clear from a careful reading of chapter 7 that
this ascetic viewpoint had its proponents in Corinth. In fact, two approaches to sexuality existed in Corinth. One group claimed that all
things were lawful (6:12; 10:23) and indulged in a new morality of
sexual freedom; another group claimed freedom from sexuality and
promoted celibacy as spiritually superior (Bartchy 1973, 132). For the
latter, sexual abstinence was their way of stepping out of the world and
up to God.

Those who argued for an ascetic life-style could appeal to isolated sayings of Jesus found particularly in the Gospel of Luke to support their case if they were aware of this tradition. In the parable of the banquet, one who has been invited to feast informs the messenger of the host—unlike the others, he does not ask to be excused—that he has married a wife and will not attend (Luke 14:20). From this example marriage can be construed as a hindrance to salvation; the guest was more interested in pleasing his new wife (see 1 Cor. 7:33) than heeding the call of God. This parable is followed by a clarification of the costs of discipleship in Luke 14:25–33: "If any one comes to me and does not hate his own father and mother and wife and children and brothers and sisters, yes, and even his own life, he cannot be my disciple" (Luke 14:26). The parallel in Matthew 10:37 mentions only father, mother, son, and daughter. Luke includes "hating" the wife as a criterion of discipleship. This idea reappears in Luke 18:29–30, where Jesus promises that those who leave household, wife, brothers, parents, and children for the sake of the kingdom of God will receive much more in this time and the age to come. "Hating" one's wife has nothing to do with psychological hate but means either "to love less" (see Matt. 10:37) or "to leave aside" or "abandon" (Marshall 1978, 592). If these sayings were known to the Corinthians, they could easily fuel the exaltation of asceticism. They could justify denying their sexuality for the sake of the greater calling and reward of the kingdom.

Luke 20:34–36 would be particularly apropos when interpreted from this perspective:

> The sons of this age marry and are given in marriage; but those who are accounted worthy to attain to that age and to the resurrection from the dead neither marry nor are given in marriage, for they cannot die any more, because they are equal to angels and are sons of God, being sons of the resurrection.

In Corinth there were those who sought to be accounted worthy of the new age by renouncing their human sexuality. Not only did they speak the tongues of angels (13:1), they were trying to live like angels by renouncing marriage and sex. They abstained from sexual intercourse with their marriage partner or divorced their spouses and dissuaded others from marrying. From their point of view, one who wanted to reach the highest spiritual plateau had to renounce his or her sexuality. Celibacy then became a badge of the new exalted spiritual state, and Genesis 2:18 was turned on its head: "It is not good for a man to be alone" became "It is not good for a man to touch a woman"—even if he were married.

Paul did not concur with this world-denying view that promoted celibacy as a higher way; he argued strongly *against* asceticism in marriage. First, he insisted, "let each one have his own wife/husband"

(7:2). By saying this Paul was not advising *anyone* to marry. Celibacy was a valid option for those with this gift (*charisma*, 7:7). The verb "to have" is another euphemism for sexual relations (see also Mark 6:18; 12:23; John 4:18; 1 Cor. 5:1, KJV), which means that Paul was addressing those already married, not the unmarried. The topic concerning those who had not yet married, "the virgins" (KJV), is taken up later in 7:25–38. The use of the present imperative in 7:2—"let every man have"—suggests that Paul was aware that some couples had already renounced coitus, and he was refuting this kind of spiritual marriage. According to Paul, marriage was to be a fully sexual relationship; he did not commend those who tried to become asexual in marriage.

Second, he warned them of the temptation of fornication (*porneia*). This is not to be construed as Paul's rationale for marriage—namely, that one ought to marry to avoid being guilty of fornication. Paul was not addressing the pros and cons of marriage in these verses but opposing attempts by some in Corinth to be celibate *in* marriage. He wanted to reel in these supernal Christians from their spiritual stratosphere and remind them of the realities of earth. Common sense made it clear that withdrawing from conjugal relations simply invited the temptation to have one's sexual needs satisfied illicitly. The church already had problems with incidents of fornication (1 Cor. 6:12–20; 2 Cor. 12:21), and the notorious city of Corinth provided abundant opportunities for this. In chapter 6, Paul reminded the Corinthians that God had not called them out of a bodily existence (6:17–20); here in 7:2 he reminded them that they were still subject to bouts with sexual temptation. Paul knew that the sex instinct was a powerful drive and that Satan was a powerful adversary (7:5). They had already had their sexual instincts awakened in marriage; they should not attempt to deny them by striving for celibacy as if it were the spiritual ideal. It was therefore *not* good for married couples to make the shift to celibacy; it would only open the door to the temptation of fornication. They should not overstrain the flesh with unrealistic demands no matter how willing the spirit might be.

Third, Paul told them not to refuse ("deprive" or "rob") one another of what is owed—namely, their conjugal rights. The use again of the present imperative, "do not refuse one another," suggests that this was exactly what they had been doing. Paul countered that sexual intercourse in marriage was not only spiritually permissible, it was obligatory. It was a right that was owed to the spouse, since each spouse, according to Paul, had authority over the other's body. One spouse therefore should not deprive the other of a fully sexual relationship in marriage. This does not mean, however, that one can demand sexual relations from a spouse. The right of sexual access to each other is to be governed by loving concern and can never be something demanded or forced or, for that matter, offered as some kind of reward. Paul did allow for the possibility that a married couple might withdraw from conjugal relations, but only on three conditions (7:5). The first was that it be done only by mutual consent. One spouse may not disregard the sexual needs of the other in a selfish pursuit of some spiritual discipline. Religious devotion was not to be used as a pretext for withholding sex from one's partner. The second condition was that the withdrawal be for a season of prayer. It was not that Paul believed that one could pray better when one refrained from sexual activity. Instead, he recognized that there might be times when a couple was so overwhelmed by spiritual concerns that retreat in prayer might be expedient. Paul would have agreed with 1 Peter that one's prayers are hindered by mistreatment of a spouse (1 Peter 3:7), but he never hinted that they would be hindered by sexual activity with a spouse. The third condition he laid down was that if a couple did decide mutually to withdraw for prayer, it was to be for a limited time only. Paul did not want them attempting to set endurance records.

It must be admitted that Paul did believe that marriage was inadvisable, but his arguments were not based on a devaluation of marriage as a spiritually inferior state. He did not agree with those Corinthians who believed that sexual union contaminated the Christian's life in the Spirit. He vigorously disagreed with those in Corinth who thought that celibacy enhanced one's spiritual standing with God (see D. E. Garland 1983, 356–358; Bartchy 1973, 138–140). Instead, Paul discouraged marriage for quite pragmatic reasons. Marriage was not recommended by Paul primarily because of his concern for the eschatological urgency of the hour, which he believed required the focus of all one's energies (7:29–31). Paul thought that one would have distress enough in the last days without also having the burdens of marital responsibilities. Second, he took it for granted that marriage brought with it troubles in the flesh (7:28); it was not a romantic haven from the problems of the world. Perhaps he would have agreed with the rabbi who said:

> A young man is like a colt that whinnies, he paces up and down, he grooms himself with care: this is because he is looking for a wife. But once married, he resembles an ass, quite loaded down with burdens. (Midrash on Ecclesiastes 1:2)

Third, Paul assumed that marriage also divided a person's allegiance at a time when singleness of purpose was most needed (1 Cor. 7:32–35). The married man and wife must be concerned with how to please each other, while single Christians can devote all their attention to the affairs of the Lord. Finally, Paul considered marriage to be an institution that, as a part of this world, was passing away (7:31). The claim of marriage ended with death (7:39; see also Rom. 7:2–3); the claim of Christ extends beyond death and this world and therefore should have priority.

It was for these practical reasons that Paul considered it inadvisable for those who had never married to marry and better for those who had been widowed to remain unmarried (7:8–9, 38–39). Nevertheless, he asserted that marriage was not a sin (7:36). If the widower or widow could not exercise control over his or her desires, marriage was recommended (7:9; see also 1 Tim. 5:11–14). The same thing applied to those who were betrothed; if their passions were strong, let them marry and enter into a fully sexual relationship (7:36–38; this passage is a notorious crux; see Kümmel 1954). There was nothing wrong with choosing to marry; what was wrong was the vain attempt to enhance one's spiritual standing with God through celibacy. Those who attempted this misunderstood both the nature of salvation, which comes by grace alone and not through some supererogatory spiritual achievement, and the nature of the sexual relationship in marriage. It was intended by God to be a part of the marriage experience and was therefore good (1 Tim. 4:1–3). Paul recognized that not all persons had the charisma for celibacy, nor should they have it (1 Cor. 7:8). He had his personal preference (7:7, 32), but he did not impose this on anyone and never suggested that those who were not celibate but fully sexual were in any way spiritually tainted.

In this discussion, Paul made it clear that he was offering his opinions on the matter: "I wish" (7:7), "I think" (7:26). They are the opinions of one who has been counted by the Lord's mercy to be trustworthy, but they are still *his* opinions. He based them pragmatically on what he believed would be to the Corinthians' advantage and would "promote good order" or seemliness (7:35), given his assessment of the hour. He was convinced that the celibate life was less anxious (7:32), more ordered (7:35), and happier (7:40), but there have been many other Christians through the ages who have found this to be just as true of the married life. Experience shows that both the married and the unmarried can be anxiety ridden and distracted. In spite of his personal preferences, Paul allowed for each individual to decide for himself or herself how to live in obedience to God's call when it came to marriage and did not dictate that others imitate his example. Each was considered able to make responsible choices, and Paul would not "cast a snare" on them (7:35, KJV) or pronounce *ex cathedra* how they were to order their lives.

Although there were those in the early church who frowned on human sexuality (see Von Campenhausen 1949; Vööbus 1958), we conclude that Paul cannot be numbered among them. On the contrary, he radically opposed this attitude when it surfaced in Corinth. It should be clear from the opening verses of 1 Corinthians 7 that Paul did not consider sex and marriage to be an obstacle to the spiritual life or the lesser of two evils—marriage or fornication. One also need not appeal outside 1 Corinthians to see that marriage was normative for him (see 9:5, 11:7–9). Although he personally preferred celibacy (possibly as one who had been widowed or even divorced), he never disparaged sexuality in marriage. On the contrary, he insisted in 1 Corinthians 7 that marriage was to be a fully sexual relationship. He was forced to give so much attention to this aspect of marriage in this chapter because this was what was being denied in Corinth. It does not defile the couple, nor does it distract them from their calling in Christ any more than other normal activities such as mourning, rejoicing, or dealing with the outside world (1 Cor. 7:30–31).

Later Christians may have appealed to isolated passages in Paul to support their ascetic inclinations, but in so doing they misinterpreted and misused him. As Collins recently states, "Nowhere in Paul is there the slightest hint that human sexuality is evil." Paul was not worried that Christians might express their sexuality; his concern was only that they express it fittingly (Collins 1978, 11).

In 1 Thessalonians 4:3–8, this concern comes to the surface. He wrote:

> For this is the will of God, your sanctification: that you abstain from unchastity; that each one of you know how to take a wife for himself in holiness and honor, not in the passion of lust like heathen who do not know God. (1 Thess. 4:3–5)

God's will, as Paul defined it here, is that Christians not be guilty of fornication and that they be sanctified. One can infer from this with Collins (1983, 423) that "a sexually active marital relationship is a means of fulfilling God's will." Marshall thoughtfully comments, "Holiness does not exclude sexual activity . . . but controls its character" (Marshall 1984, 107). Paul did not warn against sex; he warned against lust infecting the sexual relationship between husband and wife so that the spouse becomes nothing more than an object for sexual release. He also resolutely insisted that sexual contact be limited to the marriage relationship.

It is self-evident for Paul and the rest of the New Testament that sex loses its meaning outside of marriage. As Furnish notes, "Sex is a meaningful part of marriage, but it is meaningful only within marriage" (Furnish 1979, 35). In the Greco-Roman world, a man might keep a mistress, own a slave concubine, and visit a temple prostitute without incurring a moral stigma. The New Testament contends that sexuality can be properly channeled only in a marriage relationship that is based on a permanent and total commitment.

The New Testament condemns any behavior that is exploitative of

another. This includes sexual encounters that treat a partner as an object
to gratify one's lust for pleasure and excitement or to compensate for
some sense of personal failure in other aspects of life. The partner is
to be treated with honor as a holy thing (1 Thess. 4:4) and may never
be held cheap as something expendable or interchangeable. The New
Testament ethic is based on the command to love thy neighbor as
thyself (see Matt. 22:39; John 13:34–35; Rom. 13:9–10; Gal. 5:14;
Eph. 5:2; James 2:8). This requires respect for the personhood of
others and concern for their welfare. Sexual union for the Christian
therefore entails responsibility and commitment to the other and to any
child who may be produced from that union.

The sacred character of this commitment requires absolute fidelity.
It is this that generates trust between partners. Paul rejected casual
sexual encounters with prostitutes in 1 Corinthians 6 because he believed that a sexual encounter can never be casual. It is not something
that only involves the genitalia and does not affect the deepest recesses
of the soul (see Matt. 15:19; Mark 7:21; sexual sins come from the
heart). Today many remain unconvinced of this. For example, a husband in Gay Talese's best-seller, Thy Neighbor's Wife, derides his wife
for her unwillingness to become more venturesome in her sex life. He
accuses her of being a typical woman who cannot have sex without
becoming emotionally involved. But sex does involve emotions, and
also our deep-seated attitudes about ourselves and others. Paul in-
timated in 1 Corinthians 6:16 that sexual intercourse was far more than
simply a collision of bodies. It is not merely a bodily function such as
eating (see 1 Cor. 6:12–13) that does not affect the very depths of one's
being. Union with a prostitute, for example, was compared to union
with Christ; when one was joined to a prostitute he became one body
with her (1 Cor. 6:15–16). The phrases "one body," "one flesh," and
"join" ("cleave," see Matt. 19:5) make clear that Paul believed that
sexual intercourse involves more than one's physiological parts; it involves the total self.

Sexuality Is a Shared Relationship

Paul considered sexual relations to be something owed to the partner
(1 Cor. 7:3). It is a debt. In other words, when one assumes a marriage
commitment, one also assumes a commitment to the sexual needs of the
partner. In writing this, Paul implicitly acknowledged that the wife also
had sexual desires and was not simply to wait for and be a passive
recipient of her husband's sexual overtures. Paul also wrote, "The wife
does not rule over her own body, but the husband does; likewise the
husband does not rule over his own body, but the wife does" (1 Cor.
7:4). This means that Paul considered the sexual relationship to be "a

shared relationship of two persons of equal standing" (Furnish 1979, 35). It does not mean that one may dictate to the other. As Foerster recognizes, having authority over the other does not mean that each partner now has a right to the other's body but that each forgoes the right freely to dispose of his or her body and gives that right to the other (Foerster 1964, 574–575). Each thereby becomes vulnerable for the other. Although the word "love" never appears in 1 Corinthians 7, this is in essence what a loving commitment to another entails (Friedrich 1977, 80). Sexuality in marriage is not to be self-centered so that the spouse becomes an object for self-gratification. It is never to be a question of What do I need and how will my needs be met? but What can I give to the other? The sex act is something that is done with and for the other.

This may be considered by some as too modern a reading of Paul's statements. Keck, for example, maintains that Paul did not give sex a positive assessment as a means of enhancing mutuality or of expressing love and tenderness but excuses him by claiming that this is primarily a modern perception (Keck 1979, 113). Sex as a means of expressing love and tenderness, however, was not at issue in 1 Corinthians 7. The point of controversy centered on the attempt of some Corinthians to enhance their relation to God by withdrawing from sexual relations with their spouse or by renouncing marriage altogether. The problems he tackled in the letter therefore did not call for him to state specifically that a married couple's sexual activity was a means of expressing love and enhancing mutuality. But this idea is not so modern as some might believe. For example, Josephus claimed that sexual relations were a mingling of souls—the soul of each was shared with the partner (*Against Apion* 2.25)—and there is no reason to doubt that Paul would have agreed with this assessment. From what he did say in 1 Corinthians 6 one can infer that he would have recognized that sexual relations served this purpose. The body can become a channel by which one communicates one's whole psychological, physiological, and spiritual being to another. He affirmed that the body can and should be used as an instrument to glorify God (1 Cor. 6:20). This would include the sexuality of our bodies. Therefore, one way that the body can be used to glorify God is by using our God-given sexuality to communicate love, belonging, and acceptance in the intimacies of sexual embrace.

The companionship that grows out of the sharing of self with another, sexual intercourse, is viewed as a primary function of sexuality in our culture. One of the key elements of companionship is knowing each other and understanding each other. It is this belief that another knows me "inside and out" that assuages my aloneness. Sexual intimacy provides a couple with ways of knowing each other and sharing with each other that are not available in other modes of communication. It is certainly more delicate and sometimes more articulate than speech. The joining of two persons in sexual love is a powerful means of overcoming the differences of experience and thought between two people, of moving from our loneliness and isolation as individuals into togetherness, sharing, and unity despite differences—even because of differences. Hollis and Clendinning state:

> In intercourse a couple surrender the mystery of their selfhood to each other. They share with each other their most cherished secrets. The woman allows her partner to know her as she really is. The man reveals to his mate the full knowledge of his identity. The nakedness of the couple is symbolic that nothing is hidden from the other. If this revelation about one's partner is given within a covenant, there can be feelings of mutual trust and wholesome acceptance. (Hollis and Clendinning 1970, 5)

Ironically, it is this "knowing" that trips up many couples. Granting that knowledge of sex and skills in bed are important, these are not usually what is lacking when couples are dissatisfied with their sexual relationship—at least in our society with its plethora of how-to-do-it manuals. Lack of knowledge about sexual functioning is relatively easily remedied. Sexual problems for a couple result more often than not from their inability to share with each other, to risk with each other, to allow themselves to become vulnerable, and to be sensitive to the vulnerabilities of the partner. In short, they are unable to commune with each other. It is not length of foreplay or creative positioning for intercourse that is crucial, but developing companionship. This is particularly critical in the early years of marriage, although it can be a problem throughout a marital relationship. Maddock tells us:

> The marital bed is expected to reflect the dynamics of the rest of the marital system. Often it does, to the dismay of one or both partners. Erotically, they are challenged to adjust not so much to each other's sexual behavior as to each other's—and their own—sexual expectations. Complex messages and memories from families and early life experiences lurk in the background or come unexpectedly to the fore. Variations and discrepancies in their sexual desires begin to surface and require negotiated adjustments into a mutually satisfying pattern. Sharing of sexual meanings becomes more important over time than the logistics of sexual activity. (Maddock 1983, 21–22)

If sexual adjustment depended merely on knowledge of the anatomy and physiology of sexual response and on skills of arousing and satisfying a partner while at the same time experiencing arousal and satisfaction, partners could be interchangeable like musical instruments that require only minor tuning adjustments. Sexual adjustment, however, is obviously much more. It is a microcosm of the marital relationship itself, reflecting the degree to which roles are flexible or established by gender, the power arrangements of the marriage and who controls the action, the means by which conflicts and desires are resolved, and the degree to which all these processes can be changed as the needs and hopes and fantasies of the partners change.

Research, in fact, demonstrates that sexual adjustment and a happy, satisfying marriage cannot be separated. The correlation between sexual adjustment and general marital adjustment has been apparent in nearly all investigations of marital adjustment (Udry 1974; Fields 1983). If problems in the sexual relationship develop, they are much more likely to be solved if relations in a partnership are otherwise good. For this reason, most marriage counselors will not tackle sexual problems when other relationship issues prevent the couple from communicating care for each other and resolving conflict.

Although sexual problems can exist in an otherwise happy and satisfying marriage, the sexual relationship is usually a sensitive indicator of the strength of the marital relationship. As Lederer and Jackson conclude from their observations of couples in counseling:

> What is special about sexual intercourse, a highly satisfying male-female symbiosis, is that it requires a higher degree of collaborative communication than any other kind of behavior exchanged between the spouses. Sex is consequently precious, but also perilous. It is the only relationship act which must have mutual spontaneity for mutual satisfaction. It can only be a conjoint union, and it represents a common goal which is clear and understood by both. (Lederer and Jackson 1968, 117–118)

Schrenk, Pfrang, and Rausche found in their research that no relationship exists between the personality traits of spouses and satisfaction with the sexual relationship; sexual satisfaction was found instead to depend more on the quality of the marital relationship. They conclude:

> In marriage, sexuality is a means to express the continuously more pronounced feelings of appreciation toward the partner. This holds true even for men, who are sometimes suspected of merely satisfying physiological needs in sexual intimacy. (Schenk, Pfrang, and Rausche 1983)

Sexuality, then, cannot be separated from the relationship that gives it meaning. Often, the helping professions distinguish between the terms "sex" and "sexuality." For example, Hartman, Quinn, and Young define sexuality as including "feelings of warmth, closeness, comfort, touching, security, support, love, affection, and mutuality" and sex as "genital behavior and reproduction [which] may or may not include these feelings" (Hartman, Quinn, and Young 1981, 11). Sexuality is an expression of self-concept, including gender and the history of personal and, most importantly, relationship development. Sex is the behavior chosen to express sexuality and resolve physiological drives.

The two, however, are inseparable. Sex expresses the purpose and meaning of our sexuality; it cannot be otherwise. One purpose of sex is the sharing and companionship that we have discussed in this section. Another purpose is procreation, which unfortunately has been mistaken by some as its sole purpose and to which we now turn.

Procreation or Pleasure?

In his treatise *On the Good of Marriage,* Augustine argued that marriage was a check against illicit intercourse and that sexual intercourse was religiously sanitized only when it takes place for the sake of begetting children. If sexual relations were engaged in solely to satisfy sensual pleasure, it was labeled a venial sin—a pardonable offense, but nevertheless an offense (the wife, however, was not considered guilty since it was assumed she was only rendering her "marriage debt"). This jaundiced view of human sexuality cannot be supported from the New Testament. Procreation is never appealed to as the sanctifying purpose of intercourse; in fact, it is never mentioned at all. This is all the more striking given the Jewish background of the New Testament.

The basic purpose of marriage in Judaism was to obey the command to multiply and have children. A sampling of opinions from Jewish sources reveals how deeply seated was the concern for procreation. In Mishnah *Yebamoth* 6.6, the rabbis stated that a man must not abstain from sexual relations unless he has two children (they disagreed over what constituted two children—two sons, or a son and a daughter). Rabbi Eliezer was said to have argued, "He who does not engage in the propagation of the race is as though he sheds blood" (M. *Yebam.* 63b). The logic behind this assertion was that he took the life of his potential child and thereby also diminished the image of God in the world. As a consequence of this attitude, contraceptive measures were forbidden; a man could not marry a barren or old woman, a woman could not marry a eunuch, and divorce was recommended after ten years of a childless marriage (M. *Yebam.* 8.4).

In the *Testament of Issachar* 3.2, it was claimed that God favored Rachel with two sons: "For he perceived that she wanted to lie with Jacob for the sake of children and not merely for sexual gratification." Philo reflects this same view in asserting that when persons copulate for pleasure instead of for procreation "they are like pigs and goats" (*Special Laws* 3.36, 113). Josephus also claimed, "The Law recognizes no sexual connections, except the natural union of man and wife, and that only for the procreation of children" (*Against Apion* 2.199). The Essenes at Qumran were celibate; according to Josephus, there were other Essenes who married, but only after proof of the woman's ability to menstruate normally and presumably to be able to bear children.

They refrained from intercourse during pregnancy, "thus showing that their motive in marrying is not self-indulgence but the procreation of children" (*Jewish War* 2.160–161; see also *Against Apion* 2.202). One could go on and on with more citations, but these suffice to contrast what is found, or rather not found, in the New Testament.

For the Jews of Jesus' day, the goal of marriage was that the two become at least four; otherwise it had failed its purpose. For Jesus, marriage found its highest fulfillment in *the two becoming one* (Matt 19:6; Mark 10:8; see Eph. 5:31). Nowhere is Genesis 1:28 cited in the New Testament with reference to marriage or sexual intercourse. Meeks theorizes that Paul's eschatological expectation made the question of procreation moot for him but notes that it is significant that Paul nevertheless endorsed normal sexual relations between husband and wife (Meeks 1983, 101). Paul encouraged marriage for those who had sexual desires and insisted that marriage partners be sexually active. This means that he did not consider conceiving children to be the sole purpose of sexual intercourse, nor did it sanctify what was otherwise a blameworthy act.

The sexual relationship between a man and a woman is undeniably a means for sharing in God's work of creation, but the pleasure dimension of sexual contact should not be devalued. The means of procreation has been combined by God with interpersonal behavior that is by its very nature playful, enjoyable, and focused on you and me in this moment. In the sheer abandon of caressing, holding, touching, talking, and experiencing climax and the climax of our partner, we are renewed. The whole of the Song of Solomon as well as some proverbs express the beauty and pleasure of sexuality:

> Three things are too wonderful for me;
>   four I do not understand:
> the way of an eagle in the sky,
>   the way of a serpent on a rock,
> the way of a ship on the high seas,
>   and the way of a man with a maiden.
>   (Proverbs 30:18–19)

The function of pleasure in sexuality is built in, not an added cultural definition or, as some have said, a distortion of the procreative function. Biologically, human behavior is governed by dual steering mechanisms: the avoidance of pain and the seeking of pleasure. For example, eating is pleasurable; but it also avoids the pain of gnawing hunger. Sexuality is unique in that it is dominated mainly by the seeking of pleasure. Unmet sexual needs do not create pain in the same sense that hunger, sleep deprivation, or an overextended bladder do.

Kaplan concludes from research and clinical evidence that of all the human functions, sexuality is uniquely and intensely pleasurable. In MacLean's research with monkeys, sexual expression is associated with a tranquil and nonaggressive mood that often lasts all day in otherwise unpleasant monkeys (Kaplan 1974, 44). Many will attest to the truth of these observations from their firsthand experiences with otherwise unpleasant spouses. In human subjects, orgasm is connected with electrical discharges in a region of the brain that is associated with intense pleasure and feelings of love and affection as well as the reduction of anger and irritability. Sexual satisfaction and feelings of love and affection are therefore physiologically intertwined (Kaplan 1974, 44). Unlike other drive states, sex is pleasurable and savored even when tension is building, not just in the release of sexual tension in orgasm. The progressive distention of the bladder or building hunger is hardly experienced as pleasurable the way sexual arousal is.

We have been biologically designed, then, to enjoy the expression of our sexuality. The pleasure we experience in sex is the physiological ground for love and intimacy. It functions to reduce feelings of anger at irritations and differences, and as a result walls of alienation are broken down. Sexual pleasure enhances companionship. It also reinforces the sexual relationship and brings us back again and again into sexual intimacy. To deny that this is the case or to subjugate sexual pleasure under the task of procreation is seriously to misunderstand our sexuality.

God could have chosen another way to perpetuate humanity than sexual union between man and woman. However, we have been made as we are, not only requiring that two be joined to create another, but also with physiological mechanisms that nurture intimacy and companionship through sexual union. The intimacy and renewal of commitment to each other that are the fruits of sexual union is God-created and was not an unfortunate mistake. Sexuality was intended by God to be a source of intimacy and pleasure for the married couple and not just a means to propagate the species. God did say be fruitful and multiply, but conception is not the only means of creativity in the sexual relationship. From the companionship and shared pleasure of sexual expression a man and a woman can then turn outward as partners in the task of caring for God's world. Even contraception can be a means of fulfilling God's command to subdue nature and to exercise control and care for God's garden.

Sexual expression varies in the actual role it plays in the relationship of the partners. It can be a sharing of one's deepest unspoken longings and joys, or a playful renewal that walls off the worries of life. It can be a simple touching and holding when words will not say what needs to be said, or a reluctant fulfilling of duty to each other. It can be a recommitment to each other after a time of alienation, or one more piece of evidence that proves the lack of love or sensitivity of the partner, another issue in a boiling caldron of dissatisfaction. It can be "good" or "bad." What makes sexuality "good" or "bad" is the degree to which it fulfills or detracts from its purposes in God's creation.

We identify three purposes for sexuality in the lives of marriage partners: companionship and intimacy, pleasure, and procreation. A fourth function also operates in our culture that unfortunately has come to play a more dominant role for many than the other three. It is the desire to prove one's self-worth through sexual skillfulness.

Sexuality and Self-Worth

In discussions of sexuality in popular literature today, a major focus is on successful sexual performance. The marriage bed has become a place to demonstrate one's adequacy as a person. Men have traditionally felt this more keenly than women, but now women are also feeling the need to prove themselves to be sexually skillful as well as sexually attractive. In the past it was believed that sex was something initiated by and for men, and women simply fulfilled their wifely duty. Most couples in our culture, even if they embrace traditional values in the rest of their relationship, tend to believe that sexual expression is to be mutual. Even the "total woman" seduces her husband by meeting him at the door clothed only in plastic wrap, hardly the prototype of the submissive wife who waits for her husband to take the initiative and pliantly allows him to satisfy his sexual urges. Much of what we read in books and see on television and in the movies implies how important it is for both the man and the woman to be sexual and to be good at it. Reed notes:

> The glut of sex manuals on the market indicates our fascination with sex, our voyeuristic impulses seeking gratification through reading or seeing how others act in bed, and for the male the subconscious opportunity to compete. There is a cult of the "Big O," where couples are in search of bigger and better orgasms which are to be delivered to liberated women by dedicated men. (Reed 1977, 211)

In our achievement-oriented culture the emphasis on male sexual performance predates women's liberation and companionship marriage. The advent of companionship and egalitarian concepts of male-female relating has not eliminated this emphasis but upped the ante, since the female must also perform well. Again, Reed observes, "It was difficult enough when sex was something one did *to* a woman or *for* a woman; it is even more apprehensive when it is *with* a woman" (Reed 1977, 212). The increased stress on sexual performance is most apparent in the emphasis on simultaneous orgasms as the ideal, although virtually impossible for many couples to achieve. The emphasis is not on intimacy so much as it is achievement and demonstrating skillfulness.

This concern for sexual performance in our culture has laid the ground for alienation and deceit between partners. For example, John wants Judy to be orgasmic. He thinks he owes it to her, and it will also prove to him and to her that he is a good lover. During intercourse with her he tries to distract himself by thinking about anything else but their sexual embrace so as to delay his own climax. Judy intuits how important this is to John and feels guilty that she does not meet his needs better. He seems distracted; and she interprets this to mean that he is bored with her and tired of her taking so long to reach climax, so she fakes an orgasm. This leaves her frustrated, but she dare not tell him for fear that he will be crushed or angry. She learns to become quite an actress, since Jim makes several comments about how "good" she is in bed. This makes it virtually impossible for her to tell him what she is feeling and to seek his help in what is becoming a more and more anxious situation for her. Both John and Judy each experience themselves as separated from their bodies during their lovemaking, as though they were standing by the bed, observing and evaluating their own sexual performance and grading themselves. Judy hopes against hope that John will not read anything about the potential of women for multiple orgasms and raise the grading scale.

Sex, then, can become work. John and Judy have developed a sexual relationship that is one more place where they have to prove their worth and worry about whether they are good enough. They begin to feel a deep sense of loneliness when they want most to feel close to each other.

Lewis and Brissett have written a funny yet sobering review of marriage manuals entitled "Sex as Work: A Study of Avocational Counseling" (Lewis and Brissett 1977). According to their evaluation of these manuals, sex is something to be studied and learned much as one would study for an examination. The manuals include diagrams of the genitalia of both sexes to dispel ignorance so that mistakes will not be made. One author, they note, not only provides a sketch of the woman's genitals but also advises that it should be compared by the husband with his wife's genital region on their bridal night (Lewis and Brissett 1977, 427). That advice has the makings for a comic farce. These manuals, they point out, also contain lists of "necessary activities" with time limits for the absolute minimum of foreplay and intercourse necessary if one is to be an adequate lover. It almost reads like a pilot and copilot who are going through their checklist before takeoff rather than a loving couple who are giving and receiving pleasure.

Again, sex becomes work. Just as the goal of work is to produce a product, so the goal of sex has become to produce an end product, orgasm, preferably simultaneous. There is particular irony here because the orgasm is an individual experience, in which the man or woman is keenly tuned to individual sensations and not to the partner. It is the caring and caressing that come before and after orgasm that are relationship-building, yet they are ignored in comparison with the emphasis on orgasm as the product—goal—of sexual expression. In an article on sexuality in America, Slater says:

> Discussion of sexuality in America has always centered on the orgasm rather than on pleasure in general. This seems to be another example of our tendency to focus on the *product* of any activity at the expense of the *process*. It may seem odd to refer to an orgasm as a product, but this is the tone taken in such discussions. Most sex manuals give the impression that the partners in lovemaking are performing some sort of task; by dint of a great cooperative effort and technical skill (primarily the man's), an orgasm (primarily the woman's which masculine mystification has made problematic) is ultimately produced. The bigger the orgasm, the more "successful" the task performance. (Slater 1977, 118)

Perhaps that is why we use the phrase "making love" rather than simply "loving." We talk of "having sex" as well as "making love" as if they were consumer goods, and we would hardly think of "having" or "making" anything but the best.

What is particularly sad about the misplaced emphasis on performance is that the intentions for sexuality—companionship, pleasure, and procreation—are lost. Instead of risking vulnerability with the partner and experiencing companionship and sharing, partners may find themselves trying to impress each other, even if it is with a false impression. The function of recreation is overshadowed by the concern for performance and the evaluation of that performance. Sexual expression can even become a means for evaluating marital success instead of a means for cultivating intimacy and sharing. Couples find themselves keeping a tally on the number of times per week they make love or the number of orgasms they have to see if they are "normal"—translated "acceptable, we have an okay marriage."

With the emphasis on performance, the pleasure of sex is eroded. One common behavioral pattern of couples who have sexual difficulties is that instead of abandoning themselves to the intimate sharing and pleasuring of the sexual encounter, they mentally stand back, as spectators, watching and evaluating their own performance (Masters and Johnson 1966). This not only significantly reduces the intimacy and pleasure of the encounter but can also lead to or complicate sexual difficulties. Slater maintains:

Leisurely pleasure-seeking is brushed aside, as all acts and all thoughts are directed toward the creation of a successful finale. . . . This insures against too much pleasure obtained in the here and now, since one is always concentrating on the future goal. In such a system you can find out how much you're enjoying yourself only after it's all over, just as many Americans traveling abroad don't know what they've experienced until they've had their films developed. (Slater 1977, 119)

Perhaps it is the function of pleasure, the playfulness of sexuality, that is most damaged by demands for performance. Garvey (1977) describes five characteristics of play. First, it is enjoyable. Second, it has no extrinsic goals. Third, it is spontaneous and voluntary, not obligatory. Fourth, it involves active engagement; one cannot be a passive observer or nonparticipant. Finally, it contrasts with other goal-oriented aspects of life. It is, in other words, the opposite of work.

With all this hoopla over sexual performance, one would think that there was some objective standard against which couples could compare themselves. But no standards for optimal sexual functioning exist. Of the variety of sexual behaviors in marriage, none have been found by objective standards to be "healthier" or "better" than others. Masters and Johnson's research indicates that an orgasm is an orgasm; there is no physiological difference between orgasms that are experienced simultaneously or separately, during intercourse or during another form of stimulation.

There are no standards for optimal frequency either. In conducting research on the frequency of intercourse in marriage, Greenblat reports that during the first year of marriage, couples reported having intercourse from one to forty-five times per month. During the following five years, the frequency decreased somewhat for most couples; the range was one to twenty-five times per month. In their study of healthy families, Lewis and his colleagues found wide variations in the frequency with which spouses had intercourse. These optimally functioning families reported frequencies that ranged from once a month to five or more times each week (Lewis 1979). Yet these couples repeatedly told researchers that frequency and expertise in sex are not necessarily what made sexual expression a strength in their relationship.

It is apparent, then, that satisfying sexuality involves far more than technique and frequency. The emphasis on achievement and proving oneself, with the accompanying fear of appearing to be inadequate both to oneself and and to one's partner, actually blocks the potential for satisfying sexuality that leads to intimacy. Arbes comments:

> As a result of . . . trial and error learning and the fear of inadequacy, many couples develop a highly structured set of sexual behaviors in order to achieve orgasm. This structuring of sexual intimacy negates most pleasura-

ble behaviors other than intercourse and orgasm, easily breaks down if one thing goes wrong, and the repetition frequently leads to boredom. (Arbes 1977, 252)

Our concepts of normality and abnormality, even of satisfaction and dissatisfaction, are strongly influenced by our culture, for good or for ill. We are often more tuned in to its dictates as to what optimal sexual functioning is supposed to be than we are to the needs and uniqueness of each other. That cultural expectations override individual needs is not a new state of affairs. In the nineteenth century, many physicians were performing clitoridectomies on women who were "too" sexually responsive. In just the last decade scores of American wives underwent surgery to redesign the coital area so that the clitoris would be more easily contacted by the penis in the traditional male-above position (Reiss 1981, 277). These kinds of practices are unusual in American culture but not elsewhere. The Sudanese not only amputate the clitoris but sew up the labia, leaving a small opening for the menstrual flow, in order to ensure virginity at marriage. It was reported in 1977 that as many as thirty countries practice such sexual mutilation (in Saxton 1980). Thus, "the ideological dictates of a culture can pressure our bodies, as well as our acts and thoughts, toward conformity" (Reiss 1981, 278–279).

By comparison, American culture seems relatively free of restraints and certainly of such mutilations; anything goes between consenting adults. Sexuality has not lost its cultural significance and value, however, and it is not easy to escape strong pressures to conform to majority expectations. A century ago, cultural expectations closely governed sexual expression; today partners closely govern themselves, evaluating performance, checking to see that they measure up. Anything goes, but we are never quite sure that anything is good enough. We worry about performing well enough to earn our partner's admiration and appreciation and to satisfy our need to feel good about who we are and to feel "fulfilled." Epstein has identified roles that we expect sex to play:

> Sex is asked to provide all that religion, work, and the family once provided—something greater than oneself, a means of relief from worldly concerns, a way of getting out of oneself and onto a higher plane of existence. Instead sex today does the very reverse: the relief it offers from the world is only as great as one's physical stamina, nothing is more sharply calculated to remind one of human limitations, and the completion of no other act so quickly brings one back to reality. . . . Instead of deepened and enriched relationships, instead of shedding guilt and developing inwardly, we have the bedroom Olympics, with its accompanying tyranny of performance, unreal expectations, and misplaced salvationism. (Epstein 1974, 277)

This topsy-turvy confusion of what sexuality is and what its function is to be in marriage relates integrally to the earlier discussion of the loss of a sense of joint task in marriage. Once the vows are said, what is a couple to do? Be intimate, be close, commune with each other. Intimacy—including sexual intimacy—has become the task of marriage. Sexual expression has become the work of the marriage to be evaluated. The intention for sexuality in creation used to be buried under the demand that it be used only for procreation; now it is buried by the onslaught of anxiety about personal image and worth. The rugged individualism and achievement orientation of American culture have invaded the marriage bed.

Sexuality in the marriage relationship is important, but it in itself is not all important. A satisfying sexual relationship is most likely to happen when it is not made the primary goal of the relationship. Baker identifies the proper role of sex in marriage:

> Sex is not the "pièce de resistance" of the good life, and our present concentration upon it often prevents people from developing other aspects of personal functioning which will produce a good life. The best sex, I believe, flows spontaneously out of a life and a relationship filled with love, joy, struggle, growth and intimacy. (Baker 1983, 299)

The expectation that sexual expression will solidify personal identity or bolster sagging self-esteem, or that it is a significant evaluative mechanism for individual achievement and marital success, warps its intended function. These are false expectations that myopically lose sight of the larger aspect of marital relating. Sex is good, but it is not *the* good. Sexuality is a means for a couple to care for each other, deepen intimacy and companionship, and refresh both for the tasks they face in life. We are to meet each other's needs, not the norms of the latest research study on the sexual behavior of the human species.

When sexuality is made an end in itself, it separates the sex organs from personhood. Our genitalia and erotic zones become objects to be loaned out rather than integral parts of the self to be shared in ongoing communion and commitment with another. The objectification of sex is apparent in the image that the sex partner is like a musical instrument to be played. This image implies a degree of separateness between the partners since one is to be acted upon and, in some sense, used.

Rightly understood, sexuality is the centerpiece in the development of intimacy between husband and wife. It ideally includes the kind of relating and caring for each other that restores intimacy when we feel alienated and renews and reinvigorates us when we are tired and discouraged. It should not be based on what others may or may not do in their own sexual expression, even if they are the "average American couple." We may find in the research and clinical studies some help for deepening our intimacy and satisfaction with our sexual expression, but these do not become the norms by which we measure ourselves.

Sexuality and Intimacy

Sexuality involves much more than our sex organs. We have seen that in his objection to casual fornication with prostitutes (1 Cor. 6: 15–17), Paul recognized that our sexuality engages all of us, our wholeness, a joining of one's self with another self. It involves intimacy from other spheres of our lives besides sex. The genitals are only 1 percent of our body mass, and sex most of the time is only about 1 percent of our relationship with each other (Pittman 1984). It therefore can never be a substitute for intimacy in all its dimensions.

Tolstedt and Stokes identify three types of intimacy between couples —affective intimacy, verbal intimacy, and physical intimacy. They define them as follows:

> Affective intimacy is the perception of closeness and emotional bonding, including intensity of liking, moral support, and ability to tolerate flaws in the other.
> Verbal intimacy is the depth of verbal exchange, including sharing of self and expression of emotions, judgments, and opinions.
> Physical intimacy is sex and other physical expressions of love. (Tolstedt and Stokes 1983)

They found that verbal and affective intimacy made stronger contributions to the satisfaction of partners with their marriage than did physical intimacy, although all three types of intimacy were important. They concluded, "Independent of verbal and affective intimacy, physical intimacy plays only a small role in determining perceived marital satisfaction and is not an important factor in determining actions that lead toward separation and divorce" (p. 578).

Intimacy has often been defined narrowly as communication patterns in marriage. Lewis, for example, defines intimacy as a description of "those moments when there has occurred a disclosure of deep and private feelings and thoughts" (Lewis 1979, 74). The equation of intimacy with communication is not without basis. Repeatedly, the sharing of information about one's self, self-disclosure, has been demonstrated to be a major ingredient in marital intimacy and satisfaction (Waring and Chelune 1983). The studies of Tolstedt and Stokes, however, expand the meaning of intimacy beyond these narrower definitions of intimacy as sexual expression or communication. As significant as communication is, their tripart typology of intimacy is helpful in keeping in mind that intimacy is more than communication, just as it is more than sex (see also Waring 1984). In fact, their research indicates that affective intimacy is just as important as communication or sex if not more so, yet it has received the least attention in discussions of marital intimacy. Affective intimacy reflects the commitment of spouses to each other, the sense of bondedness to each other, the toleration of each other's "flaws" and differences.

It is quite possible for couples to have a satisfying relationship that is functional without any emphasis on intimate sharing of self with each other. Mutual soul-baring is not as critical as the sense of belonging to each other, mutual affection, and the toleration of differences. In their study of well-functioning working-class black families, for example, Lewis and Looney (1983) found that verbal intimacy and even satisfaction with their sexual relationship were not the keys to these couples' satisfaction and marital strength. What we usually think of as intimacy was not important to these couples because of their *contextual* difference. These couples grew up in poverty in a racist society, and their goal was not to develop intimacy so much as it was to survive and to see that their children flourished and had the opportunity for a better life. Lewis and Looney summarize: "Their mutual struggle and ultimate success in surviving, establishing an economic foothold, starting a family, purchasing a modest home, and generating an income to assure the survival of the family were the elements of their relationship which they reported with greatest pride" (p. 152). The satisfaction with their relationship was based not on the degree to which they felt intimate with each other but, rather, on whether together they accomplished the tasks before them.

For many, the ability to take care of their own and their children's needs, to provide children with educational opportunities and a home in which they feel the strength of parents' love for them and for each other, is the minimal expectation for what life owes them and from which they can work to achieve mightier goals and visions. These families, struggling on the edge of survival, have strong marriages, even though they may not possess the characteristics our culture prescribes for marital success.

A couple's sense of intimacy is subject to the changes and fluctuations of the marital context. A couple with two careers, a new baby who cries to be fed every two hours around the clock, and a preschooler still in diapers may not feel very intimate with each other. Little time, energy, or inclination for sexual expression or long soul-searching discussions is available. Each may feel lonely and yet frustrated when the other implies that they need more time to be together; where is the time going to come from? It is not the most intimate of times in their marriage. The situation, however, may not be as critical as it appears to be. If their children and careers are important to them and provide meaning for their relationship, an undercurrent of satisfaction helps them to "endure all things."

Although physical intimacy and verbal intimacy may not be high, the third type of intimacy, affective intimacy, is present. They may not be able to identify it with the term "intimacy," but affective intimacy involves the bonding of one to the other—commitment. It is unfortunate that this intimacy has been labeled "affective," for it is not a feeling so much as it is a decision to stand by the other in spite of problems and stress and to support each other when the chips are down. With this kind of intimacy mature love flowers. Love is not a feeling but a commitment. Clinebell and Clinebell note that intimacy is not dependent on the absence of hostility, resentment, and anger, or even alienation from each other. "If it were," they go on to say, "there would be *no* intimacy, since negative feelings are persistent and valuable threads in the cloth from which all close human relations are cut" (Clinebell and Clinebell 1970, 51). The key to intimacy is the commitment to love the other in spite of negative feelings and to care enough about the other to tackle the sources of these feelings.

We are commanded in scripture to love our neighbors as ourselves. This is impossible if we define love only in terms of feeling. We cannot normally will the physiological changes that are involved in experiencing a feeling. What we can will is our behavior, our choices of what we will do. Love is action, not feeling. Jesus recognizes this:

> Greater love has no man than this, that a man lay down his life for his friends. You are my friends if you do what I command you. (John 15: 13–14)

Laying down one's life for a friend is not feeling—who of us feels like doing that? Even Jesus in the garden did not feel like going through with the act of love that lay before him; he asked that it be taken away. Nevertheless, he was willing and acted on his choice. He does not call us his disciple if we feel what he commands us to feel, but if we do what he commands us to do.

It is this kind of love that is expected of Christians in marriage. It requires an act of will, a decision to commit ourselves to each other. This is not a grit-your-teeth-and-stick-it-out kind of commitment, or a commitment only to maintain marital stability at all costs—"I'll stay with you no matter what you do." Commitment based on obligation is often mistaken for fulfillment of the marriage contract. The spouses remain faithful to each other and meet their mutual responsibilities, but the commitment is only to the institution of marriage and not to the partner as a unique, special person (Masters and Johnson 1970). The commitment to partnership is based on the personal commitment of

one person to another. It is love of one for the other because of who
that other is.

Married love is a commitment freely chosen. Because it is freely
chosen, however, does not mean that our love is based on our feelings
at any particular time. In short, both in our commitment to each other
and in the living out of that commitment, our actions need to be based
on decision rather than emotion. As Peck sees it:

> Couples sooner or later always fall out of love, and it is at the moment
> when the mating instinct has run its course that the opportunity for genu-
> ine love begins. It is when the spouses no longer feel like being in each
> other's company always, when they would rather be elsewhere some of
> the time, that their love begins to be tested and will be found to be present
> or absent. (Peck 1978, 118)

Truth to tell, many times arise when we do not feel loving or intimate
with our partner. What then? As we saw in the last chapter, feelings are
transitory, but they are important as indicators. They can give us important clues about problems, needs, and even strengths in our relationship
with each other. What is important is to keep the feelings in perspective
as indicators, not controllers. The young couple with the new baby, the
preschooler, and two careers needs to pay attention to feelings of
loneliness, alienation, and frustration with each other. The wife faking
orgasm because she does not want to hurt her husband's male pride is
in fact not acting lovingly by ignoring her own needs and depriving
both partners of the intimacy that comes with sharing vulnerabilities
and needs.

Sexual expression, intimacy, and love are foundational in a Christian
perspective on marriage. They are the companionship function that
God intended for marital union; "it is not good that the man should
be alone." Marriage is a place of service, but it is also a place of
"at-homeness." Marital couples cannot carry out their calling without
a firm commitment to each other and the bonding of companionship
that is enhanced by shared pleasure and intimacy. On the other hand,
couples cannot maintain the intimacy and bondedness of companionship without a task, a calling to give definition to their relationship.
Sexuality symbolizes these two functions in unity and interdependence
—communion, including intimacy and shared pleasure, and creation.

7

What God
Has Joined Together

When a rabbi stated that God made the heavens and the earth in six days, he was asked what God has done with his time since then. The rabbi answered, "He brings marriage partners together" (*Pesiqta* 11b). But the cement that God uses to join couples together unfortunately is not impervious to the weight of human sinfulness or the tempests of life. Marriage partners can and do become disjoined. The hurt in the lives of families who undergo divorce is a familiar topic in our culture, and no other statistic seems to draw more attention and concern than the divorce rate. It has been estimated that 40 percent of all marriages begun in the 1970s will end in divorce (Glick and Norton 1977), and one child of every five today has a stepparent (Visher and Visher 1983). In this chapter we will attempt to understand some of the processes at work in the experience of divorce in our own culture. We will then examine divorce in biblical times and in the New Testament. Finally, we will explore current sociological and psychological understandings of the processes of divorce that we think relate to God's intention concerning marriage and divorce in our own context.

Behind the Divorce Statistics—Divorce Today

The divorce rate in America today can be read as both bad and good news about marriage. Since so much attention is focused on the bad news of divorce and the apparently weakening fabric of family life, it perhaps would be more helpful to begin with the positive implications that can be drawn about divorce in our culture.

The divorce statistics do not indicate that people are giving up on marriage as a commitment—that would be reflected by a sharply declining marriage rate. Instead, the rising divorce rate reflects the great expectations that couples have for marriage. Many people marry today with the expectation that their partner will meet all their needs for emotional support and nurture, stimulating social interchange, friendship, partnership in shared activities, sexual stimulation and satisfaction, and family belonging. When marital conflict arises and intensifies, or attraction wanes, or common interests become no longer common, it is taken as evidence that this particular match was an unfortunate mistake. The partners usually do not bring their expectations for marriage into question. These expectations are not reexamined because many married couples do find their married life together to be increasingly satisfying and intimate. Bernard claims, "Just as revolutions do not come in times of the most abject misery but rather in times of better and improving prospects, so discontent with marriage is expressed today not because it is so bad but because it is better than ever" (Bernard 1982, 281).

Many researchers have noted that good marriages tend to end in divorce more often than bad ones (see Bernard 1982; Farson 1977). This is because couples who are caught in vicious patterns of injuring each other psychologically, and perhaps even physically, are often too dependent on each other for protection from the unknown and fear a worse fate if they let go and begin anew. Their egos are not strong enough or have been so weakened by the psychologically debilitating relationship that they are unable to strike out alone. It is the marital partners who have found some sustenance in the marriage who are strong enough to allow themselves to recognize its problems. Farson concludes, "The couples who get in the most trouble are those who know enough to see the things that are wrong with their marriage. And, ironically, it takes quite a bit of success in a marriage to make that understanding possible" (Farson 1977, 251).

Farson discusses a number of reasons for the paradoxical rise in the divorce rate when marriage appears to be "better than ever." First, as the basic needs of the family are met—food, shelter, financial security —couples soon take them for granted and then expect the more complex needs in Maslow's hierarchy to be fulfilled. Maslow's hierarchy of needs has therefore been transformed into the hierarchy of demands on marriage. The most basic are the needs for safety and survival— physical sustenance, adequate shelter, and protection from outside threats. When these are cared for, spouses expect marriage to provide them with a sense of being loved and wanted, a sense of "family." Since the fulfillment of the basic needs is simply taken for granted, being loved and wanted are usually the primary expectations when couples commit themselves to marriage. When this next level of needs is being reliably met, however, spouses begin to grow restless with feeling only secure and expect instead to have their marriage reinforce or help them develop a sense of personal identity and self-esteem. Finally come the expectations for self-actualization we discussed in chapter 4. The more "successful" a marriage is in meeting spouses' needs, then, the more additional needs are expected to be fulfilled by the marriage relationship. Each higher layer of needs ups the ante and requires ever more complex interpersonal skills and adaptability of the relationship to the individuality of the partners (who are always developing and changing). The sexual relationship exemplifies this process; the more partners experience a gratifying sexual relationship, the greater their expectation that it will always be this satisfying and could probably be improved even more.

Lasch also suggests that discontent in marriage is increased by cultural norms that set the calibration for measuring marital satisfaction too high as it is idealized by the entertainment industry. Americans are too often limited in their attitudes and expectations about marriage to what they read in popular novels and to what they see on television and the movies. Here they are offered a steady diet of romantic and highly charged sexual relating interspersed with dramatic crises that portray life as anything but ordinary and hardly reflect the day-in day-out living of most marriages. The only real-life marriage that most people have been exposed to in any depth is that of their parents. Yet parents' marriages are usually dismissed as not normative; it is even hard for many to accept that their parents have a sexual relationship, despite evidence to the contrary. Because of the influence of the media, young adults accept only with difficulty that the unromantic, mundane relationship that characterizes what they know of their parents' lives is really the norm and not unique to Mom and Dad. They naively assume that their married life with their partner will be better and will assuredly have more pizzazz, but as the years go by they find themselves looking more and more like Mom and Dad. When this happens they experience a sense of failure because their fantasy about what married life should be like proves to be just that—a fantasy.

Marriage counseling and other efforts to improve married life may even reinforce misconceptions about the intensity of marriage and consequently add to the disillusionment of the couple. The focus in counseling is on working toward desired changes rather than accepting and appreciating what is. Farson argues:

> Any effort to improve life, whether by education or religion or philosophy or therapy, seldom makes life simpler. In fact, it makes it more complex. Just as labor-saving devices have caused us more labor and complicated our lives, so counseling has further burdened our marriages by asking us to live up to what we know to be our best relationship that is achievable only under the special circumstances of the psychotherapeutic hour. . . . Perhaps most serious, counseling gives a person the feeling—much more than is probably true—that he is in charge of his own life, that his problems are basically of his own making, and that their solutions are

within his control. . . . Constant attention to our problems as personal
rather than as universal (which happens in counseling) has given us a
highly distorted picture of what we can do about the problems we find
in marriage. (Farson 1977, 251)

Discontent also builds in a marriage when spouses compare their
relationship as it presently is with how it was in the past in different
circumstances. Parents of preschoolers may remember wistfully the
romantic excitement of courtship or the relative freedom and financial
well-being of early marriage when both were working and had no
children to support. Middle-aged partners may longingly recall the
intimacy, enjoyment, and sexual abandon they experienced on vacation
together and wonder why they cannot maintain that in their everyday
life. For some, wistfulness may lead to open dissatisfaction with the
marriage and to attempts to blame the partner for a seemingly less-than-
ideal relationship. In conclusion, the better we think other marriages
are than ours, or the better our own marriage has been at some time
in the past, the worse we are going to feel about our marriage as it is
now. Thus, for some, discontent with the marriage does not arise so
much from its failures as from comparison with its successes in previous
times or from heightened expectations of what should be.

A second inference that can be drawn from the high divorce rate in
our nation is that improved health and living conditions have increased
the likelihood of divorce. Life is no longer as nasty, brutish, and short
as it once was. It has been only during this century that a majority of
people could expect to live through a life cycle that includes leaving
home, marrying, having children, and surviving to age fifty as a couple.
Before 1900 only 40 percent of the female population experienced this
life cycle (Skolnick and Skolnick 1980). Most died either before they
were married or during childbirth, or they themselves were widowed
while they still had young children. When life was shorter, a vow to
commit oneself till death do us part was not such a lengthy commitment. In pioneer days a man might go through several wives in his
lifetime because of the high mortality rate during women's childbearing years. We now speak of serial polygamy in connection with divorce
and remarriage, but a similar pattern existed in the past. The difference
is that the spouse was buried, not divorced. Bernard observes, "Nowa-
days, people have a much longer time in which to discover how unhappy their marriages are" (Bernard 1982, 98). Today, couples can
expect to have as long as thirty years together after their youngest child
leaves home, and marriages that last half a century or more before the
death of one of the partners are now commonplace.

The positive implications of divorce—that it is caused by rising expectations of what marriage is supposed to be and that it is more likely

because couples live longer than they used to and are therefore married longer—do not in any way assuage the pain or justify divorce. These explanations of the higher divorce rate do counter arguments that marriage is becoming obsolete as a viable institution, but they in no way imply that divorce is a "positive" experience. Divorce is unpleasant for all involved. It grieves the partners, their children, their families, and the community of which they are members.

Because this book deals with the partners in marriage, we will focus on the marital partners' experience of divorce and leave the effects on children, family, and community to others. Many couples who go through divorce find it more painful than the death of a partner. They undergo grief because of dashed dreams and the loss of one who has been a part of their life and memories, even if the choice to divorce was more or less voluntary. Partners often discover the full significance of their relationship with each other only after divorce. They may have gone to great lengths to end the relationship because they believed they desperately wanted out, only to find that they miss the spouse and at times fervently wish they could restore the marriage. During the process of deciding on separation and divorce, the conflictual interaction in the marriage and the individual's own internal thoughts center on what is wrong in the relationship to build up motivation and a rationale to take the final step of divorce. It is only afterward that the comfortable, useful, and "right" aspects of the marital relationship begin to creep back into awareness. Divorced persons often feel overcome by the extent of the stress and grief they feel as a result of their disengagement from what they perceived was a totally dysfunctional relationship.

Divorce is a wrenching experience regardless of the amount of love that partners may or may not have felt toward each other (Berscheid 1983). No matter what the relationship was like, it was the pattern for living one's life; the partners became bonded to each other, molding their lives to fit the other's idiosyncrasies and needs. Even if they hated each other, they had to adapt in some fashion, if only by developing habits to avoid each other. Like a tree on a mountainside that twists itself to fit around a boulder and retains that shape long after the boulder has been washed away by a torrential rain, each partner has been shaped by the marriage. The patterns of living developed in the marriage seem suddenly strange when the partner is gone.

Despite current studies claiming that single parent and blended families are healthy family forms and that divorce can be a potentially "creative" response to a difficult situation, divorce is hardly a welcome experience. As surgery is useful in removing an organ that cannot otherwise be healed through less drastic measures, so divorce can be useful in ending the progressive dysfunction and pain of a relationship that cannot be healed by other means. It is seldom a choice made gladly.

Experiencing divorce as an unhappy but functional alternative to dysfunctional marriage is certainly not unique to our culture. It has been around as long as marriage and is addressed in the Bible as a problem that needed to be controlled.

Divorce in Biblical Times

In biblical times, divorce was not a judgment awarded by a court but an independent action taken by a husband against his wife. Deuteronomy 24:1–4 contains two stipulations regarding divorce: the husband was to give his wife a bill of divorce, and he was forbidden to remarry his wife after she had become the wife of another man who later divorced her or died. Remarriage to a former wife after she had been "defiled" by another husband was considered an abomination. This law was primarily concerned with preventing such an abomination but also may have been intent on protecting the wife. With a written certificate of divorce, a wife could not be charged with adultery should she remarry. Because the husband relinquished forever all rights to her, it may also have averted some rash decisions on the part of the husband to divorce a wife as well as eliminating any temptation for him to interfere in her second marriage.

Deuteronomy 24:1–4 does not prescribe grounds for divorce. It impassively notes that if the wife finds no favor in her husband's eyes because she is guilty of some indecency (Deut. 24:1), or if he simply dislikes her (Deut. 24:3), he puts her away. It does not say anything about whether the husband ought to, or is permitted to, divorce in such cases; it only places restrictions on what the husband is to do and not do should he divorce his wife. The practice of divorce is simply taken for granted. The abomination is not divorce but remarrying the first wife (Atkinson 1979, 102–103). Divorce was so accepted as a part of life that even God is said figuratively to have divorced: "Thus says the LORD: 'Where is your mother's bill of divorce with which I put her away?' " (Isa. 50:1).

In the Mishnah, divorce is also accepted as a fact of life. Tractate *Giṭṭin* ("bills of divorce") addresses the proper and valid means of giving the wife the legal notice of divorce, her marital pink slip, in accordance with the provisions of Deuteronomy 24:1. It carefully outlines the procedure concerning witnesses, content, manner of delivery (for example, he is not to slip it in her hands at night while she is asleep), and the possibility of withdrawing it. Despite the isolated comment of Rabbi Eliezer, "For him who divorces the first wife, the very altar sheds tears" (B. *Sanh.* 22a; *Giṭ.* 90b), divorce was viewed as an accepted part of life that needed to be controlled only by due process.

According to the Gospel of Mark, the Pharisees probed Jesus with the question, "Is it lawful for a man to divorce his wife?" (Mark 10:2). Most commentators have claimed that this is a Marcan formulation, since it is assumed that no Jew would have doubted whether divorce was legal or not and would not have been likely to pose this question. Consequently, it has been suggested that the question would have been more relevant in Rome, for example, where divorce had become epidemic (see Anderson 1976, 240; Nineham 1978, 264). All Jews, however, were *not* unanimous that it was permissible to divorce a wife, given the evidence from the recently published Temple Scroll where it is commanded that the wife of the king (and therefore every commoner's wife as well) should be with him all the days of his life (11Q Temple 57.17–19; see Fitzmyer 1978, 103–110). One therefore cannot dismiss the question as it is framed in Mark as unhistorical. Nevertheless, the question as it is phrased in Matthew's Gospel, "Is it lawful to divorce one's wife for any cause?" (Matt. 19:3), is considered by many to be more relevant to the Palestinian context. The phrase "for any cause" was a catchword in a raging debate in Jesus' day (see Philo, *Special Laws* 3.30; Josephus, *Antiquities* 4.253).

According to Mishnah *Giṭṭin* 9.10, a difference of opinion existed between two schools of thought on the grounds for divorce. The debate turned on what weight to give the components of the ambiguous phrase in Deuteronomy 24:1, "a matter of indecency" (*'erwat dabar*). The school of Hillel stressed the word "matter"; grounds for divorce could be over any matter that provoked the husband's displeasure, such as the wife's ruining a dish that had been prepared for him or even his finding a prettier woman (see also Josephus, *Life* 75–76). The school of Shammai, however, stressed the word "shame" or "indecency"; one could divorce his wife only if he found some indecency in her. The shameful behavior of the wife included, in addition to adultery, such violations of sexual propriety as conversing with men, spinning in the streets with bare arms, being loud-voiced in sexual embrace (M. *Ketub.* 7.6), or loosening her hair in public (B. *Giṭ.* 90b), as well as deliberate transgressions of the law.

Most Jews in Jesus' day therefore assumed that men had an inalienable right to cut their wives adrift: "The man that divorces is not like to the woman that is divorced; for a woman is put away with her consent or without it, but a husband can put away his wife only with his consent" (M. *'Arak.* 5.6; see M. *Yebam.* 14.1). The rights of a husband were akin to his property rights since the wife was in effect a possession. This prerogative to rid oneself of unwanted property was restricted only in certain cases: if the wife were insane (M. *Yebam.* 14.1), or in captivity (M. *Ketub.* 4.9), or if the husband had brought false charges of premarital fornication against her or had been forced to marry her because he had violated her virginity (Deut. 22:13–19, 28–29). In such cases he was not permitted to divorce her. The real obstacle to divorce, however, was the rabbinical development of the marriage contract *(kethubah)* in which a sum, settled on before the marriage, was to be paid the wife should her husband divorce her. It was forfeited only if the wife was guilty of serious misconduct. The cost of the *kethubah* dissuaded many in economic straits from divorcing their wives (see B. *'Erub.* 41b) and provided wives with some measure of protection against the threat of divorce.

Wives, on the other hand, had no power to divorce their husbands on their own but, in certain circumstances, could sue for divorce in a court that could force the husband to give her a divorce as well as her marriage settlement. The circumstances, however, were most limited. Only if the husband was afflicted with a skin disease or a morbid growth or engaged in a disgusting trade that caused him to smell (such as dung collector or tanner) or was impotent could the wife obtain a divorce. The reports in Josephus of two ruling-class women who divorced are considered by him to be flagrant violations of the law. He wrote that only men have the right to divorce, and that the divorced woman may not even remarry without her former husband's consent *(Antiquities* 15.259). With this background in mind, we can turn to the issue of divorce in the New Testament.

The Question for Jesus

Both Matthew and Mark agree that the question about divorce was put to Jesus by the Pharisees to "test" him (Matt. 19:3; Mark 10:2); that is, to ensnare him in some way. The question of the legality of divorce and remarriage had become politically hot since John the Baptist had publicly rebuked Herod Antipas for divorcing his wife to marry Herodias, the wife of his brother whom she had divorced. The denunciation of the ruler of Galilee led to John's subsequent imprisonment and death (Mark 6:16–29). This past history could therefore explain the territorial note in Mark 10:1 that has puzzled many commentators. Jesus was asked the question about divorce by guileful opponents (possibly collaborating with the Herodians; see Mark 3:6; 12:13) within the territorial jurisdiction of Herod Antipas. It is conceivable that they posed this question to him suspecting that his position on divorce would be no different from that of John's and that it would be voiced no less stridently. This, they may have hoped, would have rewarded Jesus with the same fate as that of John the Baptist.

Jesus immediately lifts the question of divorce out of the crossfire of human controversy and places it in the sphere of the will of God. First, he reaffirms the lifelong character of the marriage bond as being God's intention from the beginning:

> But from the beginning of creation, "God made them male and female." "For this reason a man shall leave his father and mother and be joined to his wife, and the two shall become one." So they are no longer two but one. (Mark 10: 6–9)

Matthew has a slightly different version. He emphasizes that it was the Creator who from the beginning made them male and female (Matt. 19:4–6). Marriage was designed by God and was designed to be indissoluble. It was to be characterized by a loyalty to the partner that is even greater than loyalty to one's parents. Jesus' conclusion from this is the familiar passage: "What therefore God has joined together, let not man put asunder" (Matt. 19:6; Mark 10:9); Aside from the treachery involved in the question put to Jesus, it was based on a false premise. As Anderson notes, the questioners began with Deuteronomy 24:1–4 and assumed, as nearly everyone did, that God approved of divorce: "They acted as if God only gave commandments concerning the legal aspects of family dissolution and forgot that he originated and purposed the couple's union" (Anderson 1976, 241–242). The correct starting point, according to Jesus, was not the later concession to human sinfulness but what God intended from the beginning.

A corollary to this is that Jesus implies that one does not find God's intention for marriage in Deuteronomy 24:1–4 but in Genesis 1–2. He thereby sets Genesis over Deuteronomy and God over Moses (Matt. 19:8). In Mark 10:3, Jesus asks the Pharisees, "What did Moses command you?" They respond, "Moses allowed a man to write a certificate of divorce, and to put her away" (10:4). Jesus reminds them of Genesis 1:27 and 2:24, which all Jews believed Moses also wrote; these verses contain Moses' real command and reflect the unadulterated will of God regarding marriage. In Matthew 19:7, the Pharisees ask Jesus, "Why then did Moses command one to give a certificate of divorce, and to put her away?" Jesus clarifies for them that Moses *permitted* this only because of hardness of heart. It was a concession to sinfulness, not a command. The issue in Deuteronomy 24 had moved away from God's will for marriage to an attempt to stem the damage wrought by divorce. To say that divorce is a concession permitted by Moses because of hardness of heart (willful obstinacy) undercuts any notion that divorce accords with God's will or was a special privilege granted to Israel, as some later rabbis supposed (Greeven 1969, 377; see P. *Qidd.* 1.58c; *Gen. Rab.* 18:5).

Second, Jesus specifically condemns the initiative of a husband to break up his marriage union. There is to be no divorce; a wife may not be jettisoned as if she were only a piece of property that has outlived its usefulness. By doing this, "Jesus brushes aside not merely the question of the meaning of Deuteronomy 24:1ff. but also the sacred text itself" (Manson 1949, 293). Jeremias also claims that this saying "is not an accentuation of the Torah but an annuling of it" (Jeremias 1971, 225). This may be another possible reason why his opponents posed this question to trap him (Meier 1981, 215). Simply choosing between the reputable positions of the two camps of Hillel and Shammai would hardly bring Jesus under reproach. The opponents may have suspected that Jesus' response on this question would openly abrogate a divinely inspired institution of the Mosaic law, and this would be something else indeed.

Jesus therefore takes a stand against legal provisions that would make divorce legitimate—even those with a biblical warrant—and that mislead a husband to believe that everything is fine as long as it is performed according to the proper procedures. The husband could confidently conclude that he was a righteous man because he fulfilled his legal obligations and gave his wife a bill of divorce. This, in Jesus' view, is only a "self-legalization of sin" (Schweizer 1975, 126); the husband has no right whatsoever to dissolve the bond. "What God has joined together, let not man put asunder." According to Jesus, it is God who has joined the couple together. The husband is not the lord of the marriage and therefore has no right to dispose of his wife as if he were (Friedrich 1977, 128).

Anderson comments that the response of the Pharisees in Mark reveals that they sought what was permitted to them: "they reckon less with God's will for them than with their own rights within the limits of what is permitted" (Anderson 1976, 241). According to Jesus, one can no longer ask what is permitted or forbidden by the law and where the loopholes are. God's will as revealed by Jesus invades even the areas of what is legally and culturally accepted and permitted.

The Exception Clause

The puzzling question of the exception clause that appears only in Matthew (5:32, "except on the ground of *porneia,*" and 19:9, "except for *porneia*") has absorbed attention and taxed people's ingenuity for centuries. It allows an exception to the absolute prohibition of divorce. Two questions have arisen: Does it go back to Jesus himself, or is it an addition by the Evangelist? And what precisely does *porneia* mean?

Many believe that this exception to the rule of no divorce does not go back to Jesus for the following reasons:

1. Jesus' statements in the other Gospels allow no exception (see Mark 10:11–12; Luke 16:18). Paul also seems to be unaware of an exception clause as a word of the Lord (1 Cor. 7:10–11).

2. The exception clause contradicts Jesus' argument for the permanence of the marital bond based on God's design in creation. It would seem to say that the relation between man and wife is permanent until *the wife* does something that nullifies that permanence. It also allows divorce on demand (for the man!), with the proviso that some sexual sin had to be committed by the wife. This would only perpetuate the unjust treatment of wives.

3. If the exception clause, allowing for divorce in cases of unchastity, were original in Matthew 5:32, it would not stand in antithesis to the words of Moses in 5:31: "It was also said, 'Whoever divorces his wife, let him give her a certificate of divorce.' But I say to you . . ." The exception clause essentially brings Jesus' statement in line with Deuteronomy 24:1 (Guelich 1982, 208).

4. In cases of adultery, a Jewish man was obliged to divorce his wife because she had been defiled by sexual relations with another man (see Deut. 22:20–22; M. *Yebam.* 2.8, *Soṭa* 5.1, *Ned.* 11.12; *Num. Rab.* 9:12; see also Isaksson 1965, 23). As a righteous man, Joseph determined to divorce Mary on learning of her unexpected expectancy and was prevented from doing so only by angelic revelation (Matt. 1:19–20). Jesus' pattern throughout his ministry, however, was to make radical demands that challenged time-honored norms of behavior. The idea of remaining with a wife guilty of adultery was considered to be absurd, which is why Hosea conveyed God's love for Israel in the most striking terms by pointing to a love that remained faithful and forgiving in spite of adulterous behavior. Jesus would have expected no less from any husband; as Jesus' disciple, he was expected to forgive without limit (Matt. 6:14–15; 18: 21–35).

5. If the exception clause allows for divorce on the grounds of unchastity, the shocked reaction of the disciples in 19:10, "If such is the case of a man with his wife, it is not expedient to marry," would not make sense. Their response implies that they understood Jesus to forbid divorce on any grounds and feared being stuck with a lemon. They are portrayed as considering marriage to be a reasonable proposition only if one could easily rid oneself of an unsatisfactory wife.

It has consequently been argued by many that the clause "except for unchastity" was added by the church or by the Evangelist on the basis of the authority "to bind and to loose" (Matt. 16:19; 18:18). Of the several hypotheses that have been offered to explain why it was added,

162 Beyond Companionship

we will mention only three. It has been suggested that the severity of Jesus' statement, reflected in the dismay of the disciples, was watered down to allow for divorce in cases of unchastity. It has also been suggested that Matthew wanted to make explicit what was tacitly assumed in the tradition in Mark and Luke. Jesus forbade divorce on grounds less grievous than adultery and simply assumed that adultery nullified the marriage bond. Matthew added the clause to make clear that adultery remained grounds for divorce (Charles 1921, 18–24).

An increasing number of others have accepted the conclusion that the Greek word *porneia*, usually translated "fornication" or "unchastity," has a more narrow meaning here and refers to incest, marriage within the forbidden degrees of kinship outlined in Leviticus 18:6–18 and 20:17, 19–21. These restrictions were extended even further by the members of the Qumran community and the rabbis as a precautionary measure. There are four reasons for this novel opinion.

First, the word *porneia* can denote sexual sins in general and does not necessarily mean adultery; *moicheia* and the verbs *moicheuō, moichaomai* are the words used to specify adultery (see Matt. 5:27–28, 32). Matthew reflects an awareness of this distinction because *porneia* and *moicheia* occur together in the same list of vices in 15:19. *Porneia* is then something distinguished from and broader than *moicheia* (see also 1 Cor. 6:9, Heb. 13:4).

Second, Acts 15:20 and 29 (also 21:25) contain the list of the minimum requirements decided by the Jerusalem council that were to be observed by Gentile Christians before Jewish Christians would extend fellowship to them. The Gentiles were asked to abstain from the pollutions of idols, *porneia*, what is strangled, and blood. *Porneia* is usually translated "unchastity," but why ask Gentile Christians to refrain from unchastity as a minimum requirement for their continued association with Jewish Christians? Would this not be taken for granted as part of the Christian calling? Since the other requirements are related to restrictions found in Leviticus 16–18, it would seem likely that *porneia* refers to marriage to prohibited sexual partners listed in Leviticus 18:6–18.

Third, Paul uses the word with this meaning in 1 Corinthians 5:1. He was astounded to hear that that there was *porneia* (translated "immorality") among you; and this is identified as a man's having his father's wife—incest, or marriage within forbidden degrees (Lev. 18:7–18; see also *Testament of Reuben* 1.6; *Testament of Judah* 13.3).

Fourth, the *Damascus Document* discovered in Cairo and at Qumran lends further support to this interpretation (see Fitzmyer 1976, 197–226; Mueller 1980, 247–256). It explicitly identifies marriage within certain degrees of kinship as *zenut*, unchastity, a word translated as *porneia* in the Septuagint (see CD 4.20; 5.7–11).

If this is the connotation of the word in the exception clause—no divorce except in cases of marriage within forbidden degrees—it reflects a practical dilemma in the mission situation of the church of Matthew. The church had to come to grips with the problem of some Gentile converts' joining the community, who, in the eyes of Jewish Christians, had incestuous marriages (see Baltensweiler 1967, 95–101). In this case, divorce was permissible because the marriage could never have been recognized by God. The exception clause is therefore not an escape hatch for those whose wives are guilty of adultery. Jesus taught that there was to be no divorce, period. The church of Matthew later adapted this repudiation of all divorce to fit a situation that they believed required divorce. For this reason, the question concerning divorce, as it appears in Matthew's Gospel, raises the issue of the grounds for divorce and provides the answer that the only valid ground for divorce was the exceptional case of marriage within forbidden degrees of kinship.

The Question for Paul

We can also see Paul adapting the word of the Lord about divorce in 1 Corinthians 7:10–16, where he faced a situation not envisioned by Jesus. Jesus' audience consisted of Jews married to Jews; Paul was confronted by a pluralistic society. He strictly forbade Christians from divorcing their Christian spouse, with no exceptions, and punctuated this statement with the Word of the Lord (1 Cor. 7:10–11). He relaxed the prohibition against divorce, however, when he addressed the problem of the Christian married to the unbeliever (1 Cor. 7:12–16).

Mixed marriages—between Christians and nonbelievers—had apparently become a matter of concern for some of the Corinthians. They may have been worried that intimate connection with a pagan might defile them in some way. Was it similar to joining a member of Christ to that of a prostitute (1 Cor. 6:15)? Views such as those in 2 Corinthians 6:14–7:1 ("Do not be mismated with unbelievers. For what partnership have righteousness and iniquity?") may have prompted some Christians to consider divorce from their pagan partner as a Christian duty (see Ezra 10:10–11). In keeping with the teaching of Jesus, Paul forbade Christians to initiate a divorce and attempted to assure them that the unbelieving partner was sanctified by the believing partner. Therefore, they did not need to worry about being defiled by their spouse; if the unbeliever was willing to continue in the marriage, so should the believing partner. But Paul went on to say that the Christian should not feel obligated to cling stubbornly to a marriage that the unbeliever wished to dissolve. In this case the Christian was not bound (perhaps better translated "enslaved"); that is, he or she was not to be enslaved in an intolerable situation by the prohibition of divorce. Christians have been called to peace (7:15). This meant for Paul that they should not create strife by divorcing on religious grounds, nor should they obstinately attempt to salvage a marriage an unbeliever intends to end in the fond hope that the unbeliever will eventually be saved (7:16).

As Gooch perceptively notes, rules and principles need to be interpreted and sometimes modified to apply to new circumstances (Gooch 1983, 68). Jesus clearly prohibited divorce, but Paul remembered that he also has called us to peace (1 Cor. 7:15; Rom. 12:18; 14:19). Gooch maintains:

> The question is not the simple one of obedience or disobedience; the crucial issue is in *knowing how to obey*. This involves intellectual and moral judgment, not a mindless surrender of will, for it involves knowing what the rules mean and deciding what constitutes their application in a given situation. (Gooch 1983, 68)

As Paul interpreted the authoritative words of Jesus in a new situation, he concluded that the brother or sister was not bound when it came to a marriage that a pagan partner wished to end. They were free and not to be enslaved by the rules.

The Relationship Between New Testament Teaching and Today's Realities

What can be said of this rigorous attitude about divorce in the New Testament? Jesus clarifies that if one asks the question "What is God's will?" the answer is, "God wills that there be no divorce." Every marriage failure is therefore a failure to live according to God's will and contributes further to the hostility and disunity in the world. Marriage, as God intended, is not a temporary romantic alliance that may be terminated at will whenever one feels unfulfilled or unhappy. Jesus' condemnation of divorce and remarriage, however, was not addressed to people in unhappy marriages but to pettifoggers who thought they could arbitrarily put away wives and still be counted righteous before God because they followed the proper legal procedures. Jesus was intent on putting the wanton abuses of the strong (husbands) in check to protect the weak (wives) and did not intend to put another burden on the shoulders of those already weakened from the brokenness of their marriage.

When Jesus insisted that marriage should not be dissolved, he was not commenting on a particular marriage but uttering a moral challenge to perfection. As McNeile recognized, Jesus "constantly laid down principles without reference to any limitations which the complexity of life now demands" (McNeile 1915, 66). In appealing to the creation account before the fall, Jesus assumed that a new beginning was being inaugurated. In the kingdom of God, there will be no "hard hearts" and no need for concessions because God will put a new heart in the believer (see Ezek. 11:19; 36:26). But the church has the task of trying to balance what ought to be with what is, and the reality is that some marriages fail. Although God hates divorce (Mal. 2:13–16), it should also be made clear that he does not hate the divorced person. The fact is that most divorced persons also hate divorce because of its harmful effects. God hates sin because it is like a cancer that destroys persons, but God does not hate the sinner, whom he seeks to heal. The church must therefore walk a tightrope by insisting on the sanctity of marriage and the sinfulness of divorce, while at the same time extending grace to the divorced person. It must proclaim that while God is not blind to sin, neither is God unwilling to forgive when a person sins.

The Sin of Unresolved Differences in Every Marriage

Married partners sin against each other whenever the marital bond is broken by the failure to love, long before and whether or not the legal bond is broken. One cannot conclude that those who never have committed adultery or even thought of initiating a divorce have therefore fulfilled God's will for marriage (Atkinson 1979, 147). It is not the legal act of divorce itself that is the sin but the failure of the marital partners to realize God's purposes in their relationship. Partners who live in alienation from each other, angry, hurt, and convinced that the other is responsible for the pain in the relationship, are missing the mark as certainly as the couple that legally divorces. As one unhappy spouse observed, "I am not married, just undivorced."

The truth is that just as all of us sin and fall short of the glory of God, all marriages come short of God's purposes, even the most stable and fulfilling marriages. A husband of fifty years was asked by reporters if he had ever considered divorce. He replied candidly, "Never divorce. Murder many times, but never divorce" (Clinebell and Clinebell 1970, 154). In every marriage there are differences that flare into conflict. When that conflict is unresolved, a wedge of alienation is driven into the relationship. If the wedge is driven deeper by the accumulation of unresolved conflict, the process of emotional and spiritual separation— divorce—begins. A couple may live under the same roof with a legal marriage contract, but, because of the poisonous anger and alienation pervading their relationship, they are no less guilty of breaking their vows to love and cherish each other till death. God is more concerned with the hurt that we inflict on each other than with legalities. Maintaining a marriage contract is therefore no protection from committing the sin of divorce. Legal divorce is just the issuance of a death certificate, not the death itself. Or, in another analogy, it is the accident report filed with the police long after squealing tires and colliding automobiles have left lacerated casualties strewn on the highway. Legal recourse to divorce is only the final step in the total process. It is almost anticlimactic after the high-water mark of family stress and the time of separation. After the separation the brokenness of the relationship can no longer be ignored. The failures can no longer be denied. In one sense, then, the acts of separation and legal divorce can be confessional; they can be a public recognition of past failures that were allowed to gather swell without being checked.

Does Jesus' teaching require that people must remain together after their marriage has become a legal shell rather than an interpersonal commitment? The partners have been "yoked together," but what are they to do when it becomes a yoke of bondage? In his discussion of divorce, Paul was not insensitive to questions of the quality of the marriage relationship (Furnish 1979, 45); peace and harmony were also important in marriage. Does one have a right to a fulfilling relationship in marriage? Can it be that sometimes staying together is as sinful as divorcing? The New Testament does not offer explicit answers to these questions. The church must give its counsel but must also be cautious not to calcify Jesus' teaching into a rigid legalistic system. Jesus sought to correct a serious misunderstanding of God's intention for marriage that passed off divorce for God's will and caused many powerless wives untold suffering. He also sought to challenge his disciples to the highest good. His church, then, should be cautious not to get bogged down in the same legal casuistry of his opponents by becoming preoccupied with defining terms and grounds.

The Permanence of Marriage

We have suggested that divorce occurs in every marriage in which unresolved conflict is allowed to drive a wedge of alienation between marital partners. The sin of divorce and the legal act of divorce are not the same. Legal action provides legal definitions for relationships, but legal definitions are usually not God's definitions. Jesus made this clear when he condemned remarriage after divorce.

The statements of Jesus concerning divorce and remarriage may be broken down into two groups. The basic saying can be found in Luke 16:18: "Every man who divorces his wife and marries another commits adultery." In Mark 10:11 the additional phrase, he commits adultery "against her," appears; and in Matthew 19:9 the exception clause has been added. Mark 10:12 alone also mentions the wife: a wife who divorces her husband and remarries commits adultery. This was probably an expansion of the basic concept to make it pertinent for the Roman world, where wives could also initiate divorce. From these different accounts of the saying, it is clear that Jesus defines divorce and remarriage as adultery.

The second group of statements concerns the wife who has been put away. In Matthew 5:32, Jesus does not specifically accuse the divorcing husband of adultery but claims that by putting his wife away he makes her an adulteress (literally, "makes her to be adulterated"). He also adds that every man who marries a wife who has been divorced "commits adultery" (Matt. 5:32b; Luke 16:18b). Adultery here connotes any violation of the marriage bond, which explains why an otherwise innocent man who marries a divorced woman is accused of adultery. He is considered guilty of tampering with another man's marriage, since the one flesh of the marriage, according to Jesus, continues to exist. Jesus thus argues that, regardless of the legal action taken by the husband against his wife, she always remains his wife. A certificate of divorce, however sanctioned by human law, does not end a marriage.

It would seem that with this judgment Jesus compounds the woes of the guiltless wife who has been put away by making her bear the added stigma of being an adulteress should she remarry—almost a necessity if she is to survive. This was certainly not his intention. Instead, his concern was to emphasize the permanence and sanctity of the marriage bond and the husband's guilt in putting away his wife; the husband is guilty of adultery and makes his wife an adulteress. This would have met with a response of incredulity from a Jewish audience, since the essential words in a bill of divorce were, "Behold, thou art permitted to any man" (M. *Git.* 9.3). The whole point of the bill was to avoid the fear of adultery on anyone's part. It would be like saying to a modern audience, "Anyone who sells his car and buys another is guilty of theft; and anyone who buys the used car is guilty of theft" (see Malina 1981, 120). Jesus' healers also would have been surprised to learn that a man who divorces his wife and marries another commits adultery *against her* (Mark 10:11). By definition, adultery was something a man committed against another married Israelite male by violating his property or a wife committed against her husband by violating the sanctity of his bed; a husband could not commit adultery against his wife. The Mishnah tractate *Soṭa*, the Suspected Adulteress, reflects this bias. It is based on the ceremony of the bitter water found in Numbers 5:11–31 in which a suspicious husband could put the fidelity of his wife to the test. The passage in Numbers was not in the least concerned about the husband who might go astray. Consequently, there is no tractate on the suspected adulterer. The fact is that he could marry additional wives, have concubines and girlfriends, and visit prostitutes without any qualms about committing adultery as long as the women were not the wives of another Israelite. This was by no means encouraged or condoned in the time of Jesus, but it was not considered adultery. In contrast, Jesus identified the lustful leer as tantamount to adultery (Matt. 5:27–28). By claiming that a man commits adultery against his wife by divorcing her and marrying another, Jesus redressed the injustice of the belittlement of the rights of wives in marriage. The wife is treated by Jesus as her husband's equal.

Jesus' unstated premise is that it is impossible for divorce to dissolve a marriage. Sirach advises that if your wife does not go as you would have her go, cut her off from your flesh (*Sirach* 25:26). Jesus maintains, however, that the wife can never be considered a disposable appendage and that the one-flesh unity between husband and wife can never be sundered. As callous as this may sound to partners who are being psychologically and perhaps even physically mauled by a destructive marriage, the emotional reality of this premise is becoming increasingly clear in our own culture to those who counsel with troubled marriages. One of the leading figures in family therapy, Carl Whitaker, has stated flatly that there is no such thing as divorce. Family relationships involve an irrevocable investment of one's life. The trust of one's self to another can be disrupted or become destructive, but, according to Whitaker (and Jesus!), it can never cease to exist.

> The craziest thing about marriage is that one cannot get divorced. We just do not seem to make it out of intimate relationships. It is obviously possible to divide up property and to decide not to live together any more, but it is impossible to go back to being single. Marriage is like a stew that has irreversible and irrevocable characteristics that the parts cannot be rid of. Divorce is leaving part of the self behind, like the rabbit who escapes the trap by gnawing one leg off. (Whitaker and Keith 1977, 71)

The legal term "dissolution" is often used as a synonym for the act of divorce. The definition of dissolution is to decompose into fragments or parts, or to terminate or extinguish by deconcentration or dispersion. No marital relationship can be dissolved in the sense of eliminating it. The marriage relationship may no longer be visible to onlookers, but it still influences the lives of the former partners. Recognizing this, the rabbis explained the saying, "Do not cook in a pot in which your neighbor has cooked," to mean "[Do not marry] a divorced woman during her husband's lifetime. For a Master said: 'When a divorced man marries a divorced woman, there are four minds in the bed' " (B. *Pesaḥ*. 112a).

The marital relationship may change, but it cannot be extinguished. One woman who had recently gone through divorce burned all the couple's vacation pictures and other mementos of their life together in a desperate attempt to blot her former husband out of her life, only to realize that she was in the process destroying a significant part of herself. She was obliterating most of the past that provided her with roots and continuity. The only way for a relationship to end is to blot out one's past, one's mannerisms and habits that have developed in response to the other. Married partners are like two plants that have grown together in the same pot for years so that their roots become intertwined. It is well nigh impossible to uproot one without affecting the other.

When children are involved, ending the relationship becomes virtually impossible regardless of the lack of previous commitment of the partners to each other. Spouses may no longer be spouses, but they remain kin to each other as the parents of their children. They may be warring kin, but divorce cannot cancel their bond of parenthood (Atkin and Rubin 1976). Despite all the research indicating that divorce is no worse for children than an unhappy marriage, it is also apparent that the continuing relationship of parents with each other after divorce is very important for the children, as well as for the parents. More simply, the legal status of the marital relationship is virtually irrelevant to children compared to the importance of their parents' actual relationship with them and with each other. When the marriage relationship ends with no further involvement by the departing parent (usually the father), all suffer. A departing spouse who attempts to sever the relationship with the former partner completely is more dissatisfied and depressed, the custodial parent is more overburdened and depressed, and the children suffer significant development and emotional distress (see the literature review, Ahrons 1983).

The common assumption in our culture is that the marital relationship ends with divorce and any continuation of it is strange behavior, but most divorced persons have and need to have a continuing relationship with the former spouse. In a study of divorced parents, Ahrons found,

> These relationships were predominantly kin or quasi-kin in nature, based on the couple's shared history, including extended family and friendships formed during the marriage. Some divorced parents considered their former spouses to be friends, and like other friendships, these relationships were characterized by a wide range of intimacy. (Ahrons 1980, 438)

Most divorced persons are living out the reality, then, that legal action does not end the interpersonal relationship. The words of Jesus can be interpreted as not only pointing to God's intention that marriage be a lifetime commitment but also to the reality that a marriage relationship cannot be ended by a legal procedure.

The Question of Remarriage

Nearly half of all marriages currently end in divorce, and nearly 80 percent of all divorces are followed at some time by remarriage (Visher and Visher, 1979). What may be said to those today who have been divorced and have remarried or wish to remarry?

Divorce is clearly labeled a sin by Jesus, but it is not the unpardonable sin that permits no second chance. Jesus condemned those who were concerned only with the legal minutiae involving the licitness or grounds for divorce and who assumed that one could carelessly put away a wife and remain righteous. But what would Jesus have said to the divorced? The woman Jesus met at the well had five husbands (John 4:16–19, 28–30, 39–42), but he did not tell her to "get thee to a convent" or to return to her first husband. Nor did he label her an adulteress. Presumably, she continued the relationship with the man she was living with and, with the good news of the gospel, began to see evidence of the renewal of her life. Jesus also refused to join in the condemnation of the woman caught in adultery but told her simply, "Go, and sin no more" (John 8:11, KJV). When the woman's accusers melted away, she was free to go, but free to go where and free to do what? She certainly could not return to the house of her husband, who probably instigated her condemnation (see Derrett 1970, 156–188). Was she condemned to accept a life of celibacy and poverty, or was she perhaps free to find another husband who would forgive her past and support her? The text is not interested in providing any answers to these questions. Nevertheless, we may observe that, while Jesus did not condone her sin—she is told to sin no more, implying that what she had done was sinful—he did not dictate to her what she was to do. Is it illegitimate to infer from this that he offered her the opportunity to pick up the pieces of her shattered life and begin anew, including the possibility of a new marriage?

A broken marriage falls short of God's will, but this is true of any sin. The question is, once a marriage is broken, then what? Since one is unable to turn the clock back, what are the options for the future? There are some who will become as "eunuchs for the sake of the kingdom" and will choose never to remarry. What about those who are overcome by the burden of loneliness or those who, like the widowed in 1 Corinthians 7:9, burn with passion? Must they remain single until death lest they become guilty of greater sin than divorce by remarrying? Cannot one who has sinned have a second chance, or is this one sin for which a second chance is impossible? The church has too often applied the teaching of Jesus on the subject of divorce and remarriage with a legalistic rigor that it suspends when it comes to his other sayings. In our opinion, the principle that should govern our approach to these questions should be the principle of salvage and redemption that governed Jesus' ministry to people. If it is the case that marriage was made for the blessing of humankind, and not humankind for marriage, it would seem that one who has failed in marriage might have another opportunity to remarry. Any moral superiority that the undivorced might feel toward the divorced who remarry is undermined by Jesus' claim that everyone who lusts after another is guilty of adultery (Matt 5:28). Every spouse has broken commitments to the partner, and every relationship experiences alienation from unresolved differences. One may not pass judgments on others. The elder brothers and prodigal brothers are on the same footing when they come before the father who loves them both and wishes them both to be happy.

In spite of the principle of grace that should govern our attitudes toward those who experience a troubled marriage, however, we cannot simply dismiss the question and assume that with God's forgiveness the slate is wiped clean so that remarriage is no different from a first marriage. We are creatures with a history, with roots in our past. The message of redemption proclaims that we can be reconciled to God and transformed; our past failures need no longer control us and may have new meaning from the strength and growth that occurred as a result of those experiences, but they are not eliminated. We still live with the realities of our pasts. Although the new marital partners may welcome the chance to begin again, they often bring children, belongings, ex-inlaws who are still kin, and patterns of living that developed around a different partner to this "new beginning." Wisdom is needed to untangle the complex relationships and issues that are implicit in a second marriage. Remarriage often creates even more crisis and stress than the divorce for children, friends, and extended family. Lives become more complicated, ex-spouses and grandparents fear being replaced by new relatives, and children's dreams of parents' reuniting are dashed. Children particularly feel torn by remarriage and are often more emotionally distressed by this than by the divorce (Visher and Visher 1979; Sager and others 1983). They feel split apart by the need to be loyal to two sets of parents. On top of this, they often experience the turmoil of adding step-siblings, thus changing the age, sex, and role structure of the family. (See Visher and Visher 1979 for an excellent discussion of remarried families.)

The Response of the Church to Divorce and Remarriage

Jesus' teachings about divorce and remarriage heightened the sanctity of marriage and stressed God's intention from the beginning that it be a lifetime commitment. He also dismissed the casuistry that sought out loopholes in God's will. Nevertheless, Jesus had compassion on sinners of all varieties, including those who failed to live up to their commitments in marriage. He did not lightly dismiss the failure, but neither did he offer legislation about what to do or not to do, given certain failures. He spoke out unequivocally against divorce, for he recognized the pain and turmoil created by broken relationships for which legal action provides no solution. Divorce laws are merely the means by which to order material possessions and a public statement of what has occurred interpersonally between partners. For many, remarriage, despite its complexity, can be an experience of God's grace and an opportunity to use the wisdom gleaned from previous failures to create new relationships of love and commitment.

Jesus' teaching on divorce and remarriage was not a hardening of the law to prohibit remarriage; it was a recognition that no matter what the laws do or do not allow, relationships between persons cannot be formed or destroyed by legal categories. Jesus did not concern himself with legal categories (single, married, divorced, remarried) or the rites for moving from one to the other but with the will of God and the effects of interpersonal sin and alienation on God's children. All spouses fall short of God's intention for their relationship with each other. For some, the alienation and hurt continue until the radical measures of separation and legal divorce are the most appropriate step to take, and many then remarry. The church's task is not to define the rightness or wrongness of divorce and remarriage in certain circumstances. It is to proclaim God's intention and to counteract the suffering inflicted by one upon the other when they fail to live out that intention.

Second, Jesus did not say much about the marital status of persons except when he was asked to address the issue. Jesus was less concerned with marriage and kinship ties than with membership in the family of God. Yet for churches today, strengthening individual marriages and sociological families often takes programmatic precedence over developing and strengthening the family of God, the community of believers. A significant means of ministering to those experiencing the pain of divorce is to place less emphasis on marriage and more on developing the family of God, as Jesus did.

Ministry for persons experiencing divorce is certainly needed, and churches can do much more to help (see Kysar and Kysar 1978; Guernsey 1982; Lester 1976). But our ministry cannot stop in ministry to troubled family relationships or even be concentrated there. Christians belong to the household of God, not to a singles, singles-again, young-married, or any other segregated group based on marital status. Membership in this household should provide a sense of acceptance, security, and belonging, regardless of the stresses and changes in one's marriage.

Bibliography

Books dealing with communication and conflict in marriage that may be of particular interest to couples are marked by an asterisk.

*Achtemeier, Elizabeth. 1976. *The committed marriage.* Philadelphia: Westminster Press.

Ahrons, Constance R. 1980a. Divorce: A crisis of family transition and change. *Family Relations* 29:533–540.

———. 1980b. Redefining the divorced family: A conceptual framework. *Social Work* 25:437–441.

———. 1983. Divorce: Before, during, and after. In Hamilton I. McCubbin and Charles R. Figley, eds., *Stress and the family: Vol. 1. Coping with normative transitions.* New York: Brunner/Mazel.

Anderson, H. 1976. *The Gospel of Mark.* New Century Bible. London: Marshall, Morgan & Scott, Oliphants.

Arbes, Bill H. 1977. Counseling the sexually dysfunctioning couple. In Robert F. Stahmann and William J. Hiebert, eds., *Klemer's counseling in marital and sexual problems: A clinician's handbook,* 2nd ed. Baltimore: Williams & Wilkins Co.

Argyle, Michael, and Adrian Furnham. 1983. Sources of satisfaction and conflict in long-term relationships. *Journal of Marriage and the Family* 45:481–493.

Atkin, Edith, and Estelle Rubin. 1976. *Part-time father.* New York: Vanguard Press.

Atkinson, D. 1979. *To have and to hold: The marriage covenant and the discipline of divorce.* London: William Collins Sons & Co.

Bailey, D. S. 1952. *The mystery of love and marriage.* London: SCM Press.

Baker, Luther G. 1983. In my opinion: The sexual revolution in perspective. *Family Relations* 32:297–300.

Balch, D. L. 1981. *Let wives be submissive: The domestic code in 1 Peter.* SBL Monograph Series 26. Chico, Calif.: Scholars Press.

Baltensweiler, H. 1967. *Die Ehe im Neuen Testament. Exegetische Untersuchung über Ehe, Ehelosigkeit und Ehescheidung.* ATANT 52. Zurich: Zwingli.

Bane, Mary Jo. 1976. *Here to stay.* New York: Basic Books.

Bartchy, S. S. 1973. *First-century slavery and 1 Corinthians 7:21.* SBL Dissertation Series, no. 11. Missoula, Mont.: Scholars Press.

Barth, M. 1974. *Ephesians.* The Anchor Bible. Garden City, N.Y.: Doubleday & Co.

Batey, R. A. 1967. The *Mia Sarx* union of Christ and the Church. *New Testament Studies* 13:270–281.

Bayly, J. 1977. How basic the conflict? An open letter from Bill Gothard. *Eternity,* August 1977:41–43.

Bean, F. D., R. L. Curtis, Jr., and J. P. Marcum. 1977. Familism and marital satisfaction among Mexican Americans: The effects of family size, wife's labor force participation, and conjugal power. *Journal of Marriage and the Family* 39:759–767.

Beare, F. W. 1970. *The first epistle of Peter.* 3rd ed. Oxford: Basil Blackwell Publisher.

Bedale, S. 1954. The meaning of *kephalē* in the Pauline epistles. *Journal of Theological Studies,* new series 5:211–215.

Belsky, Jay, Graham B. Spanier, and Michael Rovine. 1983. Stability and change in marriage across the transition to parenthood. *Journal of Marriage and the Family* 45:567–577.

Bernard, Jessie. 1982. *The future of marriage,* 2nd ed. New Haven, Conn.: Yale University Press.

Bernard, M. L., and J. L. Bernard. 1983. Violent intimacy: The family as a model for love relationships. *Family Relations* 32:283–286.

Berscheid, Ellen. 1983. Emotion. In Harold H. Kelley and others, eds., *Close relationships.* New York: W. H. Freeman & Co.

Best, E. 1971. *1 Peter.* New Century Bible. London: Marshall, Morgan & Scott, Oliphants.

Blood, R. O., Jr., and D. M. Wolfe. 1960. *Husbands and wives: The dynamics of married living.* Glencoe, Ill.: Free Press of Glencoe.

Bochner, A. 1979. Relational bonding. Paper presented to the SCA seminar on Functional Intimate Discourse, San Antonio, 1979. As quoted in M. A. Fitzpatrick, S. Fallis, and L. Vance. *Family Relations,* 31:61–70.

Bockelman, W. 1976. *Gothard—The man and his ministry: An evaluation.* Santa Barbara, Calif.: Quill Publications.

Boucher, M. 1969. Some unexplored parallels to 1 Cor. 11:11–12 and Gal. 3:28. *Catholic Biblical Quarterly* 31:50–58.

Bowen, Murray. 1976a. Family therapy and family group therapy. In David H. L. Olson, ed., *Treating relationships.* Lake Mills, Iowa: Graphic Publishing Co.

———. 1976b. Principles and techniques of multiple family therapy. In Philip J. Guerin, ed., *Family therapy: Theory and practice.* New York: Halsted Press.

———. 1976c. Theory in the practice of psychotherapy. In Philip J. Guerin, ed., *Family therapy: Theory and practice.* New York: Halsted Press.

Broderick, Carlfred. 1979. The state of marriage and family: A progress report. In Nick Stinnett, Barbara Chesser, and John DeFrain, eds., *Building family strengths: Blueprints for action.* Lincoln, Nebr.: University of Nebraska Press.

Bronfenbrenner, Urie, and Ann C. Crouter. 1982. Work and family through time and space. In Sheila B. Kamerman and Cheryl D. Hayes, eds., *Families that work: Children in a changing world.* Washington, D.C.: National Academy Press.

Bruce, F. F. 1971. *1 and 2 Corinthians.* New Century Bible. Grand Rapids: Wm. B. Eerdmans Publishing Co.

Brueggemann, W. 1982. *Genesis.* Interpretation. Atlanta: John Knox Press.

Burgess, Ernest W., and Harvey J. Locke. 1945. *The family: From institution to companionship.* New York: American Book Co.

Burkill, T. A. 1971. Two into one: The notion of carnal union in Mark 10:8; 1 Cor. 6:16; Eph. 5:31. *Zeitschrift für die neutestamentliche Wissenschaft* 62: 115–120.

Caird, G. B. 1976. *Paul's letters from prison.* New Clarendon Bible. Oxford: Oxford University Press.

*Calden, George. 1976. *I count—you count: The "do it ourselves" marriage counseling and enrichment book.* Niles, Ill.: Argus Communications.

von Campenhausen, H. 1949. *Die Askese im Urchristentum.* SGV 192. Tübingen: J. C. B. Mohr (Paul Siebeck).

Caplow, T., and B. A. Chadwick. 1979. Inequality and life-styles in Middletown, 1920–1978. *Social Science Quarterly* 60:367–386.

Cartlidge, David R. 1975. 1 Cor. 7 as a foundation for a Christian sex ethic. *Journal of Religion* 55:220–234.

Cassuto, Umberto. 1961. *A commentary on the book of Genesis.* Trans. by I. Abrahams. Jerusalem: Magnes Press.

Centers, R., B. H. Raven, and A. Rodrigues. 1971. Conjugal power structure: A reexamination. *American Sociological Review* 36:264–278.

Charles, R. H. 1921. *The teaching of the New Testament on divorce.* London: Williams & Norgate.

Cherlin, A. 1979. Work life and marital dissolution. In G. Levinger and O. C. Moles, eds., *Divorce and separation: Context, cause and consequences.* New York: Basic Books.

Clark, S. B. 1980. *Man and woman in Christ: An examination of the roles of men and women in light of scripture and the social sciences.* Ann Arbor, Mich.: Servant Publications.

Clinebell, Charlotte Holt. 1973. *Meet me in the middle.* New York: Harper & Row.

Clinebell, Howard J. 1973. *User's guide for growth counseling.* Nashville: Abingdon Press (cassette tapes).

*———— and Charlotte H. Clinebell. 1970. *The intimate marriage.* New York: Harper & Row.

Collins, R. F. 1978. The Bible and sexuality II: The New Testament. *Biblical Theology Bulletin* 8:3–18.

————. 1983. The unity of Paul's paraenesis in 1 Thess. 4:3–8. 1 Cor. 7.1–7, a significant parallel. *New Testament Studies* 29:420–429.

Condran, John G., and Jerry G. Bode. 1982. Rashomon, working wives, and family division of labor: Middletown, 1980. *Journal of Marriage and the Family* 44:421–426.

*Crable, Richard E. 1981. *One to another.* New York: Harper & Row.

Cutright, P. 1971. Income and family events: Marital instability. *Journal of Marriage and the Family* 33:291–306.

Derrett, J. D. M. 1970. *Law in the New Testament.* London: Darton, Longman & Todd.

Deutsch, M. 1969. Conflicts: Productive and destructive. *Journal of Social Issues* 25:7–41.

DeYoung, A. J. 1979. Marriage encounter: A critical examination. *Journal of Marital and Family Therapy* 5:27–34.

Doherty, W. J., and M. E. Lester. 1982. Casualties of marriage encounter weekends. *Family Therapy News* 13:4, 9.

Doherty, W. J., P. McCabe, and R. G. Ryder. 1978. Marriage encounter: A critical appraisal. *Journal of Marriage and Family Counseling* 4:99–106.

Duberman, Lucile. 1977. *Marriage and other alternatives,* 2nd ed. New York: Holt, Rinehart & Winston.

Edmiston, Susan. 1977. To love, honor, and negotiate. In James E. De Burger, ed., *Marriage today: Problems, issues, and alternatives.* New York: John Wiley & Sons.

Elder, Glen H. 1981. History and the family: The discovery of complexity. *Journal of Marriage and the Family* 43:489–519.

Elkind, David. 1981. The family and religion. In Nick Stinnett and others, eds., *Family strengths 3: Roots of well-being.* Lincoln, Nebr.: University of Nebraska Press.

Elliott, J. H. 1981. *A home for the homeless: A sociological exegesis of 1 Peter, its situation and strategy.* Philadelphia: Fortress Press.

Epstein, Joseph. 1974. *Divorced in America.* New York: E. P. Dutton & Co.

Erikson, Erik H. 1968. *Identity: Youth and crisis.* New York: W. W. Norton & Co.

Farson, Richard. 1977. Why good marriages fail. In James E. De Burger, ed., *Marriage today: Problems, issues, and alternatives.* New York: John Wiley & Sons.

Fee, Gordon D. 1980. 1 Corinthians 7:1 in the *NIV. Journal of the Evangelical Theological Society* 23:307–314.

Fein, Robert A. 1980. Research on fathering: Social policy and an emergent perspective. In Arlene Skolnick and Jerome H. Skolnick, eds., *Family in transition,* 3rd ed. Boston: Little, Brown & Co.

Feldman, H. 1971. The effects of children on the family. In A. Michel, ed., *Family issues of employed women in Europe and America,* pp. 1107–1125. Leiden, The Netherlands: Leiden University Press.

Fendrich, Michael. 1984. Wives' employment and husbands' distress: A meta-analysis and a replication. *Journal of Marriage and the Family* 46:871–879.

Ferber, Marianne A. 1982. Labor market participation of young married women: Causes and effects. *Journal of Marriage and the Family* 44:457–468.

Fields, Nina S. 1983. Satisfaction in long-term marriages. *Social Work* 28: 37–40.

Filsinger, Erik E., and Margaret R. Wilson. 1983. Social anxiety and marital adjustment. *Family Relations* 32:513–519.

———. 1984. Religiosity, socioeconomic rewards, and family development: Predictors of marital adjustment. *Journal of Marriage and the Family* 46: 663–670.

Fiorenza, Elisabeth Schüssler. 1984. *In memory of her.* New York: Crossroad.

Fitzmyer, J. A. 1976. The Matthean divorce texts and some new Palestinian evidence. *Theological Studies* 37:197–226.

———. 1978. Divorce among first-century Palestinian Jews. *Eretz-Israel*, H. L. Ginsberg volume 14:103–110.

Fitzpatrick, Mary Anne, Susan Fallis, and Leslie Vance. 1982. Multifunctional coding of conflict resolution strategies in marital dyads. *Family Relations* 31:61–70.

Foh, Susan T. 1979. *Women and the word of God: A response to biblical feminism.* Phillipsburg, N.J.: Presbyterian & Reformed Publishing Co.

Förster, W. 1964. *"exestin . . . ."* In Gerhard Kittel, ed., and Geoffrey W. Bromiley, trans., *Theological Dictionary of the New Testament*, vol. 2, pp. 560–575. Grand Rapids: Wm. B. Eerdmans Publishing Co.

Frankl, Viktor E. 1959. Man's search for meaning: An introduction to logotherapy. New York: Simon & Schuster.

Friedrich, G. 1977. *Sexualität und Ehe. Rückfragen an das Neue Testament.* Stuttgart: KBW-Verlag.

Fromm, Erich. 1956. *The art of loving.* New York: Harper & Row.

Fullerton, H. 1980. The 1995 labor force: A first look. *Monthly Labor Review*, December 1980:11–21.

Furnish, Victor P. 1979. *The moral teaching of Paul.* Nashville: Abingdon Press.

Garland, David E. 1983. The Christian's posture toward marriage and celibacy: 1 Corinthians 7. *Review and Expositor* 80:351–362.

Garland, Diana S. Richmond. 1983. *Working with couples for marriage enrichment.* San Francisco: Jossey-Bass.

Garvey, Catherine. 1977. *Play.* Cambridge, Mass.: Harvard University Press.

Glenn, Norval D., and Sara McLanahan. 1982. Children and marital happiness: A further specification of the relationship. *Journal of Marriage and the Family* 44:63–72.

Glick, P. C., and A. J. Norton. 1977. Marrying, divorcing, and living together in the U.S. today. *Population Bulletin* 32:5. Washington, D.C.: Population Reference Bureau.

Gooch, P. W. 1983. Authority and justification in theological ethics: A study in 1 Corinthians 7. *Journal of Religious Ethics* 11:62–74.

Goodman, Ellen. 1979. The new ideal American woman. In L. Van Gelder, Ellen Goodman: A columnist you can trust. *Ms*, March 1979.

———. 1981. To work or not: Women's dilemma. *Minneapolis Tribune*, April 1981:7:10.

Gottman, John M. 1979. *Marital interaction: Experimental investigations.* New York: Academic Press.

Greenblat, Cathy Stein. 1983. The salience of sexuality in the early years of marriage. *Journal of Marriage and the Family* 45:289–299.

Greeven, H. 1969. Ehe nach dem Neuen Testament. *New Testament Studies* 15:365–388.

Guelich, Robert A. 1982. *The sermon on the mount.* Waco, Tex.: Word Books.

Guerin, Philip J. 1976. The use of the arts in family therapy: I never sang for my father. In Philip J. Guerin, ed., *Family therapy: Theory and practice.* New York: Halsted Press.

Guerney, Bernard G., Jr., and others. 1977. *Relationship enhancement: Skill-training programs for therapy, problem prevention, and enrichment.* San Francisco: Jossey-Bass.

Guernsey, Dennis B. 1982. *A new design for family ministry.* Elgin, Ill.: David C. Cook Publishing Co.

*———. 1984. *The family covenant: Love and forgiveness in the Christian home.* Elgin, Ill.: David C. Cook Publishing Co.

Hancock, Maxine. 1975. *Love, honor and be free.* Chicago: Moody Press.

Harriman, Lynda Cooper. 1983. Personal and marital changes accompanying parenthood. *Family Relations* 32:387–393.

Hartman, Carl, Jane Quinn, and Brenda Young. 1981. *Sexual expression: A manual for trainers.* New York: Human Sciences Press.

Hiller, Dana V., and William W. Philliber. 1982. Predicting marital and career success among dual-worker couples. *Journal of Marriage and the Family* 44: 53–62.

Hollis, Harry N., and B. A. Clendinning. 1970. *Sex education: Resource guide for the church.* Nashville: Broadman Press.

Hoskyns, E. C., and F. N. Davey. 1981. *Crucifixion, resurrection: The pattern of theology and ethics of the New Testament.* Ed. by G. S. Wakefield. London: S.P.C.K.

Houseknecht, Sharon K., and Anne S. Macke. 1981. Combining marriage and career: The marital adjustment of professional women. *Journal of Marriage and the Family* 43:651–661.

Howell, John C. 1979. *Equality and submission in marriage.* Nashville: Broadman Press.

Hull, W. E. 1975. Woman in her place: Biblical perspectives. *Review and Expositor* 72:5–17.

Hunt, Morton. 1977. The future of marriage. In James E. De Burger, ed., *Marriage today: Problems, issues, and alternatives.* New York: John Wiley & Sons.

Hurd, John C., Jr. 1965. *The origin of 1 Corinthians.* London: S.P.C.K.

Hurley, J. B. 1981. *Man and woman in biblical perspective. A study in role relationships and authority.* Leicester, England: Inter-Varsity Press.

Isaksson, A. 1965. *Marriage and ministry in the new temple.* Copenhagen: Munksgaard.

Jeremias, J. 1971. *New Testament theology: The proclamation of Jesus.* Trans. by J. Bowden. New York: Charles Scribner's Sons.

Jewett, Paul K. 1975. *Man as male and female: A study in sexual relationship from a theological point of view.* Grand Rapids: Wm. B. Eerdmans Publishing Co.

Judge, E. A. 1960. *The social pattern of the Christian groups in the first century.* London: Tyndale Press.

Kähler, E. 1960. *Die Frau in den paulinischen Briefen.* Zurich: Gotthelf.

Kamerman, Sheila B., and Cheryl D. Hayes. 1982. *Families that work: Children in a changing world.* Washington, D.C.: National Academy Press.

Kaplan, Helen Singer. 1974. *The new sex therapy: Active treatment of sexual dysfunctions.* New York: Brunner/Mazel.

Keck, L. E. 1979. *Paul and his letters.* Philadelphia: Fortress Press.

Kinsey, Alfred C., Wardell B. Pomeroy, and Clyde E. Martin. 1948. *Sexual behavior in the human male.* Philadelphia: W. B. Saunders Co.
———and others. 1953. *Sexual behavior in the human female.* Philadelphia: W. B. Saunders Co.
Knight, G. W. III. 1977. *The New Testament teaching on the role relationship of men and women.* Grand Rapids: Baker Book House.
Kolbenschlag, Madonna. 1979. *Kiss sleeping beauty good-bye.* Garden City, N.Y.: Doubleday & Co.
Kümmel, W. G. 1954. Verlobung und Heirat bei Paulus (1 Cor. 7:36–38). *Neutestamentliche Studien für Rudolf Bultmann,* pp. 275–295. Berlin: Alfred Töpelmann.
Kysar, Myrna, and Robert Kysar. 1978. *The asundered: Biblical teachings on divorce and remarriage.* Atlanta: John Knox Press.
LaRossa, Ralph. 1983. The transition to parenthood and the social reality of time. *Journal of Marriage and the Family* 45:579–589.
Larson, Jeffry H. 1984. The effect of husband's unemployment on marital and family relations in blue-collar families. *Family Relations* 33:503–511.
Lasch, Christopher. 1980. The family as a haven in a heartless world. In Arlene Skolnick and Jerome H. Skolnick, eds., *Family in transition,* 3rd ed. Boston: Little, Brown & Co.
Laslett, Barbara. 1977. Family membership, past and present. *Social Problems* 26:476–490.
*Lederer, William J., and Don D. Jackson. 1968. *The mirages of marriage.* New York: W. W. Norton & Co.
Leenhardt, F. 1946. *Le mariage chrétien.* Neuchâtel: Delachaux & Niestlé.
Leipoldt, J. 1962. *Die Frau in der Antike und im Urchristentum.* Gütersloh: Gütersloher Verlagshaus Gerd Mohn.
Leonard, Joe H. 1984. Celebrate Christian marriage. *Education Newsletter* (World Council of Churches) 2.
Lester, Andrew D. 1976. *It hurts so bad, Lord!* Nashville: Broadman Press.
———. 1983. *Coping with your anger: A Christian guide.* Philadelphia: Westminster Press.
*Lewis, Jerry M. 1979. *How's your family?* New York: Brunner/Mazel.
——— and others. 1976. *No single thread: Psychological health in family systems.* New York: Brunner/Mazel.
——— and John G. Looney. 1983. *The long struggle: Well-functioning working-class black families.* New York: Brunner/Mazel.
Lewis, Lionel S., and Dennis Brissett. 1977. Sex as work: A study of avocational counseling. In James E. De Burger, ed., *Marriage today: Problems, issues, and alternatives.* New York: John Wiley & Sons.
Lietzmann, H. 1949. *An die Korinther I–II.* Rev. by W. G. Kümmel. Handbuch zum neuen Testament. Tübingen: J. C. B. Mohr (Paul Siebeck).
Lillie, W. 1975. The Pauline house-tables. *Expository Times* 86:179–183.
Litfin, A. D. 1979. Evangelical feminism: Why traditionalists reject it. *Bibliotheca Sacra* 136:258–271.
Locke, H., and G. Karlsson. 1952. Marital adjustment and prediction in Sweden and the United States. *American Sociological Review* 17:10–17.

Lohse, E. 1954. Paraenäse und Kerygma im 1 Petrusbrief. *Zeitschrift für die neutestamentliche Wissenschaft* 45:68–89.

Lu, Y. C. 1952. Marital roles and marriage adjustment. *Sociology and Social Research* 36:364–368.

Luckey, Eleanor. 1970. Children: A factor in marital satisfaction. *Journal of Marriage and the Family* 32:44.

Mace, David R. 1973. *Whom God hath joined.* Rev. ed. Philadelphia: Westminster Press.

*———. 1982a. *Close companions: The marriage enrichment handbook.* New York: Continuum Publishing Co.

*———. 1982b. *Love and anger in marriage.* Grand Rapids: Zondervan Publishing House.

——— and Vera Mace. 1976a. The selection, training, and certification of facilitators for marriage enrichment programs. *The Family Coordinator* 25: 117–125.

———. 1976b. Marriage enrichment—A preventive group approach for couples. In David H. L. Olson, ed., *Treating relationships.* Lake Mills, Iowa: Graphic Publishing Co.

———. 1976c. *Marriage enrichment in the church.* Nashville: Broadman Press.

———. 1985. *In the presence of God: Readings for Christian marriage.* Philadelphia: Westminster Press.

Madden, Margaret E., and Ronnie Janoff-Bulman. 1979. Blaming and marital satisfaction: Wives' attributions for conflict in marriage. Unpublished manuscript. Department of Psychology, University of Massachusetts, Amherst.

———. 1981. Blame, control, and marital satisfaction: Wives' attributions for conflict in marriage. *Journal of Marriage and the Family* 43:663–674.

Maddock, James W. 1983. Human sexuality in the life cycle of the family system. In James C. Hansen, Jane Divita Woody, and Robert Henley Woody, eds., *Sexual issues in family therapy.* Rockville, Md.: Aspen Systems Corp.

Malina, Bruce J. 1981. *The New Testament world: Insights from cultural anthropology.* Atlanta: John Knox Press.

Manson, T. W. 1949. *The sayings of Jesus.* London: SCM Press.

Markman, Howard J., Frank Floyd, and Fran Dickson-Markman. 1982. Towards a model for the prediction and primary prevention of marital and family distress and dissolution. In Steve Dick, ed., *Personal relationships 4: Dissolving personal relationships.* London: Academic Press.

Marshall, I. Howard. 1978. *Commentary on Luke.* New International Greek Testament Commentary. Grand Rapids: Wm. B. Eerdmans Publishing Co.

———. 1983. *1 and 2 Thessalonians.* New Century Bible. Grand Rapids: Wm. B. Eerdmans Publishing Co.

Maslow, Abraham H. 1968. *Toward a psychology of being,* 2nd ed. New York: D. Van Nostrand Co.

Masters, William H., and Virginia E. Johnson. 1966. *Human sexual response.* Boston: Little, Brown & Co.

———. 1970. *The pleasure bond: A new look at sexuality and commitment.* Boston: Little, Brown & Co.

McCubbin, Hamilton I., and Charles R. Figley. 1983. Bridging normative and catastrophic family stress. In Hamilton I. McCubbin and Charles R. Figley, eds., *Stress and the family: Vol. 1. Coping with normative transitions.* New York: Brunner/Mazel.

McDonald, Gerald W. 1981. Structural exchange and marital interaction. *Journal of Marriage and the Family* 43:825–839.

McGoldrick, Monica, John K. Pearce, and Joseph Giordano. 1982. *Ethnicity and family therapy.* New York: Guilford Press.

McLain, Raymond, and Andrew Weigert. 1979. Toward a phenomenological sociology of the family: A programmatic essay. In Wesley R. Burr and others, eds., *Contemporary theories about the family,* vol. 2. New York: Free Press.

McLean, Paul D. 1962. New findings relevant to the evolution of psychosexual functions of the brain. *The Journal of Nervous and Mental Disease* 135:289–301.

McLean, Stuart D. 1984. The language of covenant and a theology of the family. Paper presented to the Consultation on a Theology of the Family, Institute for Marriage and Family Ministries, Fuller Theological Seminary, Pasadena, California, November 19–20, 1984.

McNeile, A. H. 1915. *The Gospel according to St. Matthew.* London: Macmillan & Co.

Meeks, Wayne A. 1983. *The first urban Christians: The social world of the apostle Paul.* New Haven, Conn.: Yale University Press.

Meichenbaum, Donald, and Dennis Turk. 1976. The cognitive-behavioral management of anxiety, anger, and pain. In Park O. Davidson, ed., *The behavioral management of anxiety, depression and pain.* New York: Brunner/Mazel.

Meier, John P. 1980. *Matthew.* Series: New Testament Message. Wilmington, Del.: Michael Glazier.

*Melville, Keith. 1980. *Marriage and family today,* 2nd ed. New York: Random House.

Michel, A. 1967. Comparative data concerning the interaction in French and American families. *Journal of Marriage and the Family* 29, 227–244.

Miles, Judith M. 1975. *The feminine principle: A woman's discovery of the key to total fulfillment.* Minneapolis: Bethany Fellowship.

Miller, Brent C., and Judith A. Myers-Walls. 1983. Parenthood: Stresses and coping strategies. In Hamilton I. McCubbin and Charles R. Figley, eds., *Stress and the family: Vol. 1. Coping with normative transitions.* New York: Brunner/Mazel.

Miller, Claude H. 1983. Marital concord and discord. *American Journal of Psychoanalysis* 43:157–166.

Miller, Sherod, Elam W. Nunnally, and Daniel B. Wackman. 1975. Recent progress in understanding and facilitating marital communication. *The Family Coordinator* 24:143–152.

———. 1976. Minnesota couples communication program (MCCP): Premarital and marital groups. In David H. L. Olson, ed., *Treating relationships.* Lake Mills, Iowa: Graphic Publishing Co.

*———. 1979. *Couple communication I: Talking together.* Minneapolis: Interpersonal Communication Programs.

Minuchin, Salvador. 1984. *Family kaleidoscope.* Cambridge, Mass.: Harvard University Press.

Mollenkott, Virginia R. 1977. *Women, men and the Bible.* Nashville: Abingdon Press.

Morgan, Marabel. 1975. *The total woman.* Old Tappan, N.J.: Fleming H. Revell Co.

Mosher, William D., and Gerry E. Hendershot. 1984. Religious affiliation and the fertility of married couples. *Journal of Marriage and the Family* 46:671–677.

Moule, C. F. D. 1982. *Essays in New Testament interpretation.* Cambridge: At the University Press.

Mueller, J. R. 1980. The temple scroll and the Gospel divorce texts. *Revue de Qumran,* 1980:247–256.

Myers-Walls, Judith A. 1984. Balancing multiple role responsibilities during the transition to parenthood. *Family Relations* 33:267–271.

Napier, Augustus. 1980. Primary prevention: A family therapist's perspective. In Nick Stinnett and others, eds., *Family strengths: Positive models for family life.* Lincoln, Nebr.: University of Nebraska Press.

National Marriage Encounter. 1978. *Marriage enrichment resource manual.* St. Paul: National Marriage Encounter.

Neusner, Jacob. 1979. *Method and meaning in ancient Judaism.* Brown Judaic Studies 10. Missoula, Mont.: Scholars Press.

Newbigin, Lesslie. 1978. *The open secret.* Grand Rapids: Wm. B. Eerdmans Publishing Co.

Nineham, D. E. 1978. *Saint Mark.* Westminster Pelican Commentaries. Philadelphia: Westminster Press.

Nye, F. Ivan. 1979. Choice, exchange, and the family. In Wesley R. Burr and others, eds., *Contemporary theories about the family,* vol. 2, pp. 1–41. New York: Free Press.

Ogburn, William F., and C. Tibbitts. 1934. The family and its functions. Report of the President's Research Committee on Social Trends, in *Recent social trends in the United States.* New York: McGraw-Hill Book Co.

Osmond, M. W., and P. Y. Martin. 1978. A contingency model of marital organization in lower income families. *Journal of Marriage and the Family* 40:315–329.

Peck, M. Scott. 1978. *The road less traveled.* New York: Simon & Schuster.

Peplau, Letitia Anne. 1983. Roles and gender. In Harold H. Kelley and others, eds., *Close relationships,* pp. 220–264. New York: W. H. Freeman & Co.

Peterson, Donald R. 1983. Conflict. In Harold H. Kelley and others, eds., *Close relationships,* pp. 360–396. New York: W. H. Freeman & Co.

Phipps, William E. 1982. Is Paul's attitude toward sexual relations contained in 1 Cor. 7.1? *New Testament Studies* 28:125–131.

Piper, Otto A. 1949. *The Christian interpretation of sex.* New York: Charles Scribner's Sons.

———. 1960. *The biblical view of sex and marriage.* New York: Charles Scribner's Sons.

Pittman, Frank. 1984. Into the volcano. *The Family Therapy Networker* 8:63–65.

Poloma, M. M., and T. N. Garland. 1971. The myth of the egalitarian family: Family roles and the professionally employed wife. In A. Theodore, ed., *The professional woman*. Cambridge, Mass.: Schenkman Publishing Co.

Pond, D. A., A. Rule, and M. Hamilton. 1963. Marriage and neurosis in a working class population. *British Journal of Psychiatry* 109:592–598.

Quesnell, Q. 1968. Made themselves eunuchs for the kingdom of heaven (Mt. 19:12). *Catholic Biblical Quarterly* 30:335–358.

Raush, Harold L., and others. 1974. *Communication, conflict and marriage*. San Francisco: Jossey-Bass.

Reed, David M. 1977. Male sexual conditioning. In Robert F. Stahmann and William J. Hiebert, eds., *Klemer's counseling in marital and sexual problems: A clinician's handbook*, 2nd ed. Baltimore: Williams & Wilkins Co.

Reiss, Ira L. 1981. Some observations on ideology and sexuality in America. *Journal of Marriage and the Family* 43:271–283.

Renne, K. 1971. Health and marital experience in an urban population. *Journal of Marriage and the Family* 33:338–350.

Richardson, A. 1958. *An introduction to the theology of the New Testament*. London: SCM Press.

Rollins, B., and R. Galligan. 1978. The developing child and marital satisfaction of parents. In R. M. Lerner and G. B. Spanier, eds., *Child influences on marital and family interaction*, pp. 71–205. New York: Academic Press.

Rordorf, Willy. 1969. Marriage in the New Testament and in the early church. *Journal of Ecclesiastical History* 20:193–210.

Ross, H. L., and I. V. Sawhill. 1975. *Time of transition: The growth of families headed by women*. Washington, D.C.: Urban Institute.

*Rowatt, G. Wade, Jr., and Mary Jo Brock Rowatt. 1980. *The two-career marriage*. Philadelphia: Westminster Press.

Russell, C. S. 1974. Transition to parenthood: Problems and gratifications. *Journal of Marriage and the Family* 36:294–302.

Ryder, R. 1973. Longitudinal data relating marital satisfaction and having a child. *Journal of Marriage and the Family* 35:604–606.

Sager, Clifford J., and others. 1983. *Treating the remarried family*. New York: Brunner/Mazel.

Sanders, Glenn S., and Jerry Suls. 1982. Social comparison, competition and marriage. *Journal of Marriage and the Family* 44:721–730.

*Satir, Virginia. *Peoplemaking*. Palo Alto, Calif.: Science & Behavior Books, 1972.

Saxton, Lloyd. 1980. *The individual, marriage, and the family*, 4th ed. Belmont, Calif.: Wadsworth Publishing Co.

Scanzoni, John. 1968. A social system analysis of dissolved and existing marriages. *Journal of Marriage and the Family* 30:452–461.

———. 1978. *Sex roles, women's work, and marital conflict: A study of family change*. Lexington, Mass.: Lexington Books.

———. 1979. Social processes and power in families. In Wesley R. Burr and others, eds., *Contemporary theories about families*, vol. 1, pp. 295–316. New York: Free Press.

——— and Greer Litton, Fox. 1980. Sex roles, family and society: The seventies and beyond. *Journal of Marriage and the Family* 42:743–756.

Scanzoni, Letha, and John Scanzoni. 1975. *Men, women, and change: A sociology of marriage and family.* New York: McGraw-Hill Book Co.

Schenk, Josef, Horst Pfrang, and Armin Rausche. 1983. Personality traits versus the quality of the marital relationship as the determinant of marital sexuality. *Archives of Sexual Behavior* 12:31–42.

Schrage, W. 1974. Zur ethik der neutestamentlichen Haustafeln. *New Testament Studies* 21:1–22.

Schweizer, Eduard. 1975. *The good news according to Matthew.* Trans. by David E. Green. Atlanta: John Knox Press.

———. 1983. *The letter to the Colossians.* Trans. by A. Chester. Minneapolis: Augsburg Publishing House.

Selwyn, Edward G. 1947. *The first epistle of St. Peter.* London: Macmillan Co.

Senior, Donald. 1980. *1 and 2 Peter.* New Testament Message. Wilmington, Del.: Michael Glazier.

Skolnick, Arlene, and Jerome H. Skolnick. 1980. Introduction: Family in transition. In Arlene Skolnick and Jerome H. Skolnick, eds., *Family in transition,* 3rd ed. Boston: Little, Brown & Co.

Slater, Philip E. 1977. Sexual adequacy in America. In James E. De Burger, ed., *Marriage today: Problems, issues, and alternatives.* New York: John Wiley & Sons.

Smedes, Lewis B. 1984. *Forgive and forget: Healing the hurts we don't deserve.* New York: Harper & Row.

Smuts, Robert W. 1959. *Women and work in America.* New York: Columbia University Press.

Snow, J. H. 1974. Christian marriage and family life: Biblical and contemporary view. *Christianity and Crisis* 33:279–283.

Speiser, E. A. 1964. *Genesis.* The Anchor Bible. Garden City, N.Y.: Doubleday & Co.

Stauffer, Ethelbert. 1964. "*gameō, gamos.*" In Gerhard Kittel, ed., and Geoffrey W. Bromiley, trans., *Theological Dictionary of the New Testament,* vol. 1. pp. 648–657. Grand Rapids: Wm. B. Eerdmans Publishing Co.

Stitzinger, M. F. 1981. Genesis 1–3 and the male/female role relationship. *Grace Theological Journal* 2:23–44.

Straus, Murray A., R. J. Gelles, and S. K. Steinmetz. 1980. *Behind closed doors: Violence in the American family.* Garden City, N.Y.: Doubleday & Co.

Stringham, Jean G., Judith Hothan Riley, and Ann Ross. 1982. Silent birth: Mourning a stillborn baby. *Social Work* 27:322–327.

Szalai, Alexander. 1980. The quality of family life—traditional and modern: A review of sociological findings on contemporary family organization and role differentiation in the family. Paper presented at the United Nations Interregional Seminar on the Family in a Changing Society: Problems and Responsibilities of Its Members, London, July 18–31, 1973. As reported in Arlene Skolnick and Jerome H. Skolnick, eds., *Family in transition,* 3rd ed. Boston: Little, Brown & Co.

Tannahill, Reay. 1980. *Sex in history.* Briarcliff Manor, N.Y.: Stein & Day.

*Tavris, Carol. 1982. *Anger: The misunderstood emotion.* New York: Simon & Schuster.

Thomas, Sandra, Kay Albrecht, and Priscilla White. 1984. Determinants of marital quality in dual-career couples. *Family Relations* 33:513–521.

Tolstedt, B. E., and J. P. Stokes. 1983 Relation of verbal, affective, and physical intimacy to marital satisfaction. *Journal of Counseling Psychology* 30:573–580.

Trible, Phyllis. 1973. Depatriarchalizing in biblical interpretation. *Journal of the American Academy of Religion* 41:30–48.

————. 1978. *God and the rhetoric of sexuality*. Philadelphia: Fortress Press.

Turner, Ralph H. 1970. *Family interaction*. New York: John Wiley & Sons.

Udry, J. Richard. 1974. *The social context of marriage*. Philadelphia: J. B. Lippincott Co.

Visher, Emily B., and John S. Visher. 1979. *Step-families: A guide to working with stepparents and stepchildren*. New York: Brunner/Mazel.

————. 1983. Stepparenting: Blending families. In Hamilton I. McCubbin and Charles R. Figley, eds., *Stress and the family: Vol. 1. Coping with normative transitions*. New York: Brunner/Mazel.

Vööbus, A. 1958. *History of asceticism in the Syrian Orient*. Corpus Scriptorum Christianorum Orientalium 184. Louvain: Secretariat du Corpus SCO.

Walker, Lenore E. 1979. *The battered woman*. New York: Harper & Row.

Wallach, Michael A., and Lise Wallach. 1983. *Psychology's sanction for selfishness*. San Francisco: W. H. Freeman & Co.

Wallis, Jim. 1983. *Peacemakers: Christian voices from the new abolitionist movement*. San Francisco: Harper & Row.

Ward, Dawn, and Jack O. Balswick. 1984. The church, the family, and issues of modernity. Paper presented to the Consultation on a Theology of the Family, Institute for Marriage and Family Ministries, Fuller Theological Seminary, Pasadena, California, November 19–20, 1984.

Waring, E. M. 1984. The measurement of marital intimacy. *Journal of Marital and Family Therapy* 10:185–192.

———— and Gordon J. Chelune. 1983. Marital intimacy and self-disclosure. *Journal of Clinical Psychology* 39:183–190.

Watzlawick, Paul, J. H. Beavin, and Don D. Jackson. 1967. *Pragmatics of human communication—A study of interactional patterns, pathologies, and paradoxes*. New York: W. W. Norton & Co.

Whitaker, Carl A., and David V. Keith. 1977. Counseling the dissolving marriage. In Robert F. Stahmann and William J. Hiebert, eds., *Klemer's counseling in marital and sexual problems: A clinician's handbook*, 2nd ed. Baltimore: Williams & Wilkins Co.

Willie, Charles V., and Susan L. Greenblatt. 1978. Four "classic" studies of power relationships in black families: A review and look to the future. *Journal of Marriage and the Family* 40:691–694.

Yogev, Sara. 1981. Do professional women have egalitarian marital relationships? *Journal of Marriage and the Family* 43:865–871.

Young, Michael, and Peter Willmott. 1973. *The symmetrical family*. New York: Random House.

Index of Subjects

Index of Biblical References